THE MASK

Contemporary Theatre Studies

A series of books edited by Franc Chamberlain, Nene College, Northampton, UK

**Please see the back of this book for other titles in the Contemporary Theatre
Studies series**

THE MASK

A PERIODICAL PERFORMANCE
BY EDWARD GORDON CRAIG

Olga Taxidou
University of Edinburgh, UK

harwood academic publishers
Australia • Canada • China • France • Germany • India
Japan • Luxembourg • Malaysia • The Netherlands
Russia • Singapore • Switzerland

Amsteldijk 166
1st Floor
1079 LH Amsterdam
The Netherlands

British Library Cataloguing in Publication Data

Taxidou, Olga
    The Mask: a periodical performance by Edward Gordon Craig.
    – (Contemporary theatre studies; v. 30)
    1. Craig, Edward Gordon, 1872–1966 – Criticism and
    interpretation   2. Mask   3. Theater – Great Britain –
    Periodicals
    I. Title
    792'.092

ISBN 90-5755-046-6

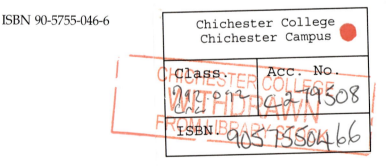

Cover illustration: Characters from the *Balli di Sfessania*, 1622 (*The Mask*, April 1911).

CONTENTS

INTRODUCTION TO THE SERIES

Contemporary Theatre Studies is a book series of special interest to everyone involved in theatre. It consists of monographs on influential figures, studies of movements and ideas in theatre, as well as primary material consisting of theatre-related documents, performing editions of plays in English, and English translations of plays from various vital theatre traditions worldwide.

Franc Chamberlain

ACKNOWLEDGEMENTS

This book has evolved over the years and many friends and colleagues have helped to shape it. Thank you to Roger Savage for being the perfect supervisor, to Peter Thomson for convincing me that it was worth pursuing further, and to Michael Walton for seeing me through the final stages. Randall Stevenson and Vassiliki Kolocotroni have fuelled many a discussion that has, I am sure, found its way into this book.

The editors at Harwood Academic Publishers have provided invaluable advice and in Franc Chamberlain I have found an editor with great knowledge, sensitivity and a terrific sense of humour.

The illustrations are reproduced, by courtesy of the National Library of Scotland, Edinburgh, from volumes of *The Mask* in their possession.

I am grateful to Ellen T. M. Craig for her kind permission to publish the illustrations.

LIST OF PLATES

FOREWORD

A review of *Romeo and Juliet* performed by the Harvey Company on their provincial tour in the autumn of 1890 concluded that in the role of Mercutio 'Gordon Craig has all the personal charm of his gifted mother, and, it is evident, heredity has done its part in endowing him with historic gifts of no common order'. Had the reviewer any inkling of Craig's subsequent career and the tactlessness of drawing attention to the unorthodox nature of Ellen Terry's domestic arrangements, he might also have pointed to the influence of Craig's father, E. W. Godwin, best known as an architect but also capable of turning his hand to the design of theatrical settings and costumes and even the production of plays. Craig was steeped in theatre from all sides and from an early age, but the combination of a theatrical childhood and this celebrated Terry charm seems to have fomented an innate quality for self-destruction to match his dramatic gifts. One result of what has often been seen as a lack of commitment to anybody but himself is the ambivalent reputation he has subsequently enjoyed.

Few of those who worked with him or have subsequently studied his writings and designs have felt neutral about Craig. Either they resented the airy arrogance with which he could make impractical and impossible demands or they have apologised for those impractical demands, as indeed did Stanislavsky, and pointed out that it was Craig himself who almost smugly labelled himself as an 'impossible'. In theatre history, no less than in his working career, he has attracted detractors and disciples (or 'zealots' as Olga Taxidou calls them). Those who have written about him in any detail have almost inevitably pitched their tents with the zealots and studied his work for the way it resurrected some of the best aspects of the theatre of the past and looked forward to what Kenneth Tynan described as 'the theatrical millennium'. The singular achievement of this book is that it creates a context for the resurrection of theatrical theatre and locates Craig as one of a number of world influences within that context.

From being a self-exiled eremite – the token Theatre Studies theorist whom nobody ever studies – Craig takes his rightful place here alongside Blake and Whitman, Beardsley and Ricketts, Wilde and Conrad, Evreinov and Meyerhold, Popova and Schlemmer. Craig's style as a graphic artist is not that of some dilettante chipping out woodcuts as bookplates for his friends' Christmas presents. It is, we can now see, part of a fashion in lettering and typography attuned to that of *The Dial*, *The Studio*, or *The Yellow Book*, a product of its age but the product too of one of nature's magazine editors who happened to be devoted to the theatre and its history as much as to publishing.

The jaundiced view of Craig's career points to a desultory ten years as an actor, an even more desultory ten or so as a director and sometime designer, followed by half a century in the wilderness during which he periodically snapped and snarled at the theatrical establishment. The charitable view allows for the conceits and absurdities of the man and looks to the visions of a visual theatre and the breathtaking redefinition of theatre space, light and mood. The accusation of impracticality against Craig is futile. Look rather to the intended resurrection of the great theatre traditions. He may have applied a romantic gloss to what he understood as the performance practice of classical Athens, of Italian comedy or 'the Theatre of the Orient'. He stood nonetheless as a rallying point for all those new voices in France, Germany, Russia and elsewhere for whom the rejection of naturalism was the necessary prelude to dragging the theatre grumbling and creaking into the twentieth century. It took a visual artist to do this – but it took the written word and all those aliases to pass the message on.

A randomly chosen copy of *The Mask*, the issue for January 1911 (Vol. 3, Nos. 7–9), has an actual mask for Arlecchino on the cover and turns out to be devoted as an issue to the Commedia dell'Arte with an incidental review of the use of Craig's screens by Yeats at the Abbey Theatre and a reference to Craig's having 'withdrawn his work for *Macbeth* at Her Majesty's'. Three months earlier Meyerhold had directed Schnitzler's *The Scarf of Columbine* in St Petersburg. He was already into rehearsal for *Harlequin the Marriage-Broker*. Meyerhold and Craig apparently did not meet at this time but they surely knew of one another's work. Craig had been a frequent, if sporadic, visitor to Moscow. His celebrated collaboration with Stanislavsky was to bring four years of preparation to fruition with the opening of the Moscow Arts Theatre *Hamlet* at the end of the year.

Another issue of *The Mask* (Vol. 14, No. 4, October–December 1928), chosen equally at random from the latter end of the periodical's twenty-year life, has advertisements for a magazine called *Old Furniture* and for a series of exhibitions at the Leicester Galleries in Leicester Square including the work of Cézanne, Degas, Epstein, Picasso and Renoir. Among the features inside there is a catalogue of the library of a comedian who died in 1858; a translation of Sabbatini with details of 'how a cloud may be made to descend straight upon the stage with persons inside it' (complete with diagrams); a review of the Folies Bergère; an open letter to Sir Thomas Beecham offering to design an opera for him on the sole condition 'that the entire scheme be British'; book reviews of, amongst other things, Eugene O'Neill's *Lazarus Laughed*, Mozart's letters and a series of woodblock prints of Venice in the year 1500. This is a journal of the living arts in which, for once, theatre claims a proper place.

What emerges from the following monograph is a fresh and immensely valuable view of Craig as a major figure in the Modernist movement. Perhaps at long last he can come to be seen not as the thwarted director who wanted to replace actors with puppets but as one of Britain's desperately few original and provocative artists who happened to want to work through the medium of theatre but found that theatre unwilling or unable to subscribe to his vision. If so, Dr Taxidou will have performed an immense service to the study of the history of the theatre as one art within a gigantic movement in aesthetics.

J. Michael Walton
University of Hull

1

THE MASK: THE PERIODICAL AS A WORK OF ART

By the time the first issue of *The Mask* appeared (March, 1908) Craig had already made a considerable contribution, through his books and essays, to the debates regarding the 'Art of the Theatre', and had established a reputation for himself on the European theatrical scene. *The Mask* came at a time in Craig's professional life when, having made his initial grand, prophetic and apocalyptic gestures, he was ready for more contemplative, analytical and scholarly research into theatre history and practice. *The Mask* stands parallel to Craig's books as their double; as an extended annotation and commentary on Craigian formulations. As such it reveals many of the contradictions and problems that Craig's particular aesthetics encapsulated. The books in their overwhelming and, arguably, over-written form tend to gloss over many of the theoretical entanglements that eventually led Craig to dead-ends and inactivity. Where Craig's books tend to exhibit a typically Modernist quality in hiding their roots and sources and highlighting their 'newness', *The Mask* recreates that bridge that connects Craigian thought with the aestheticist 1890s and helps place it within the philosophical context of Radical Idealism, as the school was interpreted in its imported form from the continent and mainly from Germany. While it links Craig's work with the past, it also locates it amongst the work of his contemporaries in a manner that highlights similarities and differences, and foregrounds respective ideologies. The physical appearance of the journal is vital in this whole venture. As an object *The Mask* is an example of the aesthetics it propagates. The synaesthetic concerns of the 'Yellow 90s' evolve, through its pages, into the Modernist concepts of 'total art', with theatre as their main platform. The Book Beautiful tradition blends with the continental Art Nouveau school. This in turn borrows elements from the pamphlet/ manifesto layout in a unique combination.

The illustrated advertisement/puff for *The Mask* published in its own pages in 1923 and reproduced as plate 30, in many ways reveals the nature, the historical background and the aesthetic ideals of the periodical, which had been running for fifteen years by then, on and off. Published with the subtitle of 'Journal of the Art of the Theatre' it bears little resemblance to other theatre journals of the period. Indeed, it sharply contrasts with most drama and literary magazines published at

THE MASK

THE JOURNAL OF THE ART
OF THE THEATRE.
VOLUME ONE, NUMBER ONE
MARCH 1908.

AFTER THE PRACTISE THE THEORY

GEOMETRY. Beauty.... or Divine Demonstration, knows no confusion. It has the perfect balance. It remains true once and for ever.... needs no proof.... can reveal itself without words or arguments, and when we see i we again see Paradise. It is the dear Heaven. Science,... or Human Demonstration,t continually calling upon proof, trusting in many words, is as a restless Balance which continually rises and falls with the uncertainty of the centuries ... the restless Terror; has become the only Evil.

1. Page 1 of Vol. 1, No. 1, 1908.

the turn of the century. As the advertisement suggests, *The Mask* can be seen as an offspring of the tradition of the Book Beautiful, a notion that sprang out of the aestheticist 1890s. Although *The Mask* was first published in 1908, its physical appearance, its layout and its whole artistic stance compare with the magazines that were conceived some years earlier as part of the Arts and Crafts movement and that later evolved into the main advocates of Art Nouveau. These were mainly fine arts magazines, all very conscious of their image since their basic guiding principle in both their form and their content was one of synaesthesia. For *The Mask* the unifying force for all the arts is provided by the theatre. There is an emphasis on the 'theatrical' quality of the journal itself and not merely of its contents; and it is chiefly this which makes it different from other theatre and literary periodicals of the period. '*The Mask* is so beautiful that even for those ignorant of English it is worth subscribing to it', says another puff.[1] Being a periodical which claims to have reached a synthesis of the arts under Craig's idea of the 'Art of the Theatre', it is mainly meant to be *seen* and not read. Hence the visual aspect of it is vital. In general the way the periodical appears to the eye is consistent with Craig's overall views on performance. In the context of his trying to establish a theory for his idea of 'the art for the theatre', *The Mask* becomes Craig's 'stage', perhaps the only one he could rely on; from it he not only writes on his theories but also demonstrates them visually. In this sense the periodical functions as a *performance*, and, as we shall see, its whole layout reinforces this effect.

The last quarter of nineteenth century Britain's cultural scene was dominated by the Arts and Crafts movement. Arts and crafts were viewed as a common front opposing mass industrial production and historical constraints and realities. The movement encompassed many different trends which had varied historical origins. The Celtic Revival stemming from Scotland and Ireland played a major role, and it was closely connected with Art Nouveau as well, its medieval motifs blending easily with Art Nouveau stylistic tendencies. The emphasis was naturally placed on craftsmanship and artistry, resulting in a great development of areas such as textile and wallpaper design and production and the illustration and production of books, the latter creating a new awareness of factors such as lettering, typography and layout. One result of the concern for well-crafted books was the notion of a periodical used not only to promote the new aesthetic ideology, but to function as an example of it.

---

[1] *The Mask*, Vol. 12, No. 4, p. II, 1927. A considerable number of the advertisements in *The Mask* refer to the periodical itself (both those originally designed for its pages and reprints from other journals favourably reviewing it). The effect smacks of Art Nouveau narcissism. [*The Mask* (Florence, 1908–1929), is quoted here from the reprinted edition (New York, 1967), but the dates given are from the original edition i.e. *The Mask*, Vol. 1, 1908, p. 1.]

The two main resources that provided a theoretical background for the design and general layout of most Arts and Crafts journals of this period were Owen Jones's *Grammar of Ornament*, first published in 1856 (which by 1910 had appeared in nine editions), and Christopher Dresser's *The Art of Decorative Design* (1862). The basic characteristic of both books is that they draw on architecture to provide a theoretical framework. Jones claims that 'all ornament should be based on geometrical construction' and Dresser concludes that 'the basis of all forms is geometry'. In general, architecture is seen as the structuring force that will achieve the unity of all the arts – synaesthesia and unification of the arts being one of the main concerns of the period. This hailing of the discipline of architecture as the archetypal model for art was reinforced by the fact that many architects themselves seemed to be involved in the whole synaesthetic project. As Watkinson writes:

> It was the architects who played the most important part. Mackmurdo and Horne of *The Century Guild*; Voysey, Ashbee and his *Guild of Handicraft*; Baillie Scott, Mackintosh, Godwin, Norman Shaw Blomfield, Lethaby not only played an important part in making the most memorable houses and public buildings of the century, but also in the great attempt at the reunification of all the arts.[2]

To the illustration and design of books, architecture introduces new concepts of the organisation and presentation of the page. The book itself is seen as an ideal material both to portray and to represent this synaesthetic approach. In 1888 under the title of *The Combined Arts* a circular was sent out seeking support to promote these ideals and as a result The Arts and Crafts Exhibition Society, which was formed in 1883, had its first exhibition in The New Gallery, Regent Street. The event was very successful and was imitated on the continent where the movement had already spread.

The roots of the revival of book illustration can be found in the work of William Blake, who is one of the figures Craig frequently refers to in *The Mask*.[3] Blake's blending of text and illustration into an integrated whole, his emphasis on lettering and the very fact that he printed his texts himself, having invented a device for simultaneous

---

[2] Ray Watkinson, *William Morris as Designer* (London, 1967), p. 69. The contributions of William Morris and the British architectural revival to the idea of the Book Beautiful are studied by Watkinson. He quotes William Morris as saying, 'I began printing books with the hope of producing some which would have a definite claim to beauty'.

[3] William Blake is seen by most art critics as a major forerunner of Art Nouveau. For his influence, see Robert Schmutzler, *Art Nouveau*, (London, 1962), pp. 35–47. Blake is quoted or referred to in *The Mask* in the following issues: Vol. 1, pp. 53–54; pp. 212–256; Vol. 3, p. 81; Vol. 4, p. 157, pp. 181–182; Vol. 5, p. 91; Vol. 8, pp. 9–11; Vol. 13, p. 40, p. 46, p. 82; Vol. 14, pp. 11–13, p. 37, p. 130.

2. Design for a stage scene by Edward Gordon Craig, Vol. 1, Nos. 3–4, p. 64b, 1908.

printing of the text and the illustrations from the same plate, make him a forerunner of the Arts and Crafts concept of the Book Beautiful. Periodicals like *The Evergreen* and *The Yellow Book* display a very strong Blakean influence. It was not only Blake's notions of obliterating the distinction between lettering, ornament and illustration and fusing them into a homogeneous ensemble, but also his very style and aesthetic mode which coincided with the aesthetics of the period.

With William Blake on the one hand providing the historical background and architecture on the other providing a theoretical context, a whole tradition of publication of 'beautiful' periodicals started. These usually rotated round a central figure who was overpowering and in complete control of every aspect of design and production. (William Morris with his Kelmscott press is a characteristic and pioneering example of such a figure.) At the same time the periodicals were very conscious of the fact that they were both promoting and representing, through their very physical existence, a particular theory of art and aesthetics. *The Mask* is a continuation of this tradition in its late Art Nouveau phase, proposing theatre as the ultimate art form, and at the same time turning the periodical itself into a kind of 'theatre'.

The Mask's connection through Craig with the new type of periodical at the turn of the century and with the more general ideas on design is two-fold. E. W. Godwin, Craig's father, was one of the main architects actually to give shape to the period's notions of design. He was the architect of Whistler's White House and also decorated the interior of Oscar Wilde's house. He was also interested in theatre and staged Greek plays in open air auditoria. His work on stage design was published in *The Architect* in a series of articles under the general title 'The Architecture and Costume of Shakespeare's Plays'. As early as 1897 Craig collected these articles and later published them as a series in the pages of *The Mask*. Godwin's notions of architectural design were to provide a framework that would help shape *The Mask*. Apart from the influence of Godwin, which can be traced on many levels both in Craig's theories and in the actual physical appearance of *The Mask*, Craig himself was involved with a number of periodicals published at the turn of the century all of which were in the Periodical – Beautiful tradition, though none was specifically devoted to any aspect of the theatre.

In 1898 Craig published *The Page*, which was primarily devoted to fine arts. *The Page* was very much within the context of the journals of the period: it was more or less a one-manned journal, short-lived (1898–1901) and was full of wood-engravings, sketches and designs, with contributions from some of the same people who wrote or designed for most of the fine art periodicals of the period (Will Rothenstein, Henry Irving, Max Beerbohm, Martin Shaw). Although *The Page* was not a theatre journal, it is interesting to see how Craig's notion of performance creeps in. He writes in his 'diary', *Index to the Story of My Days*:

> Being an actor, though now no longer acting, the need for appearing before the public was still curiously strong in me. Had I been training as a painter, or in any art and craft, I should certainly not have come out prematurely in any publication like *The Page*. But being actor-trained, I could only do my bit on a public stage – a curtain had to rise at a certain hour on a certain date, to rouse me. This curtain rising was the first number of *The Page*. Only a few copies were printed, and fewer were sold. I worked hard at its creation – many woodcuts, slight text. It appeared from 1898 to 1901 – it cost next to nothing – only life.[4]

It is characteristic that Craig never refers to *The Page* in *The Mask*. To pursue the theatrical conceit: as a dress rehearsal, having fulfilled its purpose of providing a preparatory stage, it is later forgotten about. In 1908 the pages of *The Mask*, almost literally and no longer metaphorically, provide him with a stage. He edits, illustrates and writes most of it assuming numerous pseudonyms, creating characters for each one, just like an actor. It is in the pages of *The Mask*, possibly more than in any other arena, where Craig's 'Artist of the Theatre' – the director – can take shape and exercise his power unequivocally.

Apart from editing and publishing *The Page*, Craig was involved with many journals that initially functioned as advocates of the Arts and Crafts movement and gradually evolved into the main exponents of Art Nouveau. His collaboration with these journals was mainly in the areas of design, illustration and advertising. The journals included *The Dial* (1889–97), *The Dome* (1897–1900), *The Savoy* (1896), *The Studio* (1893–1936).[5]

---

[4] Edward Gordon Craig (EGC), *Index to The Story of My Days* (London, 1957), p. 191. John Russell Taylor, talking about the layout of this particular book in *The Art Nouveau Book in Britain* (Edinburgh, 1966), p. 147, refers to it as 'the last direct issue of the Nineties book'. The book itself is not genuinely a diary as it was written in retrospect and appears more in the form of recollections. *The Page* (1898–1901), in line with the spirit of the journals of the time announces itself as 'a publication in which one finds original Poems, Prose, Music, Woodcuts, Posters, Portraits, Bookplates, and other curious things'. *The Page* (1898–1901), British Library, Department of Printed Books, 2 Vols.

[5] The most influential British periodicals at the turn of the century were:
The Dial, London, 1889–1897
The Dome, London, 1898–1900
The Evergreen, Edinburgh, 1895–1897
The Pageant, London, 1896–1897
The Savoy, London, 1896
The Studio, London, 1893–1936
The Yellow Book, London, 1894–1897.

Of these the most long-lived and influential was *The Studio*,[6] creating imitators both in Britain and on the continent that were themselves later to influence *The Mask*.

The key figure of *The Studio* was Charles Holme: a cosmopolitan like Craig who had travelled quite a lot before deciding to publish a magazine. Both *The Studio* and *The Mask* had an international character, something which makes them stand out from other periodicals of the time. Craig's initial idea was to publish his journal in German and Dutch as well as English. *The Studio* actually achieved something like this and had a French edition with a resumé of the text translated. Despite its international appeal it was mainly a European periodical, creating in a sense a whole school of imitators such as *Art und Dekoration* in Germany, and *Ver Sacrum* in Vienna. The international character of *The Studio* helped give shape to it, not only in terms of its contents but also its layout and overall aesthetic image. Appealing to a variety of audiences with different cultural backgrounds, it was mainly a visual magazine rather than a literary one. The visual aspect was promoted not only out of necessity (given the periodical's subject), but also because through it an aesthetic statement was being made on the unity of the arts. The way the idea of the periodical was conceived in 1893 is similar to Craig's initial inspiration for *The Mask*. Bryan Holme writes:

> It was during Charles Holme's trips abroad that the idea of an art magazine crystallised around his recurring observation that the chief barrier between countries was language, and his belief that the more the culture of one part of the world could be brought 'visually' to the attention of another, the greater the chance of international understanding and peace.[7]

With this belief Holme's *Studio* managed to override linguistic barriers and spread over Europe, forming a network of periodicals within the same aesthetic framework. *The Mask* formed part of this network and in

---

At the same time the most important continental periodicals were:
  Art et Decoration, Paris, 1897
  Die Kunst, Munich, 1899–1945
  Mir Isskustva, St. Petersburg, 1895–1904
  Pan, Berlin, 1895–1900
  Simplizissimus, Munich, 1896
  Ver Sacrum, Vienna, 1898; Leipzig, 1899–1903.
For further analysis and detailed index of periodicals see Robert Schmutzler, note 3.
[6] *The Studio* was the most long-lived of all these periodicals, being published until 1963 under the same title and continuing from 1964 to 1967 under the title of *Studio International*.
[7] See Bryan Holme, *The Studio: A Bibliography. The First Fifty Years* 1893–1943 (London, 1978), p. 5.

its turn aimed at creating a network of its own, proposing the 'Art of the Theatre' as its structuring unit. As Craig's son Edward Craig writes:

> It seemed to him that *The Mask* was the most urgent part of his programme to develop first; it would take the most time and depended a lot on other craftsmen. With his own magazine, he wouldn't be lost in Italy – he could keep in contact with his friends throughout the world; and by means of it, he would establish a rallying point for all those setting out in the same direction…away from a derelict art, towards a new form of expression.[8]

The parallel between *The Studio* and *The Mask* – both what they stand for and their overall impact – was noted by critics at the time. Haldane MacFall writes in *The Daily Graphic* in 1908:

> For one among us who is interested in the art of painting a dozen are beckoned to the Theatre; yet, oddly enough, while painting has its several sumptuous magazines, the Theatre has not one worthy of it. From today we are to be rid of the unseemliness, for *The Mask*, from its headquarters in Florence, makes its first appearance here and through-out Europe, to do for the Art of the Theatre what *The Studio* has essayed to do for the arts of painting and of sculpture and of the crafts allied thereto.[9]

Craig's involvement with *The Studio* stretched over 50 years, starting as early as 1898 (though there was a big gap from the early 1900s to the mid 1920s). Consequently the influence of *The Studio* on *The Mask* was not merely an indirect one simply arising from pretty much the same theoretical/sociological background. Craig had published many articles and illustrations in the pages of *The Studio*. It is also significant that in the first issues of *The Studio* Craig appears as a designer of wood plates and wood-cuts and later on as a stage designer and artist of the theatre. In many ways this reflects his gradual attempt to fuse all artisic modes that he had already mastered into an integrated ensemble, under the banner of the 'Art of the Theatre'. In addition *The Studio* is advertised in *The Mask* and it is reviewed favourably in its pages.

Some examples of Craig's work published in *The Studio* illustrate how he moved from the Arts and Crafts tradition to encompass an apparently more Modernist theory of the theatre. In 1898, in a special issue of *The Studio* (No. 8) entitled *Modern Book-Plates and Their Designers*, Craig's work is shown as 'an artist working in the field'. In 1927, his

---

[8] Edward Craig, *Gordon Craig, The Story of his Life* (London, 1968), p. 230.
[9] Quoted in *The Mask*, Vol. 1, No. 8, 1908, p. II, III.

designs are again printed in an issue (No. 128) devoted to *The Woodcut of Today at Home and Abroad*. In the same year he writes an article (in No. 130) entitled *English Designers of Sceneries and Costumes*, where he concentrates mainly on the work of Godwin. The same issue carries some of his stage designs along with others by Bakst, Derain, Goncharova, Grant, Popova, Ricketts and Schlemmer. Craig's work also appears in 1931 (No. 149) in an issue under the general title *Modern Book Illustration in Great Britain and America* together with the work of Beardsley and Whistler. In 1951 (No. 238) *The Studio* publishes more of Craig's designs in an issue tracing the history of design in the theatre. Designs by Inigo Jones, Galliari, Derain, Ricketts and Bakst are published in the same issue.

It is interesting to see how *The Studio* groups Craig with Beardsley and Whistler with reference to book illustration. *The Yellow Book* was one of the most influential periodicals of its kind. It grew out of the style-conscious 1890s with the figure of Beardsley as its centre. Although it was short-lived, its impact was great and it gathered some of the most important artistic figures of the time. Will Rothenstein (who contributed to Craig's *The Page*), Beerbohm Tree (whom Craig admired and on whom he later wrote articles, in *The Mask*) and Whistler (whom Craig often quoted in the pages of *The Mask*) all appear in *The Yellow Book*. It was also the first magazine of the period to 'display' itself consciously and narcissistically through its pages. This effect is achieved both through the layout and the designs by Beardsley. His fascination with characters from the Commedia dell'Arte and especially with Pierrot give the journal a performance-like quality, with issues being introduced by a Pierrot raising a stage curtain, illustrations of Commedia characters preparing for a performance etc. This effect, though, which is later continued in Beardsley's second periodical *The Savoy*, does not reach the degree of integration which is later to characterise *The Mask*. The distinction between text and illustration is still quite rigid. Craig manages to combine both, fusing them through his Arts and Crafts designer background and his theatrical one.

The other character with whom Craig is grouped in the pages of *The Studio* is Charles Ricketts. Ricketts also published a periodical at the turn of the century, *The Dial* (1889). On the cover he prints wood-cut vignettes in the style of William Blake, who is also quoted at the beginning of the second issue. (Craig also quotes Blake often in *The Mask*: see note 3. As mentioned earlier, Blake is considered to be the predecessor of Art Nouveau book design and illustration, obliterating the barriers between the literary and the visual aspects of text.) Reprinted issues of *The Dial* are advertised in the pages of *The Mask*, which is significant since in general Craig accepted advertisements from other journals only if he respected their work and considered them serious.

He did not have to agree with their overall views on theatre, but what always counted as a criterion was the quality of the publication of the journal. On the whole the advertising pages of *The Mask* carried as many advertisements from fine arts journals as from literary and theatrical ones.

Another magazine with which Craig had worked before starting *The Mask* was *The Dome* (1898–1900).[10] The first issue starts with an epigram about architecture, very much in the spirit of the age:

> Help us, O great Architect,
> Sure foundations here to lay,
> Though before thy shrine we slay
> Not one ox with garlands deck'd.
> As we carve for thee a throne,
> Guide the chisel o'er the stone,
> Guide it, O great Architect.[11]

Just as God is seen as an architect, architecture itself is viewed to be the highest art form, structuring and ordering all other arts. This concept of architecture providing a paradigm for any form of art runs through *The Mask*, but is slightly altered. To the geometrical conception and organisation of the page most of these periodicals share, *The Mask* adds the purely Art Nouveau mode of fluidity and plasticity, again blending the two modes. Although most of the journals at the turn of the century flirt with Art Nouveau with varying degrees of commitment, the distinctive features (flowing movement, asymmetry, the self-reflexive curving line bound together in a closed graphic form) of the movement prevail slightly later on the continent in periodicals like *Ver Sacrum* (1898–1903) and *The Mask*.

Craig was very much involved with the publication of *The Dome* as he designed the poster for it. This is done in a very Art Nouveau style and it is interesting that he undertook an advertisement as seriously as the wood-cuts and other prints he did for the magazine. Of course this is the period when advertisements themselves are gaining artistic status, and Craig shows no reluctance at all to connect his name with them. Later almost all the opening and closing pages of *The Mask* will be full of advertisements, all carefully designed and intergrated aesthetically with the general image of the periodical.

---

[10] Craig's collaboration with *The Dome* mainly consisted of illustrations, designs and advertisements. His most important work in *The Dome* was: *Dumas Papa*, a wood-cut, Vol. 11, No. 4, p. 63; *A Poster and A Pictorial Post-Card*, both from wood blocks, Vol. 11, No. 6, p. 253, p. 254.
[11] *The Dome*, Vol. 1, No. 1, 1898, p. 1.

While all these things were going on in Britain, some distance away yet another periodical was being published. This was *Mir Isskustva*, (*The World Of Art*) (1895–1904), which was published in St. Petersburg by Sergei Diaghilev and his group. Again this was in the tradition of the one-man periodical promoting the unification of the arts. Diaghilev himself was not unaware of the progress made in the field in Great Britain, and indeed there is a letter from him to D. S. McColl asking for an article on Beardsley.[12] Bakst, who later designed for the Russian Ballet, was greatly influenced by Beardsley. Diaghilev himself had considerable experience in book design and production. In 1900 he edited the Imperial Theatre's year book which he turned into a Book Beautiful, making it 'fuller and more splendid than it had ever been before – a landmark in the history of Russian book production'.[13] The innovation that *Mir Isskustva* was to introduce was that, apart from advocating a general theory of aesthetics, it actually gave practical shape to it in the form of the Russian Ballet. Diaghilev, the central figure of both the periodical and the ballet, uses *Mir Isskustva* as his first 'stage' and then proceeds to channel all his concepts on the unification of the arts into the Russian Ballet. In doing this he creates a whole new notion of dance and performance in general. Craig wanted to achieve the same thing – he wanted a whole new theatre, not just the theory for one, to spring out of the pages of *The Mask*, though he lacked the luck, the backers, the colleagues and the theoretical framework that would allow him to carry this through.

Whether Craig had actually seen copies of *Mir Isskustva* before starting *The Mask* is not quite clear, as he never refers to the periodical in *The Mask*. It is most probable though, as it was quite famous throughout Europe and as *The Mask* itself was sold in Moscow. Certainly Craig became very familiar with the work of Diaghilev and the Russian Ballet and often reviews their performances in the pages of *The Mask*, but always with a slight tone of bitterness (perhaps because Diaghilev had moved from the periodical to form his own company). He writes of the Russian Ballet:

> It is a state organization; its pocket money over a million roubles, that is to say, over one hundred thousand pounds a year. Its founders and supporters are not impelled by a great love of the nobility of art, but they wisely recognise that a great state governed by men instead of by mice and women needs a great ballet, a great Opera House, a great Theatre.[14]

---

[12] Richard Buckle, *In Search of Diaghilev* (London, 1955), p. 55.
[13] Ibid., p. 12.
[14] *The Mask*, Vol. 7, No. 1, 1914, p. 65.

The Mask
1 9 0 8

3. *Isadora Duncan Dancing* by Edward Gordon Craig, Vol. 1, No. 6, p. 126b, 1908.

Given this attitude towards Diaghilev it is highly unlikely that Craig would acknowledge *Mir Isskustva*. And even if he had not actually seen the Russian magazine, he most certainly read about it in another journal – *The Imprint*. *The Imprint* was launched in 1913 and Craig had contacts both with the periodical and its editor, J. H. Mason, as there is correspondence between the two journals. Like *The Mask*, it functions as a link between Arts and Crafts journals and those of the new movement on the continent. It does this more consciously than *The Mask*, as it is indeed chiefly concerned with matters of printing, typography and book publication in general. It heralds itself as a true successor of the William Morris tradition and the very first issue boasts a frontispiece from a colour print by William Blake. Being a periodical directly dealing with matters of printing and production, *The Imprint* cites *Mir Isskustva* as a fine example of magazine production. Within the first months of its publication it presents a long article on *Mir Isskustva*, praising its contents and its overall layout. Alex Bakshy writes in *The Imprint*:

> In the domain of pictorial arts the new movement was led by the magazine *Mir Isskustva* which gathered round itself a group of gifted Russian artists. ... It led to an introduction of considerable improvements in commercial printing and gave birth to some artistic publications, which, though not quite supreme as works of the printer's art, yet are marked with much taste and show great care given to their production.[15]

The last sentence of that quotation reflects *The Imprint's* own magisterial attitude, as it basically considers itself the authority on matters of publication and good taste in general. This is an attitude from which *The Mask* does not escape either. The same article on *Mir Isskustva* ends with an engraving by Craig conspicuously entitled *The Mask of Envy*.[16] Perhaps the editor read *The Mask* and knew of Craig's feelings towards Diaghilev!

A month later the two editors, Craig and Mason, were to meet at Weimar at the invitation of Count Kessler, who was setting up a new press there. The two men discussed their magazines and each wrote up his recollections in the editorial pages of his periodical. Mason writes:

> In Weimar I met Mr. Gordon Craig who is doing woodcuts for the Cranach Press... We got talking about *The Mask* and to my stricture Mr. Craig replied by just inviting me to go to Florence and look after it.

---

[15] *The Imprint*, Vol. 1, No. 1 (London, 1913), pp. 10–17.
[16] Ibid., p. 17. *The Mask of Envy* by EGC in *The Imprint* is a reprint of the original which first appeared in *The Mask*, Vol. 1, Nos. 3–4, 1908, p. 90.

As to the type, well all that is necessary is for someone to make them a present of a good type – this is an invitation – and *The Mask* will soon begin to shape itself into a good piece of typography. *The Mask* offers a splendid opportunity with its woodcuts – fascinating reproductions of old and modern drawings of rare interest and no little beauty. But technical knowledge of the manner in which the books were produced is indispensable, if their full possibilities are to be developed.[17]

The Mask responds to this patronizing attitude of *The Imprint* in an article by Craig where he (perhaps ironically) accuses *The Imprint* of being so obsessed with matters of form and style that it neglects the quality of its contents:

And it finds fault with *The Mask* which it says is the work of 'amateur printers'.... In fact *The Imprint* looks first at the polish on the gun and afterwards tests its firing capacity.[18]

The Imprint was first published in 1913, which means it was already too late for it to have any determining influence on *The Mask*. It is more a case of analogy with *The Mask*, and the comparison serves to bring out their two, very distinct, aesthetic positions. *The Imprint*, being a purist magazine, remains very much within the British school of Art Nouveau, emphasizing strict geometrical design, clear lines, and an overall simplicity. *The Mask*, on the other hand moves on from this tradition and in many ways typifies continental Art Nouveau. Compared with the more strict and geometrical British tradition, its continental counterpart appeared indulgent and narcissistic; this combined with his own sometimes eccentric views on design proved the perfect setting for Craigian notions on theatricality.

Another important factor to bear in mind is that Craig was mostly working on his own and that he had to face great financial difficulties. Though magazines like *The Imprint* may have focused on one person, that person had a team of skilled people supporting him. Publishing the magazine in Florence did not help the situation either, making it difficult for Craig to acquire different kinds of fonts. However, Craig managed to use what was locally available without changing his elaborate style. His son Edward writes:

The format of *The Mask* was governed by the size of the paper, which was handmade, cheap, and came from near-by Fabriano. The typography

---

[17] Ibid., p. 95. In the same number, p. 121, J. H. Mason reviews A *Living Theatre* by EGC and criticizes it along the same lines.
[18] *The Mask*, Vol. 6, No. 2, 1913, pp. 181–182.

4. The Arena Goldoni – Mr Craig's open-air theatre in Florence, Vol. 2, Nos. 1–3, p. 33a, 1909.

was dependent on what founts of type the printers had to hand. The firm of Morandi was able to produce a small quantity of Elzivere, which pleased him immensely.[19]

Despite the difficulites and the limited resources available the appearance of a typical *Mask* page was very impressive indeed. Whatever limitations were imposed on its production they didn't affect Craig's overwhelming and excessive sense of design. This is at its most apparent in the first issues of the periodical. Leaving almost no blank space, its pages seem packed with text and illustrations. Following the plant-like imagery of Art Nouveau Craig introduces each new paragraph with the drawing of a leaf. In general the overall appearance of each issue depended, to a certain extent, on its contents. The issues devoted to the study of the Commedia dell'Arte, for example, were covered in designs of Commedia masks, some reproductions and others by Craig himself. The same principle shapes those issues concerned with Oriental theatre. There Craig reproduces illustrations either from other scholarly books or from manuscripts. These aspects do not only determine the contents of the periodical but also affect its physical appearance and, to a certain degree, how it is approached by its readership. The Commedia issues, for example, extend the characteristics of that Italian theatre to the way the page is formatted and consequently read. Paragraphs are abruptly interspersed with drawings, pieces of text are laid out in diagramatic form, in combinations and fusions that help three-dimentionalize its pages. The final volumes of *The Mask* (Nos. 12, 13, 14) are the more conservative and strictly structured ones. These coincide with Craig's 'historicist' phase, as he tries to find past equivalents for much of the Modernist experimentation at the time. In these issues Craig, with the help of his son Edward, prints designs of old theatres, maps of Italian cities and devotes many pages of his journal to historical and encyclopaedic research. These seeming extreme phases of the periodical are bridged by the middle issues, which display yet another ingenious combination of necessity and aesthetic choice. Due to financial difficulties volumes 8 and 9 were reduced to a pamphlet form. This was directly in line with much pamphlet and manifesto printing going on at the time (1915–17). The layout and overall design in these appears to be much clearer and sharper than the previous ones. Still keeping in line with the magazine – beautiful tradition, these issues of *The Mask* share the more geometric, harsher elements of the pamphlet, with the design existing chiefly to promote the 'message' rather than for its own sake.

Whether in its excessively indulgent or in its more encyclopaedic form, the various sections of the periodical are consistent and clearly

---

[19] Edward Craig, *Gordon Craig*, see note 8, pp. 231–232.

marked throughout its issues. Framed at the beginning and at the end by advertisements the main core of the journal ends with the sections 'Book Reviews', 'Foreign Notes' and 'Editorial Notes'. These appear in the same place and bear the same stylistic signals.

Even though the *The Mask* was published in Florence its pages were full of advertisements from all over Europe, advertising being an aspect of *The Mask* that Craig worked hard on. The advertisements were always incorporated with the general layout and aesthetic stance of the periodical. *The Mask* would advertise everything, from restaurants to Arts and Crafts exhibitions on in Europe. There was no clear-cut advertising policy as long as the advertisements blended with the periodical as a whole. They always occupied the first and last few pages, creating a curtain-like effect before and after the main contents-performance of the periodical. Edward Craig writes about the way his father chose what to advertise:

> One day he came upon T. de Marinis in his bookshop in the Via Vecchietti, and they became friends. When Craig found that De Marinis had a large store of the blocks which he had used to illustrate his wonderful catalogues of incunabula and early Italian literature, he struck a bargain with him: free advertising space in *The Mask* in exchange for the use of any of these old blocks for illustrations. They would make excellent "padding", and "Allen Carric" – another Craig *nom de plume* – could always write something about them.[20]

The main subject of the advertising was of course Craig himself. Hiding behind the editorial pseudonym of John Semar, Craig promotes his ideas and his own image notoriously through *The Mask*. There are many instances of him writing letters to himself under different names. This mirroring effect of *The Mask* is something which also makes it differ from traditional periodicals. The modesty and strictness of the Arts and Crafts magazines is almost totally missing from *The Mask*.

The Mask emerges from the British Arts and Crafts and Art Nouveau movements, but its overall layout and general aesthetic stance is a result of the fusion between its traditional British background and the newer continental modes. It was not by sheer chance that Florence was chosen for the headquarters of *The Mask*. British Art Nouveau is a reaction in favour of spareness and simplicity after the excesses that preceded it, whereas Continental Art Nouveau is a further elaboration. Continental Art Nouveau is based on asymmetry created by the sinuous line, trying to break away from any notion of framework. British Art Nouveau, on the other hand, with its slightly curved surfaces and lines,

---

[20] Ibid., p. 232.

S T A G E   S C E N E R Y .

If scenery must be used when performing plays it is better to employ a simple background rather than an elaborate one, and to create this you do better to employ a few lines than many broken ones. Thus the simplest background is the unclouded sky and a plain wall is almost as simple.

For a perfect drama, should it be possible some day to write one, the sky must be used as the only worthy background. The manager or producer reveals his estimate of the value of Shakespeare by the elaboration or simplicity of his background.

The above design, (a wood engraving of the 16th century), is an example of a simple background. The lines are but little broken. In no way do they frustrate the dramatic intention.

Scenery has to speak as well as the actors, but it is better when it says only that which is necessary.

Here we see that we need to have it explained that it is an interior, a prison. It is a gentleman's prison, says the floor, but except for the slightly emphatic floor, window and stone bench the scene says nothing ; it leaves the stage to the Dramatist and the Actors.

Learn the essentials of stage scenery, and you will in time learn the essentials of Drama.

G. C.

5. An example of page layout: 'Stage Scenery' by Gordon Craig. Vol. 3, Nos. 1–3, p. 14b, 1910.

is mainly concerned with the arrangement of spaces *within* a particular geometric framework. As John Russell Taylor writes 'continental Art Nouveau is a reaction against form itself, while British Art Nouveau is a search for essential form by the stripping-away of inessentials.'[21] Continental Art Nouveau is considered by many critics to be a decadent style because of its ever-increasing self-indulgence, while British Art Nouveau, with its clear lines and flat surfaces is seen to express the more pure and orthodox style. *The Mask* manages to combine both modes, though not always smoothly. Although it acknowledges the past tradition and draws greatly on architectural and geometrical notions of design this is all portrayed in a framework that is highly self-indulgent. *The Mask* is elaborately patterned, fusing text and illustration in an ensemble. This combination is not merely geometrical but flowing, to the extent that words, designs and illustrations alike are blended in total fluidity. There are instances of a text being treated as an illustration and an illustration being portrayed as a text. The pages of *The Mask* are often, if anything, filled to excess.

On the whole, *The Mask* takes its shape more in the mode of the 'decadent' Art Nouveau than in the lines of the smooth British tradition. The periodical it resembles most in terms of layout and overall aesthetic stance is indeed a continental one: *Ver Sacrum*. *Ver Sacrum* was published in Vienna in 1898 and lent its name to the whole Art Nouveau movement there. From the very first issue it refers to William Blake and praises *The Studio*, acknowledging the British contribution. *Ver Sacrum* was published mainly by Klimt and Hoffmann, both painters/designers and not architects. As a result, in the format of their periodical, the severe geometrical form gives way to the gliding lasso-like line. The blending of text design and illustration into an integrated unity, creating a very strong visual effect, is comparable to that of *The Mask*. It is most probable that Craig had seen copies of *Ver Sacrum* if not in Britain or Florence, then possibly in Weimar when he was visiting Count Kessler. Count Kessler himself was interested in starting a new press, so he was very much aware of all the publications in Europe. Craig is more likely to have seen *Ver Sacrum* as early as 1903, before he started to work on *The Mask*, when he first went to Germany at the invitation of Count Kessler, to work with Otto Brahm of the Lessing Theatre. On his way to Berlin he stopped off at Weimar where he 'met many delightful people, among them Henry Van de Velde, the architect, the painter von Hofmann (sic), and poets and musicians'.[22] Both men were working on periodicals at the time. Van de Velde was working on *Pan* and Hoffmann

---

[21] See John Russell Taylor, note 6, pp. 17–20. He examines the differences between the British and the continental Art Nouveau styles.
[22] EGC, *Index to the Story of My Days*, pp. 251–252.

6. Examples of announcements, Vol. 4, No. 1, p. 80a, 1911.

on *Ver Sacrum*. Much later in his *Index to the Story of My Days* Craig acknowledges the influence in his own European project, *The Mask*:

> It was here in Berlin that I bent myself towards creating *The Mask*, so that through that publication I might in time come to change the whole theatre – not plays alone, but playing, sceneries, construction of theatres – the whole thing.[23]

To compare *The Mask* with other contemporary literary and dramatic periodicals of the period in English is to highlight their striking differences in contents and overall appearance. Periodicals like *The English Review* and *Poetry and Drama* see theatre as an extension of literature. As a result the journals themselves place all the emphasis on the written word and none on the possible visual impact. Matters of lettering, typography, illustration are of little interest to them as aesthetic qualities and are viewed only in their functional dimensions. On the other hand, the Craigian notion of theatre sees it as the epitome of total art, the absolute synaesthetic experience. Craig's attempt to formulate what he called a 'self-reliant' theatre, free from literature, is reflected in *The Mask*. In this respect it shares common ground with fine arts periodicals of the period, rather than literary ones, since it is the former that strive at the unification of the arts and present their magazines as tangible embodiments of this ideal. The Art Nouveau concepts of ornamentation, exhibitionism and self-reflexive narcissism are parallel to the Craigian idea of stressing the artificiality of the theatrical praxis. In this way Art Nouveau provides the framework, sets the stage, for *The Mask* to present/perform Craig's theatricalities.

The *Mask* was indeed Craig's permanent performance. He worked on it more systematically and for a longer period (1908–1929) than any other project in his life. The very physicality and concreteness of a periodical provided him with a permanency that a theatrical performance – as it turned out – could not. His attempt to formulate his theory of 'a new theatre', 'the theatre of the future', is not only expressed in the contents of *The Mask*, but is also in a sense enacted through its overall visual effect. Fusing Arts and Crafts notions of periodical design and publication with the more elaborate Continental Art Nouveau ones, and filtering through them his notions of theatricality, Craig sets *The Mask* up as a stage, a stage that heralds 'the theatre of the future' and at the same time acts as a paradigm of it.

---

[23] Ibid., p. 268.

2

THE MASK AND LATE NINETEENTH-CENTURY AESTHETICS: SYNAESTHESIA, PHANTASMAGORIA, THEATREMANIA

Within the project of Modernity theatre acquires a privileged position. Its synaesthetic qualities, its religious undertones, its forging of communal identities make it both the 'grand metaphor' for the concerns of the period and the perfect paradigm for the fusion of aesthetics, philosophy and politics (a central Modernist preoccupation). *The Mask* appears as one of the first journals – if indeed not the very first – to locate theatre within such a project. A model of theatre transpires throughout its pages that encapsulates the 'ideal' of totality, as this was expressed in the various versions of the 'total work of art' at the turn of the century. In this context, *The Mask* is within a specific philosophical tradition; one that has its roots in late Romanticism, spans the anxieties of the *fin-de-siecle* and finally reaches the ramifications of Modernism. As an extension of the Arts and Crafts magazine tradition, it results from the blending of English 1890s aestheticism and parallel European movements such as German Idealism and Russian Symbolism. Determined to expose its theoretical origins, *The Mask*, throughout all its issues, pays tribute to figures like Nietzsche, Schopenhauer, Blake, Wagner and Whitman. *The Mask* assimilates and appropriates, for Craig's own purposes, all these influences into a tapestry that not only clearly identifies its sources, but also heralds its role in the later more Modernist context.

The Nietzschean Cult

> Nietzsche has had an English sale such as he could hardly have anticipated in his most ecstatic moments, and in company he would not have expressly chosen.[1]

Wyndham Lewis's observation in *Blast* epitomizes the British response to Nietzsche and in general to late nineteenth-century German thought. By 1915, when he wrote, that response had started to fade, mainly due

---

[1] *Blast*, Vol. 2, No. 1, 1915, p. 1. For a further analysis of Wyndham Lewis's view of the 'Nietzschean Cult' see, 'Nietzsche as Vulgarizer' in his *The Art of Being Ruled* (1926), rpt in *Wyndham Lewis, An Anthology of his Prose*, ed. E. W. F. Tomlin (London, 1969).

to the First World War, which was seen by many as 'Nietzsche in action';[2] and Lewis belongs to a younger generation of artist/writers who, in the light of the war, became quite critical towards the 'Nietzschean cult'. Nevertheless it was a cult that had an overwhelming impact on the British artistic scene of the late nineteenth century.[3]

Nietzsche made his entry into late Victorian society like 'a bull in a china shop', to paraphrase a metaphor used by one of his reviewers at the time. Indeed, every periodical of any importance between 1896 and 1914 (when World War I started) published articles or reviews of Nietzsche. *The Mask* formed part of this trend, presenting the work of Nietzsche in various ways throughout its pages. It is also significant that the first journals and newspapers to pay any attention to Nietzsche were Scottish ones. 'Celtic Twilight' being one of the movements that was gaining in aesthetic awareness, it was open to new ideas. The Scot John Davidson was to publish the first articles on Nietzsche in *The Speaker* (1891) and in *The Glasgow Herald* (1893). Perhaps it is not unconnected with this that *The Glasgow Herald* was one of the first newspapers to praise the work of Craig and to follow favourably the history of *The Mask*.

The Collected Works of Friedrich Nietzsche appeared in 1896 and in the same year *The Savoy* published three articles on Nietzsche by Havelock Ellis, the first major reviews of his works in English. *The Savoy*, very much part of the Arts and Crafts and Art Nouveau movements, found Nietzschean aesthetics comparable to its own. It formed part of the network of periodicals whose very physical appearance exemplified their aesthetic stance; a network which *The Mask* was later to join with advertisements of *The Savoy* appearing on its pages.

---

[2] Nietzsche's polemic prose, aphoristic and visionary was seen as theoretically justifying much of the horror created by World War I. Passages like the following from *The Gay Science* were seen as heralding the Futurist idea of war as 'the hygiene of the world'. Nietzsche writes:

I greet all the signs that a more manly, warlike age is coming, which will, above all, bring valour again into honour! For it has to prepare the way for a yet higher age, and assemble the force which that age will one day have need of – that age which will carry heroism into knowledge and wage war for the sake of ideas and their consequences. To that end many brave pioneers are needed now...: men who know how to be silent, solitary, resolute,...who have an innate disposition to seek in all things that which must be overcome in them: men to whom cheerfulness, patience, simplicity and contempt for the great vanities belong just as much as do generosity in victory and indulgence towards the little vanities of the defeated:...men with their own festivals, their own work-days, their own days of mourning, accustomed to and assured in command and equally ready to obey when necessary, equally proud in the one case as in the other, equally serving their own cause: men more imperilled, men more fruitful, happier men!
See *The Gay Science*, (1882) trans. Walter Kaufmann (New York, 1974), p. 283.

[3] See Patrick Bridgwater, *Nietzsche in Anglosaxony. A Study of Nietzsche's Impact on English and American Literature* (Leicester, 1972), chapters 1–10.

Nietzsche appealed to the intellectual late-Victorian who was rebelling against the rigidity of his society, but still remained within the safety of his upper-class elitism. In a lecture given to the Fabian Society in 1896, entitled 'Frederick (sic) Nietzsche: a Child in a China-shop', Hubert Bland portrays an example of a typically English response:

> We must not take our child in the china-shop with too great seriousness, for he is a sturdy urchin whose very naughtiness comes from a superfluity of red corpuscles in the blood. If he does shatter our delicate Dresden shepherdesses...there be so much less left for the housemaid to dust. And when we have swept away the pieces...we may perhaps bring ourselves to realise that our treasures were worthless rubbish after all.[4]

Nietzsche is seen as an *enfant terrible*, a curiosity, whose 'naughtiness' is not harmful as long as it is defused and appropriated within the late-Victorian context, a context that reads any notion of subversiveness in Nietzsche as a form of upper-class eccentricity. In a society where ethics and morals were elevated to philosophical world views, Nietzsche's position against morality is easily appropriated by the anti-Victorian intellectual. At the same time, Nietzsche's vehement accusations against democracy and 'modern' politics render him harmless. In the sense that Modernity is seen as a process of democratisation, mass production, industrialisation, and levelling of class barriers Nietzsche is seen as an opponent of it. Edward Garnett writes in *The Outlook* in 1899:

> It is because Nietzsche challenges Modernity, because he stands and faces the ·modern democratic rush...because he opposes a creative aristocratic ideal to negate the popular will...that he is of such special significance.[5]

On the other hand however, Nietzsche seemed particularly attractive to the radical strand of British aestheticism as seen in the tradition running from William Morris to Oscar Wilde. His blasphemous attacks on Christianity, his anti-humanism, and his elevation of aesthetics into a philosophy made him a champion of Modernity. It is this double-faced character of Nietzsche's work that made him so attractive to British audiences; an attraction that Craig was to later adhere to as well. This ambiguity in the work of Nietzsche would in many ways make him a leading proponent of Modernity (an aspect of his work that was to be studied much later by the theoreticians of the Frankfurt School, amongst

---

[4] *Fabian News*, Vol. 8 (5 July, 1898), p. 17. Quoted in Patrick Bridgwater, p. 14.
[5] *The Outlook* (8 July, 1899), pp. 746–8. Quoted in Patrick Bridgwater, p. 15.

others). This aspect of Nietzschean philosophy that at once heralded and abhorred Modernity would appeal to Craig and leave its traces through-out the pages of *The Mask*.

In bridging the gap between late Romanticism and Modernism, the work of Nietzsche and his forerunner Schopenhauer expresses the concerns, the agonies and the fears of the transitional period. It is a period where philosophy focuses on art and aesthetics not only in order to exemplify, but also to formulate its theories. Nietzsche's view of art being (as Gottfried Benn puts it) the last metaphysical activity in European nihilism is one which helped shift and transform philosophy from a theory of rhetoric and logic to a theory of aesthetics. Nietzsche takes this view to its extreme when he claims that 'only as an aesthetic phenomenon are existence and the world justified'.[6]

This elevation of aesthetics into an all-encompassing ideology blended perfectly with 'advanced' thinking in the style-conscious 1890s in Britain. Indeed, as early as 1891 the work of Nietzsche was being reviewed in some sophisticated journals closely involved with new trends in the arts, such as *The Speaker* and *The Savoy*. At the same time, figures such as Walter Pater and Arthur Symons were formulating notions parallel to those of the German thinkers. The Arts and Crafts movement, Herkomer with his synaesthetic experiments and later Craig himself were to develop these theories, following a movement that is parallel to similar ones on the continent. If we read the 'yellow nineties' notions of the 'will to style' as an articulation of Nietzsche's 'will to power', Nietzsche himself can be seen as a figure of the 'yellow nineties'. Both his works and his image as a prophet/philosopher fit the dominant credo of the period, a credo to which Craig subscribed.

The influence of late nineteenth-century theories of aesthetics on the work of Edward Gordon Craig is twofold. On the one hand, he is very much part of the aesthetic consciousness of his age; artistically bred within the Arts and Crafts movement and matured towards the early stages of Modernism, he automatically exposes and exemplifies the concerns of his period. On the other hand, he refers to and quotes Nietzsche[7] and Schopenhauer[8] when formulating his own theories. This is true of his books,[9] but even more obvious in *The Mask*, as he uses it

---

[6] See M. S. Silk and J. P. Stern, *Nietzsche on Tragedy* (Cambridge, 1981), p. 87.

[7] Nietzsche is quoted or referred to in *The Mask* in the following issues: Vol. 1, p. 8, p. 56, p. 141; Vol. 2, pp. 94–95, p. 164; Vol. 4, p. 24; Vol. 5, p. 15, p. 77, pp. 91–92, p. 109, p. 172; Vol. 6, p. 237; Vol. 11, p. 80.
All of the above are citings by Craig himself, either under his name or one of his numerous pseudonyms.

[8] The philosophy of Schopenhauer is analysed by Craig in *The Mask*, Vol. 7, 1914, pp. 1–14.

[9] The influence of Nietzsche in Craig's early books (*The Art of the Theatre*, *Towards a New Theatre*) is of a different order. Like most of the avant-garde of the period, and mainly

as a forum, a theatrical *agon*, exhibiting and contrasting the most important movements of his time.

The nature of Craig's art provides a vital link to the aestheticism of the period. Nietzsche's insistence on all art as essentially *tragic* – a ritualistic theatrical enactment – is the most extreme example of theatre-cum-religion-cum-philosophy. He writes:

> The Dionysiac is the basic ground of the world and the foundation of all existence. In the final analysis, it must be thought of as the eternal and original power that calls into being the entire world of phenomena.[10]

Theatre is considered to be the ultimate art form. The emphasis placed on music or architecture in an attempt to map a structuring force for all art, gradually focuses on theatre as the locus of the synaesthetic ideal. Wagner's notion of the *Gesamtkunstwerk*, developed almost parallel to Nietzsche's work, is a more romantic version of the coming Modernist ideal of the total theatre. Craig's 'Theatre of the Future' provides the transition stage between the two, fusing modes of both periods. At the same time, Craig's main concern was to formulate a theory of the theatre, extensively a theory of aesthetics, one that can now properly be read within the framework of late nineteenth-century philosophy.

A principal concern of the philosophy of the time was to define the 'nature of art' and its relationship, if any, to the world. As Warren E. Steinkraus puts it, art was seen 'as a means to bring back the awe of truth to a philosophy which has become too conscious of itself'.[11] Philosophy is gradually replaced by aesthetics and the work of art itself, moving from a sensuous category it used to fulfil, now occupies a cognitive one, not only explaining the world, but also creating it. Consequently, the notion of art as mimesis is radically questioned. Nature and art are no longer seen in opposition and their boundaries begin to blur. The world itself is seen as a phenomenon, sharing the same qualities as a work of art. Craig writes in an article entitled 'In Defence of the Artist':

> The artist is comprehensible only because his thoughts and actions are natural... At the same time it is because he is part of Nature that he never *imitates Nature*. Why should he?

---

through the influence of Isadora Duncan, Craig shares Nietzsche's fascination with Greek art, but does not mention or quote the German philosopher in his books. In these Craig is mainly interested in presenting his own theories, rather than explicitly stating his sources and influences; something which he does not hesitate to do in *The Mask*.

[10] See M. S. Silk and J. P. Stern, Note 6, p. 88.

[11] Quoted by Warren E. Steinkraus in *Art and Logic in Hegel's Philosophy* (Sussex, 1980), p. 29.

> Whatever he creates will be natural: he of all men has no need to copy.[12]

The fusion of art and life, rendering 'aesthetic life' as the only real life, is a Nietzschean notion filtered to the British scene through the work of Walter Pater and Arthur Symons. Nietzsche writes in *The Gay Science*:

> We should learn from the artists while being wiser than they are in other matters. For with them this subtle power of arranging, of making things beautiful, usually comes to an end where art ends and life begins; but we want to be the poets of our life – first of all in the smallest, most everyday matters.[13]

This perception of the world as a phenomenon in a theoretical framework where the oppositions real/unreal, art/nature no longer exist – a world more or less 'created' by the 'artistic genius' is also stressed by Pater in *The Renaissance*, a work that was to influence Craig (among many others) and from which he often quotes in *The Mask*:

> The basis of all artistic genius lies in the power of conceiving humanity in a new and striking way, of putting a happy world of its own creation in place of a meaner world of our common days, generating around itself an atmosphere with a novel power of refraction, selecting, transforming, recombing the images it transmits, according to the choice of the imaginative intellect.[14]

Art no longer imitates life, or merely highlights experience; it composes it anew. It not only justifies life; it also redeems it, placing it in a locus beyond the reaches of time and space. The only way to experience such artistic works (one of which in this context is the world itself) is through ecstasy. The ideal of 'ecstasy' (etymologically meaning 'displacement') becomes the topmost goal, locating the artist beyond historical limitations and constraints. Summing up an article in *The Mask*, Craig quotes Nietzsche, exhibiting the same perspective:

> To the existence of art, to the existence of any aesthetic activity or perception whatsoever, a preliminary psychological condition is indispensable, namely *ecstasy*.[15]

---

[12] *The Mask*, Vol. 4, No. 1, 1911, pp. 22–23.
[13] Friedrich Nietzsche, *The Gay Science* (1882), trans. Walter Kaufmann (New York, 1974), p. 299.
[14] Walter Pater, *The Renaissance: Studies in Art and Poetry* (1873), rpt. Library Edition (London, 1913), pp. 213–14.
[15] *The Mask*, Vol. 4, No. 1, 1911, p. 24.

Pater, whose work is also chronologically parallel to Nietzsche's, expresses the same idea when he writes: 'to burn with this hard, gemlike flame, to maintain this ecstasy, is success in life'.[16] Success in art equals success in life, in an analogy that identifies one with the other.

In this context the definition of the artist's role changes drastically as well. It is in William Blake that the nineties image of the artist as prophet and philosopher often focuses. Blake's fusion of artistic modes and his apocalyptic writing herald Nietzsche and help create the notion of the 'artistic genius'. The English aestheticists of the nineties, and later Craig, reached Nietzsche through William Blake. Arthur Symons in his *William Blake* traces the similarities between the two writers in a comparison that is almost to become 'stock' during this period. He says of Blake:

> His thoughts are the passionate history of his soul. It is for this reason that he is an artist among philosophers rather than a pure philosopher. And remember that he is also not in the absolute sense, the poet, but the artist.[17]

Symons points out two aspects of Blake's work that help constitute the 'artistic genius': the blending of the categories 'artist' and 'philosopher' and the blending of artistic media.

It is with Nietzsche and Schopenhauer, however, that the role of the artist is formally described. Schopenhauer draws the distinction between 'the knowing individual' and 'the pure, will-less, painless, timeless subject of knowledge' that derives from aesthetic perception. The artist can transcend the limitations of ordinary thought following an intuitive process that has nothing to do with personality or acquired skill. Schopenhauer says that he may '*lose* himself, his individuality, his will, and only continue to exist as pure subject, as clear mirror of the object'.[18] This statement strongly pre-echoes Nietzsche's 'ecstasy'. The opposition of art to the world, tentative as it may be, still exists as the world continues to remain the object of art. The 'artistic genius' in the work of Schopenhauer is seen as the main resistance against the overpowering 'will'. In the work of Nietzsche the 'artistic genius' is no longer seen in battle with the 'will', but as constituting the highest form of it. The artist himself (for it is invariably a 'he') is elevated from a man endowed with special qualities to an *Übermensch*; from a gifted/chosen one he becomes a master of ceremonies, blending the real with the

---

[16] See Walter Pater, Note 14, p. 236.
[17] Arthur Symons, *William Blake* (London, 1907), p. 8.
[18] Quoted in Patrick Gardiner, *Schopenhauer* (Harmondsworth, 1971). See more generally the chapter entitled 'The Nature of Art', pp. 187–234.

fantastic, not only providing intuitive insights into the world, but also partaking in its creation. Nietzsche writes:

> With this system of thinking 'Dionysus' becomes an ideogram for sublimated will to power, and the 'Dionysian' man is a synonym for Ubermensch, the man in whom will to power has been sublimated into mastery and self-creativity.[19]

It is this very image of the artist that Craig envisages for himself, as a child of his age and as a theatre director. The art of the theatre, in fulfilling the ideal of synaesthesia and totality, becomes the ultimate art form; its master, the director, embodies the 'artistic genius'. (Of course the rise of the director owes much to broader social and political changes of the period as well, as will be investigated later.) This stance of Craig's is most obvious in his famous dialogues, most of which were first published in *The Mask*. In these he explains the art of the theatre to an unassuming and very often naive student, turning them into lessons in humility: Craig appears as the all-knowing master (in part a Pateresque Socrates-figure but also a Zarathustra one), initiating the student into the mysteries of his art. Most dialogues end with quotations from Nietzsche or Schopenhauer. One, with the characteristic title 'On Learning Magic', ends with a passage from *Thus Spoke Zarathustra*:

> Ah! Ever are there but few of those whose heart hath persistent courage and exuberance; and for such remaineth also the spirit patient. The rest however are *cowardly*... Him who is of my type, will also the experiences of my type meet on the way: so that his first companions must be corpses and buffoons. His second companions, however... they will call themselves his *believers*... will be a living host, with much love, much folly, much unbearded veneration.[20]

The artist is seen as a high priest who has to preach his art to faithful followers. The director embodies this notion of the all-powerful 'artistic genius'; and it is a concept that prevails in other aspects of Craig's work as well; his theories of acting and the *Ubermarionette* in many ways derive from the same source.

The 'artistic genius' figure is also parallel with the image of the 'aesthetic man' of the 'yellow nineties' in Britain. This (as we have seen) was a period of Arts and Crafts periodicals – often the work of one man alone – preaching the new artistic values and rallying against Modernity

---

[19] Friedrich Nietzsche, *Dithyrambs of Dionysus*, trans. R. J. Hollingdale (London, 1984), p. 17.
[20] *The Mask*, Vol. 6, No. 3, 1913, pp. 234–237.

and mass production. All over Britain small groups were formed that centred round enthusiastic and powerful figures, promoting a particular aesthetic stance. (One of the first articles on Nietzsche to be published in Britain was in such a periodical, *The Savoy*,[21] and one whose editor Arthur Symons was to be an important contributor to *The Mask*.) As early as 1898 Craig published *The Page*, an Arts and Crafts journal very much in line with the style and general concerns of the time. Craig as an 'aesthetic man', like others of his generation, proposes an artistic solution through craftwork, artistry and fine art, to the rising problems brought about by mechanisation and mass production. Later with *The Mask* a performative quality is added to his image. The modern world is seen as being vulgar and debased; the artist is called upon to redeem it.

Wagner, Symons and Phantasmagoria

Once the artist is placed beyond any notion of history or external reality, the work of art loses its mimetic function. It becomes a reality sui generis that is no longer obliged to identify its sources or its goals. The more perfect the illusion created by the work of art, the more 'real' it claims to be. Theatre, in constituting the ultimate art form that creates this semblance of a 'self-contained' world, acquires a prominent position among the arts in this scheme of things. The art of the theatre is seen as exemplifying the notion of the Total Art Work. The Total Art Work is art conceived as a phenomenon; one that can create reality anew and encompass every aspect of it. This totalizing function of this definition of theatre practice has direct political implications: on the one hand it can lead to theatre as a social weapon, theatre as a form of revolution (as in the work of the Russian Constructivists), and on the other, it creates a theatre that is a huge spectacle, a phantasmagoria with fascist under-tones as in the work of the Italian Futurists. Craig would later naively align himself with fascism and his work exhibits elements of this phantasmagoric style. In general, within all the debates on committed or autonomous art, on form and content that were to play such an important role in structuring the discourses of Modernism, theatre plays a dominant role. It is worth highlighting the fact that these debates themselves had historical precedents, and that *The Mask*, either directly or indirectly, was one of them.

Wagner's notion of the *Gesamtkunstwerk* is one of the first attempts consciously to use the theatre to bring forth this ideal. Craig shows his admiration for Wagner throughout *The Mask* by quoting him

---

[21] Havelock Ellis in *The Savoy*, Nos. 2, 3, 4, 1896. This series of three articles by Ellis presented one of the first sympathetic essays on Nietzsche in English. See Bridgwater, Note 3, pp. 12–14.

and reviewing books about him.[22] More significant is the fact that the first works Craig chose to direct were operas (Purcell's *Dido and Aeneas* and the semi-operatic *Masque of Love*) and he was helped in these productions by his friend Martin Shaw, the composer. He later said of the whole project 'without Martin Shaw I should never have thought to do this or done so'.[23] Like the work of Wagner, Craig's designs and overall scenic vision still possess a highly Romantic quality. Christopher Innes writes:

> Craig's first reaction once *Dido and Aeneas* was suggested had been to visualize not the scenery, but patterns of movement and grouping to bring out the mood of the music.[24]

Later his work was to become abstract and stylized with music not only 'setting the mood', but acting as a paradigm for artistic creation in general. The significance of music as a structuring force is something that Craig inherits from opera and mainly through Wagner.

The aesthetic theories of Walter Pater and his pupil Arthur Symons are strikingly parallel to the work of Wagner. Music for them is the essential art form. Pater's famous statement 'all art constantly aspires to the condition of music' is regularly quoted in *The Mask*, acquiring an axiomatic quality which helps Craig formulate his own theories.[25] In renouncing its relationship with the world, art seeks a medium that will substitute content for pure expressiveness, identifying its content in its form. Music provides the ideal paradigm, as it claims to be the most self-reliant and non-representational of all arts. Continuing his statement, Pater writes:

> That the mere matter of a poem, for instance, its subject, namely, its given incidents or situations – that the mere matter of a picture, the actual circumstances of an event, the actual topography of a landscape – should be nothing without the form, the spirit of the handling, that this form, this mode of handling, should become an end in itself, should penetrate every part of the matter; this is what all art constantly strives after.[26]

---

[22] Richard Wagner is referred to or quoted in *The Mask* in the following issues: Vol. 1, p. 20, p. 56, p. 89; Vol. 3, pp. 132–33; Vol. 4, pp. 255–57; Vol. 11, pp. 187–88; Vol. 13, pp. 173–74; Vol. 14, p. 36.

[23] Quoted in Christopher Innes, *Edward Gordon Craig* (Cambridge, 1983), p. 35.

[24] Ibid., p. 45.

[25] Pater's statement is used in the very first issue of *The Mask* (1908), and appears thereafter very frequently, introducing a variety of articles.

[26] See Walter Pater, Note 11, p. 134.

This concept of Pater's echoes a similar one expressed by Nietzsche in *The Birth of Tragedy*:

> The only possible relation between poetry and music...the word, the picture, the concept...seeks an expression analogous to music.[27]

For both men music provides a superior alternative to language. Music is seen as a pure medium beyond signification and representation. As Schopenhauer writes, 'music never expresses the phenomenon but only the inner essence of the phenomenon'.[28]

The ideal of self-reliance and autonomy is one which Craig uses both in trying to redefine the nature of his medium, the theatre, and in determining its content in terms of acting, stage design and directing. Just as music uses its own medium to express, Craig suggests that the art of the theatre initially try to understand and master its medium. He writes in *The Mask*:

> Think how far the condition of music in art will go if it is led by psychology... It is far better for all the arts, until they arrive at that condition to travel along and to concern themselves with nothing but the way their mere bodies are constructed. Let them get hold of THAT first. There is plenty of time afterwards for the study of the soul.[29]

If we read 'content' for Craig's use of the word 'soul', again we see the notion that art should be primarily concerned with form. Form is important because it is what chiefly defines the borders of the 'world of art' and separates it from the other 'real' world. In the theatre, defining the medium involves setting the literary and performative aspects of a play in opposition. This was one of Craig's main concerns. In his search for the ideal of self-reliance, his 'Theatre of the Future' has to be free from the 'tyranny' of a literary text. It has to create a language of its own, indigenous to its own medium. In Craig's work this process of defining the medium is parallel to his attempt at mapping out his role as director. He writes in *The Art of the Theatre* of the stage-director:

> When he interprets the plays of a dramatist by means of his actors, his scene-painters, and his other craftsmen, then he is a craftman. When he

---

[27] Friedrich Nietzsche, *The Birth of Tragedy*, 1872, sect. 4, in Vol. 1 of *The Works of Friedrich Nietzsche*, eds. A. Tille, T. Fisher Unwin 1899–1903. For the parallels between the work of Nietzsche and Pater see Wolfgang Iser, *Walter Pater. The Aesthetic Moment*, trans. David Henry Wilson (Cambridge, 1987). In particular see Part II entitled 'Autonomous Art'.

[28] See Patrick Gardiner, Note 18, p. 233. For a discussion of Schopenhauer's views on music see pp. 229–234.

[29] *The Mask*, Vol. 2, Nos. 10–12, 1909, p. 164.

will have mastered the uses of actions, words, light, colour and rhythm, then he may become an artist. Then he shall no longer need the assistance of the playwright, for our art will then be self-reliant.[30]

Form in the theatre is chiefly determined by its physical aspect, the stage. The concept and the function of the stage is constantly redefined during this period. The use of electricity on the stage provides fruitful ground for further experimentation. In an attempt to perfect the illusion of the scenic world and to establish complete autonomy, a sophisticated 'technology of the stage' develops. The works of Wagner can be seen as the first example of experimentation in this area. Adorno describes Wagner's works as 'among the earliest "wonders of technology" to gain admittance to great art'.[31] It is in the phantasmagoric style, traces of which appear in Craig's work, that we see a total fascination with the technology of the stage. Even though the classical Greek theatre and later forms such as sixteenth and seventeenth century intermedio and opera exhibit a very sophisticated use of stage technology/machinery, with Wagner we have the type of hypostasizing of technology that later leads to the adoration and fascination of the Futurists.

Craig and his contemporary Appia were to continue the experimentation in defining theatrical space. Craig re-introduces the idea of the open-space to the stage, changing it from a quasi-photographic representation of somewhere else to a setting in its own right, a *skene*. This notion of the *skene* derives from the Classical and Medieval theatres where the space in which a play was performed – amphitheatre or church – itself provided the setting, though elements of more conventional 'scenery' were used in both. It is a complete architectural and functional view of scenic space, creating an area that belongs only to the theatre. In representing nowhere else other than the place where it stands, the *skene* arbitrarily naturalizes theatrical space and helps create the illusion of a self-contained, non-representational scenic world.

Craig's architectural perception of scenic space was influenced by his father Godwin. Godwin, an architect himself, was very much a figure of the aestheticist 1890s. He designed furniture, houses (one of Oscar Wilde's included), theatrical costumes and scenery, and produced plays. Craig re-published his designs for Shakespeare plays in *The Mask*. Although they were by no means similar to Craig's designs, being much more traditional, they nevertheless influenced Craig's architectural perception of scenic space. Later, in 1923, when Craig published *Scene*, his own ideas on theatrical space were fully formulated through the use of

---

[30] EGC, *The Art of the Theatre* (London, 1905), pp. 56–57.
[31] Theodor Adorno, *In Search of Wagner*, trans. Rodney Livingstone (Manchester, 1981), p. 91.

his screens. Together with more Modernist modes of drama he continued his experimentation towards creating a 'technology of the stage'. He talks of 'scientific movement' and ultimately wants his screens to be mechanically controlled by the director off stage. This 'new technology' of the theatre seems to expand to cover other aspects of theatrical art such as acting and lighting. In many ways, it stems from his mania to re-create theatrical art totally. The actor becomes part of the 'new technology', a pure medium with no past or psychology, that can be fully controlled by the director. The director himself, in embodying the ideal of the 'artistic genius' has every right to do so.

The creation of a new technology for the theatre has its roots in the Arts and Crafts movement. Initially against mechanization, it stressed the importance of production as part of the creative process. In doing so, it inevitably led to developments in the means of production of a work of art. In relation to the theatre it meant recreating the stage altogether. Later with the Futurist movement the production process *is* the work of art; it becomes an integral part of it and not merely a means to an end. Craig uses music, dance and stylized acting to replace representation and mimesis on stage. These are for him the main 'mechanisms' of his new technology. His *Ubermarionette* can be seen as a theatrical version of Nietzsche's *Ubermensch* in an age of electricity. In this way Craig combines his Romantic past with the Modernist notions of performance that were to follow.

A Romanticized version of stage technology is what Arthur Symons was writing about in *Plays, Acting and Music*. Craig reviews it favourably in *The Mask* and often quotes from it. A quotation, which Craig also uses, shows how Symons incorporates the use of marionettes within his 'stage technology':

> The marionette may be relied upon. He will respond to an indication without reserve or revolt; an error on his part (we are all human) will certainly be the fault of the author; he can be trained to perfection... Above all, for we need it above all, let the marionettes remind us that the art of the theatre should be beautiful first, and what you will afterwards. Gesture on the stage is the equivalent of rhythm in verse, and it can convey, as a perfect rhythm should, not a little of the inner meaning of words, a meaning perhaps more latent in things.[32]

Craig continues this passage in *The Mask*, showing how he combines the notion of technology as art with the Arts and Crafts aversion to it:

> The Marionette through his two virtues of obedience and silence leaves to his sons a vast inheritance. He leaves to them the promise of a new

---

[32] Quoted in *The Mask*, Vol. 5, No. 2, 1912, p. 103.

art. What the wires of the Ubermarionette shall be, what shall guide
him, who can say? I do not believe in the mechanical...nor in the
material... The wires which stretch from Divinity to the soul of the Poet
are wires which might command him;...has God no more such threads
to spare...for one more figure? I cannot doubt it.[33]

In order to overcome his disgust with anything mechanical Craig dresses
his *Ubermarionette* with a Romantic mask. The wires that run through
him cannot possibly be made of steel, for then the person who is in
control will be seen as a technician and that is far too vulgar an image
for the director. Instead, they are made of a divine substance that
communicates directly with the Poet, who is compared to no one less
than God. The actual technology creating movement is ignored altogether. It is too crude an activity to occupy a real artist. He exemplifies a
contradiction that runs throughout Craig's work. On the one hand he is
faithful to the Romantic aesthetic, and on the other he formalizes theories
that acquire a very different framework in order to be realized. At the
same time, this is one of the most intriguing aspects of his work. The
Futurist movement managed to resolve this contradiction by creating a new aesthetics that identified technology with art. It is characteristic
that the Futurists actually produced 'robot plays', as they shamelessly called them, whereas Craig never 'gave life' to his *Ubermarionette*.
Again we seem to have an embryonic version of the debates about
technology that would be clearly articulated in the decades to follow
(in the work of Walter Benjamin, for example). Either heralded as libe-
rating and emancipatory, or as yet another *malaise* of the modern
world, depriving art of originality and inspiration, technology (and
the debates surrounding it) featured as one of the main discourses of
Modernism.

Another concept that Symons and Craig share is the absolute
obliteration of anything 'natural' on stage. If the world on the stage is to
be self-contained, it has to produce its own 'nature'. The *Ubermarionette*
is part of that nature. In this context the only thing that can have claim
to beauty is pure artifice. Artifice becomes nature for the scenic world.
The real world is not a creation of the 'artistic genius'; therefore it can
only be debased and of no interest. Art no longer refines or elevates
the world. It ignores it completely and seeks beauty and perfection
only within the boundaries of its own cosmos. The only conceivable
telos for art becomes newness. This accounts for the craze in the arts
of the period for constant self-reflexiveness and redefinition. The ideal
of the *New* is elevated to an all-encompassing ideology. As Benjamin

---

[33] Ibid., p. 97.

writes:

> Art that begins to doubt its task and ceases to be 'inséparable de l'utilité'
> (Baudelaire) must make the new into its highest value.[34]

Craig gives shape to Ezra Pound's doctrine 'make it new' as his ultimate goal is to re-create the art of the theatre altogether. In creating a new theatre he was mainly interested in sketching out and firmly establishing his role as director. It is also characteristic that the role of the director as an independent entity in the theatre is defined within this particular aesthetic mode. In replacing the playwright, he is seen to free the theatre from representation, he turns the mirror that used to reflect the 'outside world' onto the stage itself. This destruction of the old theatre is again achieved in a highly Romantic manner. Craig quotes Eleonore Duse in an epigram used in *The Mask*:

> To save the theatre the theatre must be destroyed; the actors and actresses must die of the plague. They poison the air, they make art impossible.[35]

This is not a clinical death, nor a natural one. It is a ritualistic, cathartic death that Craig preaches for the old theatre. The actors are seen as the main cause of deterioration. They must die a death of suffering that will give birth to the director. The mechanics of creating a 'new theatre' are something which he still considers too crude an operation to undertake. Although he spent most of his life writing and studying the theatre rather than producing plays, he still lacked the vocabulary that would help formulate his ideas. He writes in his Daybook of 1908–9:

> I want to study the theatre. I do not want to waste time producing plays... I want to leave behind me the seeds for the Art, for it does not yet exist. Such seeds are not discovered in a moment.[36]

This hesitancy of Craig's has often been interpreted as fear and insecurity. On one level, it also expresses the anxiety that derives from not belonging to one particular school of art. This was not necessarily something that Craig chose consciously, but more something very pragmatic, relating both to his personal artistic history and background,

---

[34] Walter Benjamin, *Schriften*, 2 Vols, Vol. 1 (Frankfurt, 1955), p. 418.
[35] Eleonora Duse is quoted in *The Mask* in the following issues: Vol. 1, pp. 12–13, p. 22; Vol. 2, p. 82; Vol. 4, p. 3, pp. 4–6, p. 33; Vol. 8, p. 41; Vol. 10, p. 41, p. 43, p. 118; Vol. 11, p. 92, p. 149; Vol. 13, p. 49, p. 157.
[36] EGC, *Daybook* 1, 1908–9, Humanities Research Centre, University of Texas at Austin.

and to the age he was working in. Remaining faithful to his Romantic roots, Craig could never actually transform his ideal of the new into an ideal of the *modern*, consequently moving into a Modernist aesthetic. The term *modern* and the modern world in general still triggered an aversion within him, even though his theories inevitably led there. He never quite manages to separate himself from the recent Romantic past. This quality in Craig's work finds unlikely allies in the Russian Symbolist tradition at the turn of the century.

Russian Symbolism/Soviet Constructivism

The hailing of Nietzsche as the prophet of the new aesthetic was not only part of the English *zeitgeist* of the period. Nietzsche's *The Birth of Tragedy*, proclaiming all art as tragic and theatre as the ultimate apocalyptic artform, created a whole school of imitators/followers in yet another far away land – Russia. Craig's connection with the theatrical scene of Russia would reach its most concrete form with the production of the 'Moscow *Hamlet*' for the Moscow Art Theatre in 1912. This odd symbiosis is not as strange as it initially may appear, as even the naturalist/ Stanislavskian experiment owes much to the 'theatremania' initiated by the Nietzschean cult.

The thread connecting the Symbolist tradition in the theatre with the more Modernist one that followed – or the old Russian tradition with the new Soviet experiment – is one heavily burdened with late Romantic and German Idealistic thought. Pamphlets, manifestos appear in Russia announcing the ritualistic death of the old theatre and the birth of the new *tragic art*. It is interesting to note that many of these debates were fought out in the pages of a journal, *Mir Isskustva* with which we have already compared *The Mask*. In line with the credo of the age a periodical appears on the forefront of the intellectual battles. Aleksandr Blok, Fyodor Sologub, Andrey Bely, Nikolay Evreinov and Vsevelod Meyerhold all partake in the formulation of the 'new theatre'. Craig's work was not unknown in this whole project. Laurence Senelick writes in *Russian Dramatic Theory from Pushkin to the Symbolists*:

> European influences were potent as ever; and such innovators as Wagner, Ibsen, Isadora Duncan, Max Reinhardt and Gordon Craig were quoted and emulated, adapted and absorbed. But unquestionably the two strongest influences on the Russian drama and its theorists at the time were Friedrich Nietzsche and Maurice Maeterlinck.[37]

---

[37] Laurence Senelick, ed., and trans. *Russian Dramatic Theory from Pushkin to the Symbolists, An Anthology* (Austin, Texas, 1981), p. xxxviii.

Indeed Craig's notions on the art of the theatre are very close to those of the Russian Symbolist school and remain so all through the twenty years of the publication of *The Mask* despite the fact that the Symbolist tradition, in the Soviet Union, filtered into a more Modernist one. *The Mask* serves to highlight these parallels much more than Craig's other writings. As a journal it constantly relied on a more general context, one that stressed the importance of Craig's influence, but also placed his work within a tradition. Fyodor Sologub's influential essay 'The Theatre of a Single Will' published in 1908, seems very Craigian indeed. It foreshadows Craig's powerful director figure and his idea of the *Ubermarionette*. Sologub writes:

> I think the first obstacle to be overcome on this trail is the performing actor. The performing actor draws too much attention to himself, and obfuscates both drama and author. The more talented the actor, the more insufferable his tyranny over the author and the more baneful his tyranny over the play. To depose this attractive but nonetheless baneful tyranny, two possible remedies exist; either transfer the central focus of the theatrical presentation to the spectator in the pit or transfer it to the author backstage.[38]

The 'author backstage' in Craigian terms can only be the director. This idea of the theatrical praxis as expressing one single artistic will is directly parallel to Nietzschean thought. More elaborately, this theory is developed by Nikolay Evreinov in 'Introduction to Monodrama', a lecture delivered in Moscow at the Circle of Art and Literature also in 1908. For Evreinov a production could only project in all its aspects the psyche of one artistic consciousness. In a highly expressionist manner this would be mirrored in every aspect of a production. Evreinov writes:

> Now by 'monodrama' I mean to denote the kind of dramatic presentation which, while attempting to communicate to the spectator as fully as it can the active participant's state of mind, displays the world around him on stage just as the active participant perceives the world at any given moment of his existence on stage.[39]

Four years later Craig would give shape to Evreinov's theories with his production of *Hamlet* with the Moscow Art Theatre, which Senelick calls 'the best example of the monodramatic principle on the Russian stage'.

---

[38] Fyodor Sologub. 'The Theatre of a Single Will', in Laurence Senelick, note 37, pp. 132–148.
[39] Nikolay Evreinov, 'Introduction to Monodrama' in Laurence Senelick, pp. 183–199.

Evreinov himself aligns his work with that of Craig:

> Therefore Gordon Craig comes close to my way of thinking, for he is
> driven frantic by the stage training in modern authors; I applaud him
> wholeheartedly when he declares: 'We shall do without them, since
> they fail to provide us with the most important thing – something that
> is beautiful in a stage sense'.[40]

Evreinov's acknowledgement is not returned by Craig, even though their
work is almost parallel chronologically. Craig's work *The Art of the Theatre*
was known at the time in Russia, but similar theories would have existed
had it been totally unknown. The parallels with the common theoretical
background of both are more than obvious. Later Meyerhold had to announce that he hadn't read Craig's work in 1905 at the time of the Theatre-
Studio in Moscow so as to avoid confusion.[41] Until about 1910–12 when
the whole experiment started to follow different strands throughout Europe
and Russia, it sounded as if the echo of Nietzsche could be heard in all the
writings of the period on the theatre. The work of Craig was no exception.

Another theatre theoretician-cum-mystic who was popular at this
time in Russia was the French author Edouard Schuré (1841–1929). His
writings ranging from works on musical history and mysticism to plays
and theory on the theatre bear the marks of his Nietzschean background
and promote the dominant 'theatrocracy' (Senelick) of the period. It is
recorded that Schurés 'The Theatre of the Soul' was Craig's bedtime
reading while he was working with the MAT in Moscow in 1912.[42] This
essay was to appear in its first English translation in *The Mask* later that
same year. In a typically Craigian manner the name of the translator, who
also wrote the introduction is omitted. The introduction reads:

> The present essay is, as so much of M. Schurés work, a vindication of
> the dignity of the Theatre, of its vital importance in the life of a people,
> its incalculable influence, whether for good or evil, upon the entire
> being of man, 'sense, soul and mind': a grave warning that, unless it
> strive to rise to the best it must sink to the worst; and, if not 'a school
> of beauty, of truth and of rebirth', be inevitably 'a school of ugliness, of
> falsehood and of death'.[43]

Theatre is seen as the purgatory that offers collective *catharsis*.
Schurés essay proceeds to present a model of a theatre based on the
tragic theatre of ancient Greece that is collective and orgiastic, enacting

---

[40] Ibid., p. 188.
[41] See Edward Braun, ed. and trans. *Meyerhold on Theatre* (London, 1969), pp. 111–112.
[42] See Laurence Senelick, note 37, pp. 289–290.
[43] Edouard Schure, 'The Theatre of the Soul', in *The Mask*, Vol. 4, No. 3, 1912, pp. 171–179.

the tensions between the Apollonian and Dionysiac elements – a model borrowed once more from *The Birth of Tragedy*. This totalising and all-encompassing view of theatrical art was to be adopted by Craig as well. The theatre-cum-temple not only restores past glories, but also helps redeem the present modern world. Schuré writes:

> The human soul, with its most profound mysteries and its most noble powers, the divine Psyche, had formerly its temples, its altars and its tripods. Today it seems excluded from our public life and driven out of our institutions. Science waves it aside; the Church oppresses it; the World, drunk with luxury and pleasures, forgets it; art, having lost its way, no longer affirms it but feebly, and, if it speak of it at all, seems but to ask pardon for even naming it.[44]

This is theatre substituting religion, aesthetics and finally politics. This is the theoretical background that gives shape to Wagner's phantasmagoria – a style that replaces history with metaphysics and considers itself to be *sui generis*. As Adorno writes 'the standing still of time and the complete occultation of nature by means of phantasmagoria are thus brought together in the memory of a pristine age where time is guaranteed only by the stars'.[45]

The Blake Revival and Walt Whitman

As with the Modernist movements in stagecraft the work of Craig can be traced to late 19th century and mainly German theories of aesthetics. At the same time, it possesses a very distinct quality that separates it from the continental schools of the period. Although Nietzsche and Schopenhauer feature throughout the pages of *The Mask*, Craig's main influence is William Blake. Like Pater and Symons Craig reached Nietzsche through William Blake. Craig writes in his *Index to the Story of my Days* of 1890:

> But what book, what author, was it that I knew better than all these – had known him since childhood and known and forgotten? The author of a book of verse and of drawings, flowing the one through the other? For it was he who was one of our family – we knew him so well – we needed not to stop when passing him in the house. This was William Blake. He was one I could not forget, since he was one of us and so I grew, without knowing it, to be part of him. But what was he to our stage? Nothing! To our house, Father's, Mother's, he was everything – but nothing to our stage. Yet in all my years he has been ever with me.[46]

---

[44] Ibid., p. 173.
[45] See Theodor Adorno, note 31, p. 87.
[46] EGC, *Index to the Story of My Days* (London, 1957), p. 106.

Later, Craig was able to give form to his Blakean background. *The Mask* in many ways embodied Blakean notions of design and layout, illustrating Craig's influence and admiration. Through his work on the theatre Craig manages to appropriate Blakean aesthetics and make them part of 'his stage'. In this way, although Blake never wrote about theatre, his work becomes directly connected with Craigian theatre theory/practice, especially as presented through *The Mask*.

Quite a while before Nietzsche made his impact on the British scene Blake had a strong influence on the so-called, movement of English aestheticism. From the mid-nineteenth century onwards Blake enjoyed an enthusiastic revival initiated by the publication of Gilchrist's *The Life of William Blake* in 1863. This was followed by Swinburne's *William Blake* in 1868. Both these works, the first biographical and the second interpretive, were crucial in establishing a reputation for William Blake. They both projected an image of Blake as the 'mad' and prophetic poetic genius – Gilchrist's version more as an apology or a curiosity and Swinburne's as, more or less, the 'natural' condition of a true poet. Later, W. M. Rossetti's edition in 1874 and the Ellis–Yeats edition in 1893 helped systematize what Yeats called Blake's 'Symbolic System' and mould his image as an artist. As is the case with Nietzsche, and will later be with Whitman, madness is raised to heights of authority. It is definitely a sign of genius and goes hand-in-hand with the aphoristic and visionary philosophies both men preached. Craig wants his share of 'madness' as well. While analyzing himself in the foreword to his *Index to the Story of My Days* he says 'my parents had bestowed on me some natural gifts – which suffered through being incorrectly understood and improperly nursed'. One of these was:

> Madness. Looking back over my eighty-four years, I should say that I had a touch of madness in me. When young I was dreadfully strung up. My dreams were often nightmares – and often I would walk in my sleep. Not like Lady Macbeth, wringing my hands and talking of blood. I was rather too young to have committed any crimes – so I must suppose my trouble was an inheritance – how or from whom I can't say, for I do not know.[47]

Craig wanted to be part of the Blakean tradition of 'mad' artistic geniuses.

Another characteristic of the Blakean revival was that those who contributed to it were at the same time concerned with formulating a theory of aesthetics of their own. Swinburne was chiefly giving shape to

---

[47] Ibid., p. 7.

his theory of art while studying Blake. The same is true of the Pre-Raphaelites and Yeats.[48] This is not as clear with Craig as his Blakean influence is an indirect one. He is aware of the Swinburne publication, which he reviews in *The Mask*. He also reviews Gilchrist's *The Life of William Blake*, of which he writes in *The Mask*:

> A REVELATION. What? How can it be a revelation? the book has been known for years. Oh yes, KNOWN,... as George III knew his foremost Poetic Genius. Known as the Blind Man sees everything, and the Deaf hear everything, yes, known as we know a storm is coming but are too lazy to really take it in. Take it in now, Children... Take it in... Out of the storm. Take in William Blake and learn as quickly as you can everything he can tell you... Quickly, quickly, believe all he tells you; it's true... He doesn't tease a tired world with Politics, nor with moralizing, nor with Patriotism based on Profit and Propaganda; nor with anything. He is a great Poet, a great Artist, a perfectly sane thinker, and about the sanest Englishman we ever had... After you've understood Blake you'll see where Whitman is; then the rest of us... And do stop thinking, and comparing and discussing the merits of Dwarfs when these Giants stand offering you a NEW WORLD.[49]

Craig sees himself as a direct descendant of Blake in a line that includes Whitman. It is also noteworthy that he stresses Blake's saneness. Of course, Nietzsche is not excluded from the family tree. In an article entitled 'On Some Great Men', in *The Mask*, Craig writes:

> For though Nietzsche never speaks of William Blake and though perhaps he may never have read nor heard of Blake he is for all that of the same family.[50]

Like most figures of the aestheticist nineties, in reaching Nietzsche through Blake, Craig stresses his British roots. Pater and Symons add to this Blakean foreground as well; so it is the distinctively British context that marks Craig's work and separates it from other movements on the continent. *The Mask*, which was to be Craig's main European project, served to underline these differences. It is this clear Blakean strand combined with Arts and Crafts aesthetics that both lead Craig to Nietzsche and separate him from the German philosopher. In a manner which stresses his past, Craig replaces German nihilism with Romantic Idealism.

---

[48] For the impact of William Blake on the late 19th century see Deborah Dorfman, *Blake in the Nineteenth Century* (London, 1969).
[49] *The Mask*, Vol. 8, No. 3, 1915, p. 10.
[50] *The Mask*, Vol. 5, No. 2, 1912, pp. 91–92.

Another outstanding figure of the period who marks the work of Craig and theoretically differentiates it from other European works is Walt Whitman. Whitman stands side by side with Schopenhauer and Nietzsche in moulding the aesthetic consciousness of the late nineteenth century. Whether Nietzsche had actually read Whitman is not clearly known, but their work seems to exhibit two opposing facets of the same theoretical tradition. Both Nietzsche and Whitman acknowledge their debts to Emerson. It is the same Emersonian drive for life that Nietzsche transforms into the 'will to power' and Whitman into a form of natural religion. Both men rode on a wave of Emersonian inspired vitalism. In characterizing himself as 'Walt Whitman, an American....a Kosmos, Disorderly, fleshly and sensual', Whitman presents a more humanist version of Nietzsche's Dionysus. It is the image of Whitman as the American Adam that stands as a counterpart to Nietzsche's image of man as divine being.

Rossetti, Swinburne and Ann Gilchrist were the main advocates of Whitman in Britain. The same group was responsible for the Blakean revival. The parallels between William Blake and Walt Whitman are drawn by Swinburne himself:

> The points of contact and sides of likeness between William Blake and Walt Whitman are so many and so grave, as to afford some ground of reason to those who preach the transition of souls or transfusion of spirits. The great American is not a more passionate preacher of sexual or political freedom than the English artist. To each the imperishable form of a possible and universal Republic is equally requisite and adorable as the temporal and spiritual queen of ages as of men. To each all sides and shapes of life are alike acceptable or endurable... Both are spiritual, and both are democratic; both by their works recall, even to so untaught and tentative a student as I am, the fragments vouchsafed to us of the Pantheistic poetry of the East.[51]

Swinburne reads Whitman within the same framework as Blake. Both men are controversial figures and often invite diverse reactions. Indeed, Rossetti was obliged to impose a sort of self-censorship so as to get the first collection of Whitman's poetry published. 'This peculiarly nervous age, this mealy-mouthed British nineteenth century', he writes, could not accept 'the indecencies scattered through Whitman's writings'. Whitman, just like Blake before him, was an awesome character, outrageous and outspoken, also labelled with what now came to be the mark of a genius – 'mad'.

---

[51] Quoted in Walt Whitman. *The Critical Heritage*, ed. Milton Hindus (London, 1971), p. 134.

In 1895 Max Nordau's *Degeneration* was published, which was to cause a great deal of commotion, because of its outright attack on modern art and its artists. This was an analysis firmly located within the anxieties of the *fin-de-siecle*. In his book Nordau sharply criticizes Whitman:

> I should like here to interpolate a few remarks on Walt Whitman who is likewise one of the deities to whom the degenerate and hysterical of both hemispheres have for some time been raising altars. Lombroso ranks him expressly among 'mad geniuses'. Mad Whitman was without doubt. But a genius? That would be difficult to prove... He is morally insane, and incapable of distinguishing between good and evil, virtue and crime.[52]

Interestingly enough, continuing his attack on Whitman, Nordau compares him to Wagner in saying that men 'under the pressure of the same motives, arrived at the same goal – the former at 'infinite melody' which is no longer melody; the latter at verses which are no longer verses'. Both men are accused of redefining their medium – a blasphemous act. The same quality of Whitman that Rossetti and the other Pre-Raphaelites found attractive and parallel to their own artistic goals is termed 'degenerate' by Nordau. (Nietzsche, of course, does not escape Nordau and is added to his pantheon of 'degenerates' in a chapter entitled 'Ego-mania'.)

In publishing Whitman's works Rossetti is moving a step closer to formalizing his own aesthetics. As a review of his book says:

> He desires to have Walt Whitman recognized, not merely as a great poet, but as the founder of a new school of poetic literature which is to be greater and more powerful than any the world has yet seen. He is not, it is true, entirely alone in this attempt. There have already been indications of a Walt Whitman movement in one or two quarters.[53]

William Blake and Walt Whitman are definitely seen as part of the same movement. The following generation of English 'aesthetes' will add Nietzsche to their list of 'prophets'. Craig follows in the same tradition focusing his interest on 'the art of the theatre', which, as Nordau would say, is no longer theatre as it is made 'infinite', total.

One aspect of Whitman that may seem to be contrary to Craig's aristocratic background and his firm credo in 'King and Country' is

---

[52] Ibid., pp. 243–245. Quoted from Max Nordau, *Degeneration* (London, 1895). See Chapter III, book V 'Ego-mania', on Nietzsche.

[53] Ibid., pp. 132–133. From unsigned review of *Poems* by Walt Whitman: Selected and Edited by William Rossetti 1868, *Saturday Review* (London, 2 May, 1868), pp. 589–90.

Whitman's 'democracy'. In the eyes of Craig, Whitman's politics are not seen as politics at all. His notions of democracy are seen as aesthetic ones that exhibit individualistic and anarchic tendencies, rather than solid and pragmatic political doctrines. Anyway, Whitman was an 'American', which for Craig meant that he had the licence to be slightly eccentric. Nevertheless, he treats Whitman with due respect, almost always grouping him with Blake or Nietzsche. He writes in *The Mask*:

> For THE CONSTRUCTORS OF THE WORLD are not Wells, not Shaw, not Clemenceau, no, nor the great Alfred...are not a Committee...rest to these perturbed spirits...but are William Blake and Walt Whitman and their kith and kin. Whitman sang songs for Democracy. How is it the swing is so regal? No one yet has ever explained this.
> William Blake didn't bother his head about Democracy...and yet good Democrats find his Songs Divine.
> Then *perhaps* p-e-r-h-a-p-s there is something which can become even more popular, less vexing and twenty times as successful as Democracy...as Aristocracy and all the rest of the Hocus-Pocus. Why not have THAT in place of Fudge as a foundation to a new world.[54]

Craig dismisses politics altogether, calling it Hocus-Pocus. Whitman is grouped as one of the 'constructors' of the world not because of his democratic beliefs, but mainly because he is a great artist. In employing the principle of universalization Craig's model, one shared with the later Modernists, views art as that which transcends history, and expresses supposed universal ideals. Shaw and the others he sneers at do have a clear political stance and it is one which Craig despises – socialism. The problem arises namely because Whitman is clearly political as well. Craig manages to defuse this. Not in an attempt to be clever, but chiefly because he *does* believe that there is *something* which can override political and historical reality – art – and the true artists should therefore be the ones to construct the world.

Whitman's Adam, in so far as he represents a more humanist version of Nietzsche's *Ubermensch*, blends in well with the heroic Romantic tradition. Whitman appears regularly in *The Mask*.[55] Craig had designed and engraved a portrait of Whitman for his first periodical *The Page*. In an article comparing Nietzsche to Whitman, Craig writes:

> Any student of Nietzsche should be a very careful student of Whitman and Blake. The first of them is of course our very own William Blake.

---

[54] *The Mask*, Vol. 8, No. 3, 1915, p. 10.
[55] Walt Whitman appears in *The Mask* in the following issues: Vol. 1, p. 123; Vol. 3, p. 88; Vol. 4, No. 1: frontispiece, pp. 1–3, p. 27; Vol. 5, p. 92, p. 273; Vol. 8, p. 4, p. 43.

Then comes the colossal mystery Whitman and then the careful arranger and builder Nietzsche.[56]

The influence of Blake is taken for granted as it is part of his own tradition. Whitman appears in a Romantic cloud of awe and Nietzsche is seen as the philosopher who moulds this aesthetic theory into form. It is characteristic that the movements immediately following Craig *did* break off from the strong Romantic tradition and managed to give form to their theories. In doing so they were mainly under the influence of the 'arranger and builder Nietzsche', within a framework that could provide them with both the vocabulary and the methodology to materialize their ideas.

Late nineteenth-century schools of aesthetics provide a very strong point of reference for the work of Craig. As an artist he is moulded within the philosophies of his time and they leave their signs on his work. As far as direct influence is concerned and especially that of Nietzsche and Schopenhauer, the effect is of a different order. Craig reaches German Idealism as it is filtered through the late Romanticism of Walter Pater and Arthur Symons. Early in his career Craig was to conceive Modernist notions of performance, but as long as he remained rooted in Romanticism, he lacked the language with which to express them.

A quotation from Pater's *The Law of Harmony* that Craig also quotes in *The Mask* serves to illustrate how determining the work of Pater was on Craig, and at the same time pre-echoes how this influence was to distance Craig from the other Euorpean movements in the theatre of the period:

> We are to become like little pieces in a machine you may complain... No, like performers rather, individually it may be, of more or less importance, but each with a necessary and inalienable part, in a perfect musical exercise which is well worth while, or in some sacred liturgy; or like soldiers in an invincible army, invincible because it moves as one man. We are to find, or be put into, and keep every one his natural place; to cultivate those qualities which secure mastery over ourselves, the subordination of the parts to the whole musical proportion.[57]

In replacing music by technology and the mechanics of construction as the main structuring unit in their work, the Futurist and Constructivist movements found formal means to articulate their theories.

---

[56] *The Mask*, Vol. 5, No. 2, 1912, p. 92.
[57] Quoted in *The Mask*, Vol. 4, No. 1, 1911, p. 7.

The work of Craig, on the other hand, deeply embedded in Romanticism and, at the same time, sharing Modernist anxieties about art, never quite manages to resolve the contradiction. His theoretical writings, *The Mask* included, are distinctly aphoristic and visionary rather than precise and practically applicable, always expressing the anxiety of a man who lacked the vocabulary to articulate his ideas.

3

THE PERIODICAL AS A MANIFESTO

Craig chose to publish *The Mask* in Italy and not in Britain, making it, above all, a European project. Europe, at the time, was a hot-house for new artistic ideas and political movements – in many cases side by side – most of which are either dealt with directly or echoed in *The Mask*. Movements like Cubism, Futurism and their main exponents are presented in the pages of *The Mask*. Craig's journal does not merely chronicle the Modernism of its time, but actively takes part in it. It compares, criticizes or advocates contemporary movements through its pages, but, more importantly, in doing so simultaneously creates a space for its own 'Art of the Theatre'. In this sense, *The Mask* assumes a manifesto-like quality and develops a rhetoric used to propagate most of the movements of the time. Revolutionary, extreme and apocalyptic, European Modernism utilised the form of the manifesto – elevating it in many cases to an 'Art form' – to express its total and absolute claims. The prophetic, romantic style of Nietzsche and the Symbolists gives way to that of the more iconoclastic and forceful manifesto. *The Mask*, whether admittedly or not, aligns itself with contemporary journals/manifestos as it not only sets out to redefine its medium, but, at the same time, encapsulates it within the broader claims of a 'grand theory'. In line with trends of its time, where artistic movements derive their ideologies from the extremes of the political spectrum, *The Mask* appears with fascist undertones and from that position presents and places the other ideologies of its time. Either as a pseudo-historical extension of Romantic Idealism, as is the case in the early volumes of the journal, or in its strictly political dimensions, later on, fascism presents Craig with a theory that can accomodate the Radical Idealist tradition of Romanticism and the aestheticism of the Arts and Crafts movement into a more extreme, totalizing, technologically informed – hence 'modern' – ideology.

Modernism as a European movement could be said to incorporate two distinct strands, one *idealistic* and the other *materialistic*. The former comes as a direct result of Romanticism while the latter is purely a *modern* form, resulting from trends and ideologies of the twentieth century. Nietzsche is the adopted prophet for both schools of Modernism, even though his work is assimilated through very different channels in each case. Idealistic Modernism filters Nietzsche's work through that of Pater and later T. E. Hulme and Wilhelm Worringer, whereas

Materialistic Modernism uses Nietzsche as the initial inspiration, something that lights the spark, and later turns to Freud and Marx. Idealistic Modernism appears mainly in the works of the British Modernists including Craig, in the work of Kandinsky and early German Expressionism, whereas Materialistic Modernism is articulated in the works of the Russian Constructivists and of the Weimar group.

The main dividing line between the two trends is drawn by the fact that one, Materialistic Modernism, is based on a historical social theory while the other derives all its ideology directly from aesthetics. Consequently, it moves towards the aesthetisation of history. Apocalypse seems to be the goal for one while revolution is the logical and desirable end for the other. *The Mask* with its Romantic past and its fascist present clearly falls heavily onto one side of this model. The framework itself can help determine its relationship with its contemporary movements and can resolve some of the seeming contradictions and difficulties in these interactions.

Abstraction – Empathy – Radicalism

Abstraction and Empathy[1] is the title of a study by Wilhelm Worringer which was first published in 1908 and was a best seller in the years to follow. Worringer's manifesto, as it is a short theoretical model he proposes, was to be for the first decade of the twentieth century what Nietzsche's *The Birth of Tragedy* was for the last decade of the previous century. Its influence was immense as it proposed a universal *urge to abstraction* as a model for a trans-historical/transcendental type of Modernism, with the contemporary trend being only one of its expressions. The urge to empathy, according to Worringer, can only produce representational art, which he considers to be of a lower order. Empathy itself is seen as a mode of being that relies on psychological identification (sympathy) with the world and art, and is based on the great tradition of European humanism. Against this Worringer proposes an 'urge to abstraction', in one of the first theoretical formulations of the radical and anti-humanist but, nonetheless, idealistic tradition in Modernism. The categories Worringer proposes are parallel to Nietzsche's *Apollonian* and *Dionysiac* modes. He writes:

> We regard as this counter-pole an aesthetics which proceeds not from man's urge to empathy, but from his urge to abstraction. Just as the urge to empathy as a pre-assumption of aesthetic experience finds its gratification in the beauty of the organic, so the urge to abstraction finds its

---

[1] Wilhelm Worringer, *Abstraction and Empathy: A Contribution to the Psychology of Style*, 1908, trans. Michael Bullock (London, 1953).

beauty in the life-denying inorganic, in the crystalline or, in general terms, in all abstract law and necessity.[2]

It is not for nothing that this is the period of the first revival of interest in Byzantine art. In general Oriental art forms, considered to be geometrical and non-representational, provide a model against the humanist and anthropomorphic modes of European Classicism. The urge to abstraction, as it is presented by Worringer is directly parallel to the German idealistic notion of the 'will to style', and provides the metaphysical structure required for an art that is without history, without 'nature', accountable only to itself and its needs. Proselytizing for this autonomy, Worringer writes:

> Our investigations proceed from the presupposition that the work of art, as an autonomous organism, stands beside nature on equal terms and, in its deepest and innermost essence, devoid of any connection with it, in so far as by nature is understood the visible surface of things.[3]

The urge to abstraction is elevated to the status of a 'world theory', one that can explain not only aesthetic but also historical phenomena:

> Whereas the precondition for the urge to empathy is a happy pantheistic relationship of confidence between man and the phenomena of the external world, the urge to abstraction is the outcome of a greater inner unrest inspired in man by the phenomena of the outside world; in a religious respect it corresponds to a strongly transcendental tinge to all notions. We might describe this state as an immense dread of space.[4]

Abstraction is seen by Worringer as the highest spiritual expression and the art it produces is of a purely ideal order. It is non-historical, as any reading of history is seen as a form of empathy, leading to mimetic art. Art is viewed as a religious act; its main function being to separate the artist from the rest of the world.

> In the urge to abstraction the intensity of the self-alienative impulse is incomparably greater and more consistent. Here it is not characterised, as in the need for empathy, by an urge to alienate oneself from individual being, but as an urge to seek deliverance from the fortuitousness of humanity as a whole, from the seeming arbitrariness of organic existence

---

[2] Ibid., p. 4.
[3] Ibid., p. 3.
[4] Ibid., p. 15.

in general, in the contemplation of something necessary and irrefragable. Life as such is felt to be a disturbance of aesthetic enjoyment.[5]

Worringer provided a theoretical framework for Idealistic Modernism; one that can also help determine the role of *The Mask* within its European context. Though at times his claims seem arbitrary, supported only by tendentious evidence, he nevertheless acted as ideological spokesperson for the movement in Europe which was certainly living through a time of 'inner unrest'. Another aspect of Worringer's thesis that was to be of great influence to the movements that followed was his anti-humanist and anti-Renaissance spirit. He used Byzantine, Oriental and primitive art to exemplify his points: the exact art forms that were to have a tremendous impact on the European art of the age. The most significant aspect of *Abstraction and Empathy* is that it constructs a theory of Modernism, still maintaining highly Romantic elements, stressing the spiritual and transcendental in preference to the real and historical, i.e. the political.

The main spokesperson for German aesthetics at the time in Britain was T. E. Hulme. To the liberal and organic Modernism that was developing at the time as a result of the Arts and Crafts movement and the work of groups such as the Omega workshop, he proposed a Radical Idealistic alternative. He published his ideas in yet another periodical of the period, *The New Age* (which is reviewed in *The Mask*). In 1913 he published a translation of Bergson's *Introduction to Metaphysics* and in the winter of 1912–1913 he went to Berlin to attend lectures by Worringer.

In January 1914 Hulme gave a lecture on 'Modern Art and its Philosophy'. The lecture itself was an exposition of the knowledge he had aquired from his visits to Germany and constitutes probably the first formalisation of Radical Idealism in British Modernism. He claimed:

> that the new art differs not in degree but in kind from the art we are accustomed to, and that there is a danger that the understanding of the new may be hindered by a way of looking on art which is only appropriate to the art that preceded it.[6]

Hulme not only imported a new way of understanding art but, also a new way of being.

Neither Hulme nor Worringer appear in the pages of *The Mask* but they provide a theoretical framework within which the position of *The Mask* can be assessed in relation to the aesthetics of other movements

---

[5] Ibid., p. 24.
[6] Quoted in Charles Harrison, *English Art and Modernism 1900–1939* (London, 1981), p. 96.

(most of which are also propagated through periodicals). With its Romantic roots, its aversion for the modern world and Modernity[7] in general, its fascination with art forms of the east *The Mask* can quite neatly be seen as an expression of Worringer's urge to abstraction. Combined with its fascist undertones it can be placed within the tradition of Radical Idealist Modernism. At the same time, it expresses some of the contradictions and dead-ends that particular strand of Modernism led to.

The periodicals/manifestos that *The Mask* best contrasts with in this area, exhibiting the two diametrically different 'schools' of Modernism, are mainly German ones. Between 1910 and 1920, amid the chaos of artistic and political factionism, two periodicals managed to prevail. They were both based in Berlin and promoted a left-wing Materialistic Modernism, which sees art in terms of the production structures of the society – as a commodity – and views progress in terms of the Marxist concept of class struggle. These were *Der Sturm* of Herwarth Walden and *Die Aktion* of Franz Pfemfert.[8] Like Craig, Walden saw the theatre as the arena where he could promote his ideas and formed a *Storm-Theatre* in 1917 and a school for the arts in 1916. These German periodicals helped prepare the ground for the development of one of the most important European movements of the period: the Weimar Bauhaus which was founded by Walter Gropius in 1919. From the *First Proclamation of the Weimar Bauhaus* we can see how art is defined in an organic, materialistic sense. In many ways it reads like a radicalised version of William Morris:

> Architects, sculptors, painters, we must all turn to the crafts. Art is not a 'profession'. There is no essential difference between the artist and the craftsman. The artist is an exalted craftsman. In rare momemts of inspiration beyond the control of his will, the grace of heaven may cause his work to blossom into art. But proficiency in his craft is essential to every artist. There lies a source of creative imagination.[9]

---

[7] The terms Modernism and Modernity are not used as synonyms here, although they certainly overlap. Modernism is used to refer to literary and artistic movements from 1900–1930, whereas Modernity refers to the overall modern experience, which covers broader changes in politics and society over the same period.

[8] The main groups in Europe of the period, usually centred round a periodical and combining aesthetic aspirations with political ones were: *The Bridge* (1905), *The Blue Rider* (1911), *The New Club* (1909), *The Storm* (1910), *The Action* (1911), Schoenberg's *Society for the Private Performance of Music* (1918), *The November Group* (1919), *Glass Chain* (1920), *The Bauhaus* (1919).

[9] Quoted from the *First Proclamation of the Weimar Bauhaus* 1919, in Barry Herbert and Alisdair Hinshelwood, *The Expressionist Revolution in German Art* 1871–1933 (Leicestershire Museums and Art Gallery, Leicestershire Museums, 1978), p. 26.

Meanwhile the English tradition in Modernism was continuing to divorce the artistic process from any notion of socio-political structure and to elevate the artist into a trans-historical transcendental figure. Clive Bell writes in *Art*, published in 1914:

> The artist and the saint do what they have to do, not to make a living, but in obedience to some mysterious necessity. They do not produce to live – they live to produce. There is no place for them in a social system based on the theory that what men desire is prolonged and pleasant existence. You cannot fit them into the machine, you must make them extraneous to it. You must make pariahs of them, since they are not part of society but the salt of the earth.[10]

Craig's work is not as aloof and unaware of the contemporary movements and ideas as Bell's writing here is (as the pages of *The Mask* clearly indicate). However, the Bell quotation, still embedded in Romanticism, does serve to exemplify the tradition that bred Craig: a tradition that he was in many ways trying to reconcile with the continual bombardment of ideas he was receiving on the continent.

Contrasts/Parallels with Contemporary Movements

The Mask partakes in the European cultural scene not only on a meta-level, but also directly through its pages. Movements, trends, schools, ideas and their advocates are presented, sometimes praised, sometimes condemned, at times totally misunderstood, but always given the limelight in a highly theatrical manner in accordance with the performative quality of the journal. Futurism is one of the main movements that occupies Craig especially in the middle years of the publication of *The Mask* (1911–1914).[11] In general, Craig is concerned with contemporary movements mainly during the same period, as it is the time most schools also publish their manifestos. Either due to the fact that he was living and working in Italy, or to other more theoretical and ideological parallels, Craig shows quite a keen interest in Futurism, publishing the first English translation of the Futurist Manifesto on the theatre. However, he is not always sympathetic, and his attitude towards them is quite ambivalent. On one level, there are striking parallels between his work and that of the Futurists. Both share an Idealistic framework with utopian notions of history. The Futurists' fascination with technology and industrialisation, however, couldn't be further from Craig's attitude.

---

[10] See Charles Harrison, note 6, p. 17.
[11] Futurism appears in *The Mask* in the following issues: Vol. 4, pp. 277–81, p. 356; Vol. 5, p. 89, p. 174; Vol. 6, pp. 188–200.

In a sense it is their very acceptance of Modernity that differentiates them from Craig. Still maintaining its Romantic roots, Futurism proves a surprising ally for Craig. In a sense Futurism appears as a Romantic reading of Cubism and Constructivism. As Fry perceptively put it:

> The Italian Futurists have succeeded in developing a whole system of aesthetics out of a misapprehension of some of Picasso's recondite and difficult works.[12]

And it is the seeming contradictions, the idiosyncracies and eccentricities of Italian Futurist theory and practice, which are exactly the elements Craig found attractive and even parallel to his own work.

'Futurism and The Theatre: A Futurist Manifesto' appears in Volume 6 of *The Mask*, in 1913. This was the first publication of this manifesto in English, in a translation by D. Nevile Lees, Craig's companion and secretary in Florence.[13] Like the general *Futurist Manifesto* which was published in *Le Figaro* in 1909, it appeared at a time when not a single work of Futurist theatre had been written or performed. As an introduction to his own commentary on the manifesto Craig writes:

> While doing this I want you to remember that it is not essential to our understanding in any way to mistake the Futurists as a band of wild madmen or silly fools. They are neither. They are quite serious and strong fellows.[14]

Nevertheless, despite the tolerance that Craig wants to show towards the Futurists, he continues in the same article:

> The Futurist Manifesto is the most impertinent piece of ignorance that ever a set of courageous and frisky young men trumped up to deceive themselves with while occupied with other and more profound thoughts.[15]

Although Craig seems very patronizing in his criticism of Futurism he could not ignore its impact altogether, especially living in Italy. The mere fact that he published the manifesto in full indicates that he took the whole affair seriously. For him Futurism was a 'phase'. He ends his article by stating that 'Finally, I do heartily approve of this queer grim

---

[12] See Charles Harrison, note 6, p. 87.
[13] 'Futurism and The Theatre: A Futurist Manifesto' by Marinetti in *The Mask*, trans. Dorothy Neville Lees, Vol. 6, 1913, pp. 188–193.
[14] Ibid., article by EGC following the above manifesto, p. 196.
[15] Ibid.

Manifesto...Futurismo in the Theatre can do no harm. More room for it, then. Let it go on...it must go on...we must get over it'.[16]

A few years later, still in the middle period of the journal, in Volume 8 of *The Mask* Craig would voice one of his main disagreements with the Futurist movement. Their adoration of technology as the creator of the new utopia was something that echoed too 'modern' in Craigian terms. Technology, for Craig, was one of the 'evils' of Modernity, causing the death of a 'grand past' and not necessarily heralding a brave new future. He writes:

> SPEED – There is still an erroneous idea fluttering around that the quickest things are the motor car, the aeroplane, the telegraph, train so forth.
> I will tell you something quicker. It is the Imagination of Man. And because Imagination outstrips all else it gets there sooner...Do you see?[17]

Craig's imagination is inhabited by Romantic ghosts rather than Modernist/Futurist machines. Indeed it is his fascination with the past rather than the future which marks another source of discontent with the more modern movements. Where Futurism had substituted utopia for history, Craig had a nostalgic, Romanticised conception of history. Both views are actually expressions of Idealism and neither sees the historical process as an interpretive device for the present. Marinetti's calls for total destruction of the art of the past sounded blasphemous to Craig. He believed he was working within a great tradition that he would gradually form part of. He writes in *The Mask* in 1914, a year after he had published the Futurist manifesto in its pages:

> That the two great divisions of time Past and Future, appeal to us as being each dependent on each other in this work of the Theatre should surprise no one. Our wish is not to startle but to go on with our work...Never did we dream we should be thought to be revolutionary, had no thoughts to deride 'the old school' nor laugh at honest failures.[18]

Despite the rhetoric here, which is quite prophetic and aphoristic – manifesto-like – Craig declares his traditionalism. His reference to the past as the old school uses just as hazy and idealised a notion as the Futurists' references to the term 'the future'. He has a natural aversion to the idea of revolution as it has a very modern/Modernist connotation for him. The supposed chasm with the past that Modernism proclaimed, the absolute 'break' with tradition is something which Craig finds

---

[16] Ibid., p. 198.
[17] *The Mask*, Vol. 8, 1915, p. 29.
[18] *The Mask*, Vol. 7, 1914, p. 133.

blasphemous. As early as 1914 looking back into the past becomes much more important for his work than prophesying about the future. It is interesting to note that during these years (1911–15), when *The Mask* is concerned with evaluating its Modernist contemporaries, it also resorts to the 'glorious past'. This Craig uses as both a personal reaction against, and as a corrective to the 'newness' of Modernism. He ends his commentary on *The Futurist Manifesto in the Theatre* with the following declaration:

> Epilogue: I'm a bit of a Revolutionary myself. Not to be in the fashion, I revolt against Revolt. I believe I want Order, and Obedience to be as natural as chaos and disloyalty.[19]

The 'Order' and 'Obedience' that Craig speaks of are not the materialistic notion of order and control that we find in Cubism and Constructivism or in its Neo-classical dimensions (as in the rather later work of Picasso, Stravinsky or Joyce). His is a metaphysical order, mysteriously uniting the art of the past with that of the present and leading it into the future. Craig uses the terms in a way that is similar to the terms 'arrangements' and 'harmonies' used by Whistler in the 1890s.

> Art should be independent of clap-trap – should stand alone, and appeal to the artistic sense of eye or ear without confounding this with emotions entirely foreign to it, as devotion, pity, love, patriotism, and the like. All these have no kind of concern with it; and that is why I insist on calling my works 'arrangements' and 'harmonies'.[20]

Whistler was one of the main exponents of the autonomy of art in the second half of the nineteenth century. The opposition to the pure aestheticism of Whistler was expressed by Ruskin and Morris, who believed that art ought to have an organic relationship with society and politics at large. Craig's roots definitely lie in the explicitly aestheticist 1890s, and not so much in the more organic and socially aware strand of that movement. This also accounts for his particular 'blend' of Modernism. If the Morris school can be seen as a forerunner to the later Constructivist and functional movements in Europe (i.e. Bauhaus), the aestheticism of Whistler can certainly foreshadow the Idealistic trends in Modernism that were to follow a generation later. It is this tradition Craig turns to in defining his position within a European context. For his final attack on the Futurists he resorts to Whistler:

> As signor Marinetti very rightly says 'The Futurists paint what they see'. And as Mr. Whistler as rightly said 'the shock will be when they see what they paint'.[21]

---

[19] See note 13, p. 198.
[20] See Charles Harrison, note 6, p. 16.
[21] *The Mask*, Vol. 5, 1912, p. 174.

Despite his ambivalence towards them, Craig shared common ground with the Futurists in at least one more aspect. Both Craig and Marinetti shared the anxiety of forming a new rhetoric for their art. Their concerns were more meta-theatrical than purely theatrical. Both men did a lot of theorising and explaining; in many ways the work came second. The Futurists would almost invariably write a manifesto first for a particular artistic mode and only then start experimenting with it. As a method of work this was similar to Craig's. However, although Craig and Marinetti work within the same general framework of Idealistic Modernism, Craig could never wholeheartedly accept Futurism.

In an attack Craig mounts against Futurist painting, through another issue of *The Mask*, he expresses the source of his reservations:

> The painter is trying to do in line and colour what movement alone can accomplish. He therefore makes a big blunder. Fancy a Futurist blundering! Surely that was not intentional. It comes from forgetting that movement is the property of another and quite different artist, namely the artist of the Theatre. And it comes from the modern lust after other people's property which has made the European quite crazy of late. Some more-than-Futurist will soon come along who will profess to give sound to pictures.[22]

He becomes all the more defensive when his role as Artist of the Theatre is threatened and falls back on his usual accusation of claiming that others 'steal' or 'borrow' his work. The above quotation ironically has a prophetic, even Futurist, ring to it as it foresees the arrival of 'talking pictures'.

Kandinsky, to whom Craig is much closer theoretically, sums up Craig's view well when he says of the Futurists:

> I cannot free myself from the strange contradiction that I find their ideas, at least for the main part, brilliant, but am in no doubt whatsoever as to the mediocrity of their work.[23]

Kandinsky and the *Blaue Reiter* circle form one of the most influential groups in the Europe of the period, and their work is significant in relation to Craig, as it too presents a type of Idealistic Modernism. The *Blaue Reiter* was a manifesto and its theoretical concerns are much closer to *The Mask* than anything the Futurists wrote, even though Craig does not directly deal with it and there is no evidence that he was even aware of it. The *Blaue Reiter* was first published in 1912 in what was intended

---

[22] Ibid., p. 89.
[23] Quoted in Umbro Apollonion (ed), *Futurist Manifestos* (London, 1973), p. 7.

to be the first of a periodical publication, which never continued. Like *The Mask* it proposed a synaesthetic model for the arts, and propagated the ideal of totality through a multi-media, theatre-type art form. Franc Marc, the co-editor, writes in the subscription prospectus:

> Today art is moving in a direction of which our fathers would never even have dreamed. We stand before the new pictures as in a dream and we hear the apocalyptic horsemen in the air. There is an artistic tension all over Europe. Everywhere new artists are greeting each other; a look, a handshake is enough for them to understand each other!
>
> Out of the awareness of this secret connection of all new artistic production, we developed the idea of the Blaue Reiter. It will be the call that summons all artists of the new era and rouses the laymen to hear... The first volume herewith announced, which will be followed at irregular intervals by others, includes the latest movements in French, German, and Russian painting. It reveals subtle connections with Gothic and primitive art, with Africa and the vast Orient, with the highly expressive, spontaneous folk and children's art, and especially with the most recent musical movements in Europe and the new ideas for the theatre of our time.[24]

The general framework of the *Blaue Reiter* is similar to that of *The Mask*. Both publications function as manifestos: they are working towards a synaesthetic artistic form, and they are both fascinated with primitive and Oriental art. Both can be seen as an expression of Worringer's urge to abstraction, substituting the spiritual and the idealistic for the material and historical, for Kandinsky shared Craig's fear of 'modernity'. To him art belonged to a higher spiritual order:

> A great era has begun: the spiritual 'awakening', the increasing tendency to regain 'lost balance', the inevitable necessity of spiritual plantings, the unfoling of the first blossom.
>
> We are standing at the threshold of one of the greatest epochs that mankind has ever experienced, the epoch of great spirituality.
>
> Art, literature, even 'exact' science are in various stages of change in this 'new' era; they will all be overcome by it.[25]

Theatre occupies a privileged position in the Almanac. It is viewed as the artistic mode that may bring back the spiritual in art through its synaesthetic nature. In an article entitled 'On Stage Production' Kandinsky outlines quite an elaborate theory for a purely abstract theatre. He proposes music, movement and colour as structuring units

---

[24] Wassily Kandinsky, Franz Marc eds., *The Blaue Reiter Almanac*, ed. Klaus Lankheit, trans. Henning Falkenstein (London, 1974), p. 252.

[25] Ibid., p. 250.

for a plotless, actionless and 'idea-less' theatre. He also presents a play entilted *The Yellow Sound – A Stage Composition*. As the title suggests it consists of very detailed directions of what might be conceived as moving tableaux. The acts are actually called 'pictures'. For Kandinsky the 'final goal' of art is knowledge which 'is reached through the delicate vibrations of the human soul'. The aim of such a theatre is to set these spiritual vibrations into motion. He writes in his theory for stage composition:

> There are three elements that as external methods serve the inner value:
> 1. The musical sound and its movement,
> 2. The physical–psychical sound and its movement, expressed through people and objects,
> 3. The coloured tone and its movements (a special possibility for the stage).[26]

Kandinsky's formulations read like more abstract and minimalist versions of Craig's ideas for theatre production. He too uses music as a paradigm for movement and action. He works towards a non-psychological (but not necessarily non-spiritual) theatre with his idea of the *Übermarionette*, which can be seen as the carrier of 'physical–psychical sound'. Craig's idea of 'painting with light' is also parallel to Kandinsky's 'coloured tone and its movements'. Regarding the experimental use of colour and music both men had similar kinds of influences, though from quite different sources. Craig was aware of Sir Hubert von Herkomer's synaesthetic attempts. In 1912 a book entitled *Colour Music* was published: it was written by Rimington, and the introduction was by Herkomer. Rimington had created the Colour-Organ for his purposes – a machine that produced colour sequences that correlated to musical scores. Kandinsky, on the other hand, had been influenced by Scriabin, on whom there is an article in the *Blaue Reiter*. He is heralded as the new prophet for the reunification of the arts:

> The time for the reunification of the separate arts has arrived. This idea was vaguely formulated by Wagner, but Scriabin expresses it much more clearly today. All the arts, each of which has achieved an enormous development individually, must be united in one work, whose ambiance conveys such a great exaltation that it must absolutely be followed by an authentic ecstasy, an authentic vision of higher realities.[27]

---

[26] Ibid., p. 201.
[27] Ibid., p. 130–1.

Scriabin, like Rimington, had worked out a spectrum according to which musical tones corresponded to colours. He used this system of correspondence in his production of *Prometheus*. Craig does not seem very impressed with Scriabin's experiments. In an article entitled 'Colorific Music' he traces the trend back to the eighteenth century. This historicity of Craig's becomes an obsession towards the last issues of *The Mask*. Repeating a familiar attack on his Modernist colleagues, he writes in 1927:

> It was, I think, in 1910, that I heard Scriabin in Moscow on his piano.... Scriabin was trying to work out, or had already worked out, some artistic problem about the relationship of colour and sound...But somewhat earlier – in 1776 – appeared a book by a certain W. Hooper M. D. in which is a chapter called 'Colorific Music'. I give it here and you can judge for yourself whether it is in any way related with the recent (150 years too late) discoveries.[28]

The article continues with a very clear diagram of W. Hooper's system of correspondences between notes and colour ranges. Naturally Hooper's experiments present a more basic and naive attempt at the sort of work Scriabin was doing, and what is more, the general framework is very different. Hooper was working more as a natural scientist, interested in how the senses function in response to various stimuli. The Modernists' experiments in colorific music encompass a very distinct aesthetic position – the attempt to create totality in art through the redefinition of the 'nature' of music. Craig's perspective was hardly sensitised towards these issues. Rather than looking for correlations with his contemporaries, many of whom, like the *Blaue Reiter* group, shared backgrounds and future aims, he almost invariably looked back for analogies and parallels. Kandinsky's and Marc's *Blaue Reiter* is the most strikingly similar contemporary publication to *The Mask*. Although not as long-lived as *The Mask*, it embodied many Craigian ideals in both its physical appearance and its contents. Unfortunately neither party was aware of the other.

Being so determined to remain faithful to his concept of 'tradition', of 'the past', Craig develops a kind of pseudo-historicity in the last issues of *The Mask*, according to which he finds historical correlatives for modern movements. It is significant that this trend develops in the late 1920s by which time the slogan 'make it new' was slightly old fashioned. Craig's ideas themselves, although revolutionary at the time of their conception, were by now almost mainstream amongst experimental theatres in Europe. Craig's Romantic belief in the uniqueness of his artistic theories and his very 'genius' as an artist helped create a

---

[28] *The Mask*, Vol. 12, 1927, p. 158.

narrow-mindedness, which is evident in the last issues of *The Mask*. This obstructs him from working creatively with fellow artists, and it shades his perception of his contemporary movements. At times it leads to misconception, oversimplification and total appropriation of Modernist trends to artistic movements of the past. When working in the opposite direction of assessing artistic movements of the past, Craig exhibits an impressive knowledge and an acute understanding of his topic. The same is not, unfortunately, true of his studies of twentieth-century modes.

Cubism and Craig's interpretation of it furnish a characteristic example of the distorting effect of his obsession with the 'traditional past'. In an article entitled 'Cubism as Old as the Pyramids' (1913), he presents his evidence as an 'outstanding discovery', in an attempt to unveil the sources of 'true Cubism'.

> In our last number we gave a series of illustrations as proof that the Cubists, who claim to be the newest of the new, the 'dernier cri' in sculpture and painting, are not really new at all; that they are merely the conceited and disorderly followers of a great master who, four hundred years ago, knew all the secrets which they profess to have discovered. This master was the German, Albert Durer...[29]

The main point that seems to bother Craig is the fact that the Cubists claim to be 'the newest of the new'. In this continual struggle for 'newness', Craig's innovation lay in the fact that he acknowledged that he was working within a tradition. His idea that Cubism somehow copied existing forms reveals his total misunderstanding of fundamental principles of the type of Modernism that Cubism represents. The idea of reinterpreting and reconstructing existing artistic modes towards new goals and with new media seems foreign to Craig. For him the past is idealised and therefore static. This is more characteristic of his perception of the arts in general, whereas, regarding the theatre in particular, he does manage to use the past organically. He also works against the very grain of Modernism when he puts forward the notion that artistic creation involves the revealing of some sort of clearly-defined and centred 'secret'. Still floating in Romantic clouds he fails to see the Neo-classicism of Cubism and claims that their ideas were 'very well known to artists, not merely some hundreds, but thousands of years ago'. He adds:

> But let us not forget that it was known with this supreme difference: ...that as Durer used his method only as a means to an end,

---

[29] *The Mask*, Vol. 6, 1913, p. 97.

doing his best, as Mr Urban wrote in July 'to hide all art by being too much of an artist to show how he was doing the thing', so did the artists of those remote times allow no evidence of effort, no desire to show how 'clever' they were, to detract from the supreme calm of their finished work.[30]

Here a noticeably more sophisticated argument is used. The artistic process itself is of no interest. Only the result counts. Craig considers it 'cleverness' when an artist reveals his methods. Cubism in deconstructing the creative process and incorporating it as part of the work of art, is being indulgent, as far as Craig is concerned. He urges the Cubists to remember a verse by William Watson:

> No record art keeps
> Of its struggles and throes;
> There is toil on the steeps,
> On the summit repose.[31]

Craig's conception of what he considers to be 'classical unity' does not allow him to see how the Cubists interpret this notion and appropriate it to their work. He ends his article with a simile: the Cubist artist, he asserts, is someone 'who goes struggling before our eyes (like a modern Sisyphus),... bearing instead of the "shameless stone" a cube upon his back'. The myth of Sisyphus was to be interpreted later by the existentialists, as a metaphor for a world that has lost all sense of intention and purpose. Craig in his usual aphoristic manner makes quite an insightful point. In trying to redefine the very nature and function of art, Cubism is only one of the movements of the period that develops a degree of self-awareness and self-reflection that previous art modes lacked. The creative process itself is accentuated because the final goal has become very obscure. The Sisyphus myth funtions very well as a symbol for that quintessentially Modernist project of having initiated a process that may not necessarily lead anywhere at all.

Meetings with Outstanding Persons

Although Craig had problems when it came to collaborating with fellow artists and only managed to work with a few, he uses *The Mask* not only to expose his views on contemporary movements, but also to highlight his sometimes uneasy relationships with his colleagues. Diaghilev is such a figure. In many ways his rise is parallel to that of Craig's, though Craig never achieved the fame that Diaghilev did. Diaghilev, like Craig,

---

[30] Ibid., p. 97.
[31] Ibid., p. 97.

was involved with a periodical early in his career, *The World of Art*. He then went on to form the Russian Ballet, which Craig reviews in the pages of *The Mask*. The Russian Ballet, among other things, touched upon a particular strand of Orientalism which was already prevalent in the visual arts of nineteenth century France. With his company's *Scheherazade* Diaghilev manifests the Orientalism that plays a special role in Idealistic Modernism. As Edward Said, among others, has shown, the Orient presents the ideal locus for sexual and political fantasy. Both the *Blaue Reiter* and *The Mask* are fascinated with oriental art forms. For Modernism the Orient becomes a new *terra incognita* whose artistic modes it can appropriate into its own theoretical framework. Craig follows this pattern with his concern for the theatre of the Orient.[32] Apart from utilising similar sources, the Russian Ballet also interested Craig in purely theatrical terms.[33] Craig's notion of theatrical movement as dance is very close to ballet. Diaghilev's increasing use of well-known artists for stage design and the changes these artists introduced to scene design as a whole, were things that Craig found intriguing, but also threatening. In an article entitled 'Kleptomania, or The Russian Ballet' he writes (in 1911 just after the Russian Ballet had made a triumphant appearance in Paris):

> There is so much Russian art being let loose into the theatres of Europe lately that it may be as well to study some specimens of it and see what has made the thing so popular and whether there is sufficient ground for so much sudden and insincere enthusiasm.[34]

Authenticity again is the criterion by which Craig attacks the Russian Ballet. Within a Modernism that has come to terms with re-working past and foreign artistic modes, and where the word 'new' has lost some of its magic power, Craig continues to seek clear-cut distinctions between old and new. He continues in the same article:

> But the Russians have done a clever thing: they have increased the value of their French Ballet by adding to it a few tricks stolen from other lands and other arts. This was clever of them, ... and highly reprehensible.
> ... While doing so they stole an idea or two from the only original dancer of the age, the American, and another idea or two from the most advanced scene designers of Europe and superimposed all these upon the wiry artificial framework of the old French Ballet.[35]

---

[32] For a more elaborate discussion on Orientalism in *The Mask* see chapter five.

[33] Craig designed a ballet, *Psyche*, for Diaghilev in 1906–7. This was turned down by Diaghilev for what could have been a number of reasons. See *Edward Gordon Craig: Designs for the Theatre* (London, 1948), p. 8, p. 18.

[34] *The Mask*, Vol. 4, 1911, pp. 97–101.

[35] Ibid., p. 98.

The American Craig refers to is Isadora Duncan, who did have an influence on the progressive Russian Ballet when she appeared in Russia. The production Craig is attacking is *Scheherezarde*, a highly Orientalist version of the Islamic myth with designs by Bakst. Craig becomes especially aggresive (always under the pseudonym of John Balance) when talking of Bakst's designs, as he considers scenic design to be his domain of artistic creation. Having already fired his accusation of theft, which, as the years go by, becomes his favourite attack, he continues:

> Although his designs are ugly, they are only ugly enough to shock Parisians. ...It is never terrible like Daumier, nor has it the irony of Beardsley's demon. Bakst is ugly on account of his clumsy sense of the sensual.[36]

What Craig calls Bakst's 'clumsy sense of the sensual' is mainly due to his Orientalism and could stand as a valid point had it been placed within the theoretical context that would account for it. However, Craig's main attack is focused on his concept of originality:

> It is not original; it is something learned and then made. They create nothing... As a work of Art then the Russian Ballet is a myth; as a work of originality it is a fraud. The dancers, painters and wig-makers of the troupe are all charming will o' the wisps and their light is certainly not to be trusted.[37]

The word 'original' aquires an almost metaphysical status. The process of influence and assimilation is considered mechanical and not creative. Art for Craig should be instinctive and apocalyptic and should leave no traces of the paths it has followed.

Craig's anger reaches its peak when the Russian Ballet performs in London with the same success it had in Paris. He writes in the editor's notes of *The Mask* this time under the pseudonym of John Semar:

> The visit of the Russian Ballet to Covent Garden has proved a grand failure.
> Englishmen are generally telling each other (and incidentally the foreigners) that fine English Dancing can only be born by asking a Russian Ballet master to come over and train our feet. Isn't it stupendous!
> Our Modern Patriotism. 'Down with England, long live the Tartars'.[38]

---

[36] Ibid., p. 99.
[37] Ibid., p. 101.
[38] Ibid., in Editorial Notes, p. 266.

In great colonial style, it seems the longer Craig remained away from England the more Victorian and xenophobic he became.

A year later, in 1913, Craig speaks in his own voice, announcing the true reason for his attack against the Russian Ballet. In reply to an announcement saying that he was going to produce a ballet he writes:

> For NO amount of Ballets which I might produce would ever be announced by me as Works of Art, and I should, as I have ever done, protest against their being so considered. Well then... where are we?[39]

Here Craig exhibits a type of small-mindedness and xenophobia which was to escalate as the years went by and shape his encounters with other artists. In a gesture that totally dismisses the synaesthesia of the whole Diaghilev project, he claims that the only true art form is the theatre (as he conceives it, of course). Any other art form that claims the stage, which according to Craig only belongs to spoken drama, is threatening. The best way to deal with it is to dismiss it from the realm of art altogether.

We know from the diaries of Count Kessler that Craig met Diaghilev at least once. This was in 1928 after a performance of *Petruschka* when they all went to dinner together. No further comment is made in the diary regarding Craig's response to the performance. Craig had a much closer working relationship with the Russian spoken theatre. During Isadora Duncan's first tour of Russia, her enthusiasm about Craig managed to convince Stanislavsky to invite Craig to Moscow to work with the Moscow Art Theatre. The combination seems an unlikely one as Stanislavsky was at the time being hailed as the high priest of naturalism. Craig first visits Moscow in 1908 and by 1912 his production of *Hamlet* is staged at the Moscow Art Theatre. The collaboration with Stanislavsky is recorded in *The Mask* through the correspondence that Craig had with the editor John Semar i.e. himself, throughout the whole period of his visit to Moscow.

Craig's ideas on the theatre were not altogether new on the Russian scene. Apart from Stanislavsky, who was concerned in scientifically formulating naturalism, the Russian Futurists and the Symbolist and Decadent movements before them were all working in more or less, the same area of experimentation as Craig. In 1908, the same year that Craig arrived in Moscow a book entitled *Theatre, A Book about the New Theatre* was published in St. Petersburg. The main contributors formed part of a group that was later to form Meyerhold's experimental studio. They were the designer Aleksandr Benois, the Symbolist poets Bryusov

---

[39] *The Mask*, Vol. 6, 1913, p. 92.

and Bely, the socialist theoretician Lunacharsky and Meyerhold himself. The book itself promoted an abstract, highly stylized theatre under the control of a single artistic consciousness. 'The drama is the product of a single concept, just as the universe is the product of a single creative idea' wrote Sologub in his essay in the same book.[40] Acting would have to be so precise and schematic that only a puppet could perform ideally in this type of theatre. From its very title to the concepts it includes the book could have easily been written by Craig. And in a sense it was since the Englishman's influence was profound in this circle. Craig's first dialogue had been pirated and published in Russia in 1906. Meyerhold wrote of Craig in 1909:

> It is remarkable that in the very first year of this new century E. G. Craig flung a challenge to the naturalistic theatre...therefore, this young Englishman is the first to set up initial guideposts on the new road of the Theatre.[41]

It was not Meyerhold that Craig had come to work with though. Meyerhold had been fired and, despite the similarities in their work, the two men did not meet until 1935. Craig was supposed to design for the theatre that possibly more than any other had helped to create a language for naturalism on the stage: the Moscow Art Theatre. Stanislavsky was having problems at the time with his 'system'. In an attempt to expand the company's aesthetic concerns he invited Craig. Unlike Meyerhold, he was not informed of Craig's work and knew of him only through fame and rumour. Their approaches to theatre were diametrically opposite and this obviously caused problems in their working relationship. This working relationship was extensively documented in *The Mask*. Craig's correspondence (with himself) all the while he was in Russia is published in his journal. Despite their enormous differences *Hamlet* was staged and Craig maintained his respect for Stanislavsky and the Russian tradition in the theatre. In his correspondence with Semar (himself) in *The Mask* he would dispel all rumour and suspicion of disruption in their working relationship. He writes:

> You ask me how I feel after my third visit to Moscow. I feel tremendous for I feel that I have found friends... In the production of *Hamlet* in Moscow we are all doing as we think best. We have experienced several

---

[40] See Fyodor Sologub, 'The Theatre of a Single Will', in Laurence Senelick, ed. and trans. *Russian Dramatic Theory from Pushkin to the Symbolists, An Anthology*, Chapter 2, note 37, pp. 132–148.
[41] Quoted in Laurence Senelick, 'Moscow and Monodrama: The Meaning of the Craig–Stanislavsky Hamlet', in *Theatre Research International*, Vol. 6 (1981), pp. 109–124, p. 114.

attempts to break this harmony on the part of envious creatures who
have nothing better to do than create discord, but so far every attempt
has broken itself against itself.[42]

The almost apologetic tone of the above statement reveals its true
function. It is a fact that Craig did not work well with Stanislavsky. He
managed to work harmoniously with the Art Theatre's producer
Nemirovitch Danchenko. This was mainly because Danchenko did not
interfere with Craig's creative process. Craig had not come to Moscow
to be merely a designer. He wanted to be responsible for every aspect of
the performance. Also it is possible that Danchenko took Craig's side in
the quarrels as part of his personal feud with Stanislavsky. He saw it as
an ideal chance to weaken Stanislavsky's influence in the Moscow Art
Theatre, and, through Craig, to strengthen his own. Craig quotes
Danchenko in an attempt to dissolve the rumours of his disagreement
with Stanislavsky:

> Now Craig unites in one person the director and the artist. All rumours
> as to any misunderstandings between Craig and Stanislavsky are false.
> On the contrary, Stanislavsky is quite under the fascination of what he
> calls 'Craig's genius'.[43]

Craig's admiration and respect for Stanislavsky is not consistent
throughout all of his personae in *The Mask*. Under the pseudonym John
Balance, who, as the name suggests, always manages to keep a cool,
distanced perspective on things, he discreetly launches his attack on the
Russian theatre:

> Mr Gordon Craig has told us that the Moscow Art Theatre is the first
> in Europe, but I have noticed that when writing of that theatre he has
> invariably treated it as an organization and made no mention of its art.
> He has been very particular upon this point and his discrimination is
> significant.[44]

John Balance once again uses originality as the ultimate criterion of true
art, in a pattern that follows the same line of argument as his attack
on the Russian Ballet. Like the previous article, this one is called
'Kleptomania, or the Russian Theatre'.

In many respects Craig's attack on the Moscow Art Theatre can
be theoretically justified as it represents the kind of theatre that Craig

---

[42] *The Mask*, Vol. 3, 1910, pp. 34–35.
[43] Ibid., pp. 41–42.
[44] *The Mask*, Vol. 4, 1911, p. 97.

wanted to destroy. On the other hand, Craig could not help but admire the organization and dedication of the Russians. He believed that the work Stanislavsky was doing was like a historical phase in the development of the theatre: a phase which had to be passed in order to reach his own areas of experimentation. He writes in his review of *My Life in Art*:

> It has been proved by you, more than by anyone else at any time, that the artist may only (can only) work in a material which is 'dead' material (I search for a better word in vain) if he will create a work of art... Your book must live because of the sincerity which breathes out of every page of it. You have raised the entire profession of Theatrical workers to a position it cannot recede from. You have at last made it impossible to retreat. We salute you with affection and with reverence.[45]

Had Craig worked with Meyerhold the result would have been interesting indeed. The two men represent two very different, almost conflicting, schools of Modernism in the theatre. Their concepts are parallel but derive from opposing theoretical backgrounds. Meyerhold, with Dialectical Materialism as a guideline, deconstructs his initial ideas and moves towards the formulation of a theory that can put them into practice. He acknowledges the modernity of his age and assimilates the changes his medium has undergone. At the same time he sees his art as part of a society that was itself swept by the tumult of revolutionary change. This helped to define very clearly the relationship of his art to society and history in general. Like other movements in Europe, it does not consider aesthetics to be its grand theory. Art is subjugated under a more general world theory (Marxism). The artistic process is seen as a dialectic which can be analysed and studied.

Craig stands on the other side of the spectrum of Modernist trends. His theoretical background is an Idealistic Romantic one. Craig had visions where Meyerhold had specific plans for the theatre of the future. Craig's work appears prophetic where Meyerhold's displays methodological precision. Craig envisaged the *Ubermarionette* before Meyerhold but, it was Meyerhold that worked towards a specific system of exercises for the human body (*biomechanics*) that would help transform it into a fully controllable object on the stage. Many of Craig's designs and his conceptualisation of scenic space could have benefited from experimentation in the cinema at the time. Meyerhold's student Eisenstein carried many of his ideas onto the screen. Craig's background could never allow him to make the leap from theatre to cinema.

---

[45] *The Mask*, Vol. 10, 1924, p. 188.

Another influential theatrical figure of the time who appears in the pages of *The Mask* is Max Reinhardt. Craig's main accusation against Reinhardt again is his lack of originality. This time he considers himself to be the originator of most of the ideas Reinhardt brought to the stage. This is partly true. Craig had been experimenting in the same field and in similar style before Reinhardt worked on his successful productions. It is also true that after 1910–12, these ideas were simply 'in the air' as part of the general cultural and artistic consciousness of Europe of the age. Nevertheless most of the articles on Reinhardt in *The Mask*, either signed by Craig himself or by his collaborators, are strikingly bitter and at times very aggressive. John Semar, Craig's editorial mask, writes a review of a book entitled *The Theatre of Max Reinhardt* by Huntly Carter:

> By the way, it is worth noting that, while the book takes its name from Professor Reinhardt, we find on no less than 46 pages that the centre of interest is Mr. Gordon Craig and his work... Surely too significant a straw for either Germans or Britons in doubt which way the wind blows.[46]

The author of the book replies to Semar in an apologetic manner and adds that, in the meantime, he had revised the book to acknowledge Craig's influence on the European scene. He explains:

> However I completed the book and added some 40 illustrations and a number of charts... very important ones forming synthetic summaries and some of them showing at glance your *position* and your *influence* on the European theatre.[47]

Reinhardt is presented in *The Mask* mainly in an attempt to 'get the facts right' and establish 'who came first'. In a review of Reinhardt's production of *Sumurun* Craig writes:

> Of course the production is as Mr. Paul Konody, writing in the *Daily Mail*, rightly points out, 'merely the latest development of the stage reform initiated by Mr. Gordon Craig'. This is a fact which will naturally increase the pleasure of the public since Mr. Craig is an Englishman.[48]

As was the case with the Russian Ballet, Craig's criticisms become extra sharp when foreign companies prove to be successful in his country.

---

[46] *The Mask*, Vol. 7, 1914, p. 85.
[47] Ibid., pp. 86–87.
[48] *The Mask*, Vol. 3, 1910, p. 189.

In 1927 there is a comprehensive article on the Reinhardt company and its history by Antonio Galli. Again the importance of Craig is assessed. Reinhardt is praised for his organisational skills, for his ability to adapt ideas, for his professionalism, but not for originality of ideas. The company is referred to as a firm and a business:

> But still this firm has no IDEA of its own: borrowed notions or notions bought and paid for is the most it ever has to offer. As perhaps will be seen more clearly if the accompanying designs are looked at curiously.[49]

The author of the article continues by stressing the significance of Craig in the new movement. 'What Craig dreams Reinhardt practises' quotes Galli and answers this accusation by stating that 'Craig began by *doing* the thing in 1900 before anyone else, and damme if he isn't called theorist'. Galli touches upon one of the main criticisms against Craig. His work, conceived in Romantic aspiration, was almost impossible to realise practically. The process of creation is somehow not artistic enough to occupy him. His attack on Reinhardt brings to the surface another aspect of Craig's work that impeded the fulfillment of his ideas. Craig could only work alone. The artistic creation had to be the result of a single consciousness. Reinhardt is severely criticised for working with a group as an ensemble. 'His second talent is an astounding capacity to listen to suggestions and to pick up ideas from other people, and apply them'[50], says the article. Craig could not possibly do this as it was against his notion of the artistic genius. Count Kessler tried to engage Craig in working with Reinhardt but, the project fell through. Later Craig regretted not having worked with Reinhardt. Kessler writes in his diary:

> He expressed regret that he and Reinhardt never collaborated: Reinhardt, precisely because the differences between them are so great that they would complement each other, is the only producer with whom he could have worked. Stanislavsky, the Russians as a whole, and the Americans as well, are impossible. 'I don't want to have anything to do with Russians or Americans. I cannot abide them.' Reinhardt, he went on, has the hard-headed commonsense which he himself lacks.[51]

Craig's imaginary collaboration with Reinhardt is still biased. There is a huge division in the kind of work the two men will do. Reinhardt is seen as the organizer, the practical man, whom Craig can use to realise his

---

[49] *The Mask*, Vol. 13, 1927, pp. 102–5.
[50] Ibid., p. 103.
[51] Harry Kessler, *The Diaries of a Cosmopolitan. Count Harry Kessler, 1918–1937*, trans. Charles Kessler (London, 1971), p. 194.

ideas. The responsibility for artistic creation still falls upon Craig. The two directors would probably have worked successfully, if it hadn't been for personal differences. Theoretically Craig is much closer to Reinhardt than he ever was to Stanislavsky.

The Mask seems oblivious to all the other movements in Germany at the time. It is mainly because they derive from a very different ideological background. The Expressionist and later Bauhaus theatres of the Weimar Republic do not interest him at all. They represent the materialistic school of Modernism. Their art was seen as part of a more general historical process. At the same time, they were highly experimental with the nature of their medium as well. Political commitment did not exclude formal experimentation, and indeed dictated it. This was the climate that bred perhaps the most representative figure of this school of Modernism: Bertolt Brecht.

Even though it is surprising that Weimar receives no attention whatsoever in *The Mask*, it is, nevertheless, in line with the journal's overall theoretical context. Craig was certainly aware of the happenings in Weimar and particularly in theatre. He was a personal friend of Count Kessler. This friendship is difficult to understand, as the ideologies of the two men could not be more conflicting. Count Kessler was known as 'the red Count', and he was the main patron of the leftist artistic movements in Weimar. Yet he was the first man who invited Craig to work in Germany. Kessler was interested in publishing Craig's designs for *Hamlet* (the Moscow production) on his newly formed Cranach Press. The two men kept in touch and visited each other frequently. Kessler remains Craig's friend and firm supporter of his work, even though he is aware of their differences. Kessler sees Craig as an eccentric Romantic. He describes Craig's life-style on one of his visits to Florence in 1922:

> Light and spare, dedicated with almost religious fervour to a single purpose in life, the rooms are like monastic cells. I cannot help feeling that this single-mindedness is, in our age, somewhat childish. It was like paying a visit to a nursery, particularly when Mrs Craig and the son Teddy suddenly came out with some bloodthirsty Fascist Opinions.[52]

Kessler was a dear friend of Craig's and his criticisms are not ill intended. He manages to point out what is possibly the source of many of Craig's agonies and frustrations. He belonged to another age. He never properly became part of the 'modern' world. In Kessler's terms

---

[52] Ibid., p. 194.

7. Mask of the Fool in *The Hour Glass* by W. B. Yeats, designed and engraved by Edward Gordon Craig, Vol. 3, Nos. 10–12, p. 147a, 1911.

he never grew up. Despite his caution, Kessler still acknowledges Craig as the main inspiration for the developments in Modernist stagecraft. He writes:

> It is close on tragic to see this undoubted genius, whose vision and ideas have for the past twenty years inspired the theatre the world over, from Russia via Germany and France to America, not exercising his gifts but living like an island exile while festival playhouses, international drama exhibitions, and revolutions in theatrical production still draw on his capital.[53]

Craig's ideological limitations kept him tied up in the late 1890s, while others could expand and formally systematize his initial ideas, utilizing Modernist method and ideology.

Literary movements are conspicuously absent from *The Mask* as well. Craig's insistence on a non-literary theatre, that would be the creation of the director and not the playwright, led him to totally discard the literary aspect of Modernism. In an attempt to secure his own artistic integrity he was indifferent to Modernist developments in literature. One of the few literary figures that appeared regularly in *The Mask* was W. B. Yeats. Also Yeats was one of those rare people whom Craig openly admired and respected. His use of the mask as a metaphor for the role of the artist, and his conception of theatre as a paradigm for art, were notions that sounded very Craigian indeed. Craig worked with Yeats in the Abbey Theatre. He writes in *The Mask*:

> January 12th was a memorable occasion in the history of the Abbey Theatre...in the history of the modern theatre as a whole, being the occasion of the first public use of the new scene for the poetic drama conceived, constructed and patented by Mr. Gordon Craig... The method of decoration employed for the two former was invented by Mr. Craig and used by him for the famous Art Theatre in Moscow.[54]

Yeats contributes many theoretical articles in *The Mask*[55] on theatre. Craig considers him to be the only worth-while director in 'England'.

---

[53] Ibid., pp. 194–5.

[54] *The Mask*, Vol. 3, 1910, pp. 190–1.

[55] W. B. Yeats appears in *The Mask* in the following issues: Vol. 2, p. 148; Vol. 4, p. 61, p. 161; Vol. 5, p. 2; Vol. 7, p. 139, 174; Vol. 9, p. 50; Vol. 10, p. 66; *The Hour Glass*, vol. 3, no. 4, frontispiece; Vol. 3, pp. 190–92; Vol. 5, pp. 327–46 (play and preface printed); Vol. 7, p. 174; *Per Amica Silentia Lunae* (rev), Vol. 8, p. 39; *Plays and Controversies* (rev), Vol. 10, p. 90; *Plays for an Irish Theatre*, illustrated by Gordon Craig Vol. 4, pp. 342–43 (rev); Vol. 7, pp. 139–40; 'The Tragic Theatre' (article), Vol. 3, p. 77.

8. 'Henry Irving', by Edward Gordon Craig, Vol. 3, Nos. 10–12, p. 184, 1911.

In a prologue to an article explaining the impossibility of work for conscientious directors in England, John Semar writes:

> The only man we know of working today as a director of a theatre in whose conscience is his armour and not his pyjamas is W. B. Yeats.[56]

He stresses the fact that this is true of England and adds: 'Lest this be misunderstood let us hasten to remind our readers that Mr. Gordon Craig is at work in Paris, Mr. Allen Carrick is in Persia and John Balance in Krakow'.[57] Craig would seem quite generous here, acknowledging other directors, if it weren't for the fact that all the names he mentions are pseudonyms for himself. Given this egotism it is surprising he acknowledges Yeats as a theatrical person at all. In the same issue (1912) Yeats's *The Hour Glass* appears with positive commentary.

Despite his general acceptance of Yeats, Craig does not spare him a bitter attack when he believes that Yeats is taking over ground that he considers his own. In his review of Yeats's *Plays and Controversies* he writes in *The Mask* in 1924, after his close collaboration with Yeats had long ended.

> I cannot pretend to admire Mr. Yeats when he assumes the virtue of knowing all about the Theatre, for he is no better a dramatic poet for his little stage theories. If he only could laugh heartily at himself when he has put forth some thrilling...(and often incorrect) statement about the playhouse and its people. His power over magical words no one can be slow to acknowledge. This poet has suffered in having been born in a century when we had no Theatre to put at the service of the poets.[58]

Yeats and Craig are in many ways parallel figures. What Yeats was for literary Modernism, Craig was for Modernism in the theatre. Both men were rooted in Romanticism and never quite came to terms with their Modernity. Yeats's Irishness was as significant as Craig's Englishness. Both men shared a love/hate relationship with their inheritance, and never quite managed to break away from it.

Craig's relationship with Modernism, as it was articulated mainly in Europe, was one of tension. He never managed to appropriate the purely 'modern' developments in his art, for he was not theoretically

---

[56] *The Mask*, Vol. 5, 1915, p. 2.

[57] Ibid., p. 2.

[58] *The Mask*, Vol. 10, 1924, p. 90.

9. Edward Gordon Craig, by Max Beerbohm, Vol. 6, No. 3, p. 185a, 1914.

equipped to do so. Many of the Modernist trends in theatre (Constructivism, the Bauhaus and even the application of cinema techniques) are foreshadowed in the work of Craig. Nevertheless, he could not see them as a solution to many of the 'dead ends' that his experimentation led to. Almost purposely his work remained elusive, ambiguous, with an unfinished 'utopian' quality about it. As such, its impact is sometimes better felt and understood in his successors and in the schools he inspired (rather than analysed directly through the work itself). He has been rightly hailed as one of the great prophets of European Modernism in the theatre, rather than one of its exemplary practitioners.

4

ORIENT AND ORIENTALISM

The Orient, not only as a removed and remote world that provides an ideological framework for much of the theorising in its pages, but also as a specific locus for particular artistic forms, is dominant in *The Mask* and throughout Craigian thought. In its real, historical dimension or in its reconstructed, and to large extent fantasized one, the Orient and its theatre prove a rich source for much of the material published in *The Mask*, and set another example for Craigian notions of theatricality. This constant borrowing from and reinventing of the Orient towards its own ends is not a venture undertaken by *The Mask* alone; it partakes in the general fascination that most Modernist schools of performance share with Oriental theatrical practice, and provides for Craig yet another point of reference and contrast with his contemporaries.

The Orient as 'Other'

> The dangers of knowing are ever increasing. The danger of knowing all about the East... what a danger! The more we know the more we lose. The East seemed so far off once upon a time; to some it still seems as far... as far as the stars. How they shine... and how the East shines... in their distances. Instruct some of us in the stars and their light goes out, nor is there more light in us.
> So it is with the Holy East. Come to us, then, with your banners and your music, sweep past us with your dancers and divinities and go; do not deceive us by such flattery: let us remain ignorant, leave our hands untied. If you will conquer us do it like conquerors. So shall we (some of us) remain to the end affectionately yours.[1]

In reviewing E. Clements's *A Study of Indian Dance*, in the pages of *The Mask*, in 1913, Craig exposes his general attitude towards what he terms 'the holy East'. Despite the vagueness of the term, the 'East', or what Craig conceives as such, plays a determining role in the formulation and articulation of Craigian theories for the theatre throughout the pages of *The Mask*. This influence works on two levels: on a direct historical intercultural level, and on a mythological one. On the one hand, real information about eastern theatrical modes appears in *The Mask*.

---

[1] *The Mask*, Vol. 6, 1913, p. 81.

An immense number of articles about oriental notions of performance is spread throughout its issues, covering the whole spectrum of the performing arts from theatre and dance to puppets and masks. They are either written by Craig himself, who exhibits a surprisingly comprehensive knowledge of the field, or by pioneers of the study of oriental art on English, such as Ananda K. Coomaraswamy.[2] On the other hand, *The Mask* also maps a mythology of the East: the East as it is conceptualized by traditional western thought. This is the East of the Orientalists. Whether dark, mysterious, seductive and wise as in Craig's quotation, or threatening and barbaric, the East of Orientalism presents an alternative, an 'other' for Eurocentric art and thought in general. In this sense *The Mask* has influences both historical and ideological, and appears both as Oriental *and* Orientalist.

Much of the material about oriental theatrical modes presented in *The Mask* was new for most western audiences – certainly for English speaking ones – and consequently very important historically. Craig is meticulous and systematic in presenting his material, making the 'oriental' (as opposed to the 'orientalist') aspect of *The Mask* one of the most scholastic and academically sound, second only perhaps to the treatment of the Commedia dell'Arte. Nevertheless, Craig does not manage to escape what V. G. Kiernan called 'Europe's collective day-dream of the Orient'.[3] Whether Romantic or Modernist, this day-dream sees the Orient as a blank screen, existing primarily for its own solipsistic projection. As Edward W. Said says in his extensive study *Orientalism*:

> In the system of knowledge about the Orient, the Orient is less a place than a topos, a set of references, a congeries of characteristics, that seems to have its origin in a quotation, or a fragment of a text, or a citation from someone's work on the Orient, or some bit of previous imagining, or an amalgam of all these.[4]

It is this use of the Orient as a *topos* which in part defines Craig's work and, in many ways limits the potential which oriental theatrical modes presented for his own theories. As long as the East remained *exotic*, it

---

[2] Ananda K. Coomaraswamy, one of the authorities of the period on Indian Theatre and arts in general, was a regular correspondent of *The Mask*. His contributions include: 'Arts and Crafts of India and Ceylon' (extract), Vol. 6, pp. 270–72; 'Dance of Siva', Vol. 8, p. 31; 'The Mirror of Gesture' (rev), Vol. 8, p. 52; 'Sati: A Vindication of the Hindu Woman' (rev), Vol. 6, pp. 79–80; 'Visvakarama, Examples of Indian Architecture, Sculpture, Painting, Handicraft', Vol. 6, p. 272; 'Visvali – One Hundred Examples of Indian Sculpture' (rev), Vol. 7, p. 177. See also notes 18 and 28.

[3] V. G. Kiernan, *The Lords of Human Kind: Black Man, Yellow Man, and White Man in an Age of Empire* (Boston, 1969), p. 55.

[4] Edward W. Said, *Orientalism* (London, 1978), p. 177.

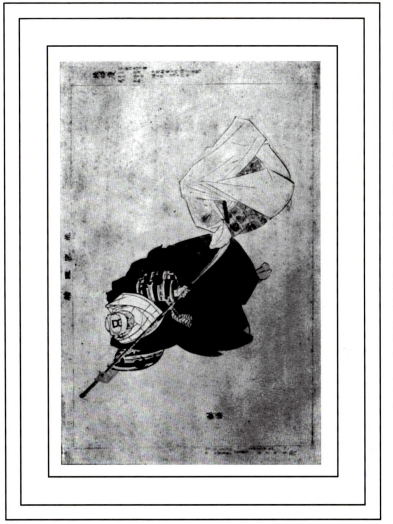

10. 'Benkei on the Bridge' (a Noh dance), Vol. 3, Nos. 4–6, p. 76b, 1910.

could not be appropriated to help form a new theatrical language. Seeing the Orient within the scope of Orientalism, as Said defines it, is a process which strips its object of any notion of history, and ultimately obscures and exoticizes it. A metalanguage of a different order is required to de-exoticize the Orient, a metalanguage which Craig lacked. Again Modernity provides such a model. Meyerhold, Brecht and Artaud had a language for their medium and an ideology to contextualize it, and so arguably made more vital use of oriental forms and techniques. Craig, to do him justice, identifies the potential the Orient presents for reviving theatrical art much earlier than his European counterparts do. Lacking the language with which to process, appropriate and eventually de-exoticize it, he enters into yet another of the conflicts which run throughout his work. All his knowledge and admiration of the East, essentially Romantic, never quite plays the determining role it could. Covered by a cloud of awe and fascination, the Holy East is somewhat fetishized and never quite appropriated. This conflict will generate more ideas, more schemes and dreams that will never be realized.

Orientalism and Modernism

A gradual, though not always successful, process of historicizing Oriental artistic modes and finally de-exoticizing them starts at the turn of the century and reaches its peak with late Modernism. In search of alternatives to Eurocentric humanism, Modernism, both in its Idealistic and Materialistic form, turns to the East for paradigms. The Russian Futurists, Kandinsky and the *Blaue Reiter* group, Craig and later the Russian Ballets all re-defined their art through re-writing what they conceived as being Oriental.

Oriental artistic modes presented the ultimate dehumanized art form. Abstract, stylized and highly conventional, they provided Modernism with a language which was the antithesis of humanism and naturalistic mimesis. It was the purely stylized formal language that Modernism required to redefine art and its role. However, the appropriation of oriental artistic modes by Modernism was not a straight-forward process. Historical and ideological parameters created differences between the various schools of Modernism.

Keeping the main categorization that we have been working with – that of distinguishing between an Idealistic and a Materialistic trend in Modernism – Craig's Orientalism can be more clearly interpreted. For Idealistic Modernism the Orient remained essentially 'other'. It presented a regenerating force for Europe. Its art was magic, wise, sensual and ritualistic. Rooted in ancient myth and archetype, it was seen as the force which would oppose the mechanization and the technology of the modern world. At the same time, Eastern art was not

Classical and humanist. It presented the ideal model for the anti-humanist Idealism promoted by T. E. Hulme in *Against Humanism* and Worringer in *Abstraction and Empathy*. This was the Orientalism of the *Blaue Reiter* and of the Russian Ballets. A very different type of Orientalism is found in the work of Brecht. It is not only time that separates Diaghilev's *Scheherazade* (1910) from Brecht's *The Good Woman of Setzuan*, or Max Reinhardt's production of *The Chalk Circle* (1924) from Brecht's reworking of the same theme. It is the ideological framework which accounts for the two antithetical interpretations of Orientalism; one that today maybe read within the complex workings of interculturalism rather than the more direct notions of influence and appropriation.

The work of Meyerhold, who had a great influence on Brecht, can be seen as a paradigm of Materialistic Modernism in the theatre. His application of Oriental theatrical modes helped him shape his own theory for acting. At the same time, his ideology contextualized and historicized modes which would be considered 'other'. The work of Craig is on the opposite side of the spectrum. His Orient is an Idealistic one. His vast knowledge of Oriental theatre at times almost succeeds in de-exoticizing the Orient, but this is never quite achieved. His ideas on theatre are Modernist in their conception, but not in their execution. Again the lack of a technology for his art form presents problems when it comes to actually giving shape to ideas. The formulation of such a technology or language could have been helped by his knowledge and experience of eastern theatre; in the same way that Meyerhold and Brecht used Oriental notions on theatre to articulate their own theories. Craig, on the other hand, approaches the Orient as a late Romantic, seeing it as the last salvation from the ever-increasing modernization of the age. He writes in *The Mask* (1914) in an article reviewing Coomaraswamy's *Arts and Crafts in India*:

> There has been of late years a revival of Arts and Crafts in Europe and America. We have all heard about the revival, . . . but where are the Arts and where the Crafts?
> How is it that man is not a scrap revived by this Revival?

The answer is provided by the frontispiece of Coomaraswamy's book which bears the Head of Krishna and the following quotation (deriving from the lament of the milkmaids in Hindu mythology):

> Have you left us, O Krishna, because we took you for a common play-fellow and did not pay you the tribute of worship that you deserved at your hands?
> How often, when playing, we quarrelled and abused you.

> Did you take these things to heart, and desert us, though we were so
> deeply devoted to you?
> We often beat you, or carried you on our shoulders, and rode on yours,
> often we ate first and gave you the remnants, calling you by all familiar
> names.
>
> Have you, for all these forsaken us, oh beloved Krishna?
> It is not wise to quarrel with the Ideal, . . . with God.
> We in Europe and in America have taken our Krishna out in motor cars
> for joy-rides, . . . while attempting the 'Revival' of the Arts and Crafts.
> Can crazyness(sic) go further . . . or dream a lower dream?
>
> We put on our Arts and wear our Crafts.[5]

The Orient here is seen as a muse who will breath the air back into
Western culture. Indian religion itself is seen as some sort of Oriental
version of Christian pantheism. The image of Krishna is borrowed, adding
an air of distance and authority. The fear of Modernity appears again with
the images of fast cars and fashion. On another level Craig's comment can
be seen as a criticism of Futurism and Constructivism and its application
of dehumanized Oriental art forms. It also foreshadows the Oriental craze
in fashion, which was to follow in a few years time, initiated by Bakst
through the Russian Ballets and popularized by Paul Poiret.

    As was the case with the Arts and Crafts movement, which
borrowed Oriental artistic modes and used them as an antidote against
the all menancing modern world, so is the case with *The Mask*. The
Orient never quite fuses with Modernity to produce an entirely new
artistic form. The distinction between Occident and Orient remains
clearly fixed. As long as the two worlds are seen in opposition and
defined against each other, the assimilation and appropriation processes
that later Modernism was to achieve remain impossible. Craig writes in
the same review:

> To look at the illustrations in this book of Dr. Coomaraswamy's after
> looking at the work of the Futurists is like looking forwards instead of
> backwards.
> These works of sculpture these paintings and cabinets, these gestures
> of actor or dancer are all so young, and really refreshing after the aged
> Futurists.[6]

Keeping the two worlds distinct and separate, Craig fails to realize
that many of the Futurist notions of abstraction, stylization, and dehumanized art in general have very clear Oriental counterparts.

---

[5] *The Mask*, Vol. 6, 1914, p. 227.

[6] Ibid., p. 270.

Also remaining faithful to his motto 'the old is better than the new', he continues to see Oriental theatre as a historical phenomenon, definitely worth studying as such, but not easily assimilated by today's all too modern world.

Oriental Theatre as Paradigm

The holy East and its dramatic arts comprise a good deal of the articles in *The Mask*, especially in the first 10 volumes of the periodical. Craig's study of eastern drama had almost certainly influenced his ideas on the 'Art of the Theatre'. Even if he considered Oriental drama as one of the great theatres of the past and studied it mostly under a historical perspective, it nevertheless helped shape Craigian notions on theatre. Apparently quite removed from a psychological theatre of ideas and from naturalistic representation through ritualistic stylization, Oriental theatre provided a model for Craig. Although this model *did* remain exotic and consequently Orientalist it still created fertile ground for Craigian analysis and speculation. His extensive studies on Noh plays, Javanese puppets and Indian dance are paradigmatic and expose his great knowledge of the field. Many of the conflicts in Craig's theories could have been resolved had he seen the possibility offered by Oriental dramatic modes, not merely as an admirable exotic theatre of the past, but as a form of theatrical discourse that could have helped him re-write his own medium.

Craig's attraction to and fascination with Oriental theatre is more than obvious. Theatre as religious ritual; stylized acting; the prominence of puppets and of the puppet-master; the wearing of masks: all these are ideas which seem very Craigian indeed. And the total aspect of this type of theatre seems to require a unifying force, an artist who will create a synaesthetic effect. So, in shaping his role as the total 'Artist of the Theatre', Craig finds a paradigm. As early as 1914 he is noting that:

> The stage manager (in fully developed Indian drama) is called, as in the puppet-play, sutradhara, 'thread holder'. From this fact, as early as 1879, a native scholar of European education Shankor Pundurang Pandit by name drew the reasonable conclusion that performance by puppets and paper figures must have preceded those by human beings.[7]

The notion of the puppet-master acquires quasi-religious qualities. The puppet-master is not only an artist, but also a high priest. Within the context of a religious, ritualistic theatre the puppet-master is seen as a

---

[7] Ibid., p. 211.

master of ceremonies, and this is exactly the role that Craig had envisaged for himself. His artistic status fluctuates between that of the Romantic stage-manager and the Modernist director, but in the guise of a high priest of a theatre which is seen as religious ceremony that will uphold tradition and eventually save the world. The director of such a theatre acquires super-human attributes. Craig continues in the same article, praising the virtues of the Japanese puppet-master:

> Their art is unique, and while they pull the strings which make the dolls move and act like creatures of real life they are able to completely efface themselves so that their faces are masks. No interest in the movements of the dolls is written there, no hint of self so that the puppets become so absorbingly interesting the audience is lost in the story they tell. 'Korombo' wear black masks, but those who are able to obliterate all trace of personality do not need a covering and their achievement is certainly worthy of the greatest admiration.[8]

The illusion is created through stylization and ritual, rather than representation. The more explicit, it seems, the creative process the more the audience is drawn into the illusion. The director himself, totally removed from his own psychology, enters into the ritual. This process of de-humanization is helped by the use of the mask. As Craig believes, quoting Nietzsche, 'every great spirit needs a mask'. The director for Craig is such a spirit. The title of his magazine is also suggestive of this role he assigns to himself.

The image of the puppet and the puppet-master is not only used as a metaphor, but acquires very real dimensions when seen in the light of Craig's theories on acting. The actor as a psychological entity is banned from the stage and is replaced by Craig's *Ubermarionette*. This idea was created by Craig in an attempt to do away with the theatre of ideas. The *Ubermarionette* was to redefine the art of acting altogether. On a stage where psychology and personality have no place the *Ubermarionette*, under the control of a masked director/priest, would be the ultimate symbol of the New Theatre. Again the puppet-master provides the paradigm:

> These men are able to vanquish the common desire of actors, in whatever part of the world they are to be found, to allow their own personality to dominate and to project themselves into the character they assume, that they can make it possible for the audience to enjoy their art which is concentrated in the dolls and at the same time be perfectly oblivious of the man behind.[9]

---

[8] Ibid., p. 217.
[9] Ibid., p. 219.

The fact that the audience would be oblivious of the 'man behind' might sound slightly simplistic and naive, especially with the rise of the director as an artistic figure that was to follow. It is interesting to note what misreadings and misconceptions Craig applies in this analysis of the role of the puppet-master. Especially so are his allusions to the Japanese Bunraku theatre which omit (perhaps strategically) the role of the narrator-reader, whose presence stresses the literary character of the Bunraku plays. In an example of Orientalism Craig re-writes or re-reads a theatrical tradition in a manner that best suits his needs.

The Cult of the Eastern Puppet and his Western Poor Relative

The artistic character of the puppet is revived throughout late Romanticism and Modernism. It is seen as the ultimate creation, not bound by psychology or history and not having to represent anything other than itself and its art. In this context the puppet-master/artist acquires divine qualities, for he literally breathes life into his creation. The European tradition in puppet theatre is not discarded by *The Mask*; it is merely considered to be inferior to the Oriental: 'Punch and Judy are the last of their proud race', writes Craig. This aura of awe and wonder that surrounds the marionette as the ultimate artifice is made very clear in a quotation from Joseph Conrad that Craig prints in *The Mask* under the title 'Flesh Blood and Marionettes – A Nineteenth Century Note':

> The actors appear to me like a lot of wrong-headed lunatics pretending to be sane. Their malice is stiched with white threads. They are disguised and ugly. To look at them breedsd in my melancholy soul thoughts of murder and suicide, – such is my anger and my loathing of their transparent pretences. There is a taint of subtle corruption in their blank voices, in their blinking eyes, in their grimacing faces, in their light false passion, in the words that have been learned by heart. But I love a marionette-show. Marionettes are beautiful, – especially those of the old kind with wires, thick as my little finger, coming out of the top of the head. Their impassibility in love, in crime, in mirth, in sorrow, – is heroic, superhuman, fascinating. Their rigid violence when they fall upon one another to embrace or to fight is simply a joy to behold. I never listen to the text mouthed somewhere out of sight by invisible men who are here today and rotten tomorrow. I love the marionettes that are without life, and that come so near to being immortal![10]

It is not only the Eastern notion of the puppet theatre – even though it is in the East where it still remains holy – that inspires Craig. In seeing

---

[10] Joseph Conrad quoted in *The Mask*, Vol. 14, 1928, p. 76. For a further discussion on the importance of puppets see chapter 7.

the marionette as the purest of artistic forms he was also working within a late Romantic tradition which in essence did not need the Orient but was happy to appropriate it. Conrad expressed his admiration for puppets as early as 1890. In search of a dehumanized, non-representational art form he chooses the marionette as a model. The art of the human actor is considered to be ugly and corrupt as it only consists of grotesque mimicry and pretence, according to Conrad. The human actor cannot by definition create real art, for he is doomed always to represent rather than to create. In this sense the marionette in all its artificiality, and because of it, is true art. The fact that they are 'without life' as Conrad suggests gives them the opportunity to be immortal. The other interesting aspect of the above quotation is its sub-title – 'A Nineteenth Century Note' – explicitly noting that Craig was working within a tradition which he was bringing into the twentieth century. He designed that 'heroic, superhuman, fascinating' creature that Conrad had only dreamt about. In doing so he based his ideas on the puppet theatre of the East, as it was still in practice the way he envisaged his theatre to be.[11]

Craig could also seek refuge in the puppet theatres of the Holy East when defending his *Ubermarionette*. From the characters of the Javanese Wayang Shadow Theatre he borrows the pseudonym for *The Mask's* editor: Semar.[12] In a series of letters to the editor (Craig writing to Craig) he proposes:

> that all the adverse critics of my suggestion should read two books on the Theatre of Japan:
>
> 1. KABUKI, the Popular stage of Japan, by Zoe Kincaid (Macmillan, 1925).
> 2. MASTERPIECES OF CHIKAMATSU, the Japanese Shakespeare, by Asataro Miyamori (Kegan Paul, 1920).
>
> Having read the former my antagonists will be bowled over; on reading the latter they will come and beg my pardon. Or they are dishonest men and all, i.e., they have no sense of humour left.[13]

By 1927, when this appears, quite a few books on Oriental theatre had been published in English. This is very different from the situation in 1908 when the essay on 'The Actor and the *Ubermarionette*' first appeared in *The Mask*. During those early years of the century and because of the lack of other relevant material, Craig's essay sounded very radical

---

[11] For a discussion on the influence of the Romantic tradition in puppets (i.e. Kleist) also see chapter 7.

[12] See chapter 8 for the significance of the Wayang puppet Semar in the construction of an editorial mask for Craig.

[13] *The Mask*, Vol. 12 bis, 1927, p. 33.

indeed. In the twenty five years that passed, and within the general atmosphere of Orientalism, much more information about Oriental theatre was made available to European audiences. But in the whole run of *The Mask* Craig takes particular delight in reviewing books on the theatre of the East, and when doing so he always makes sure to point out to his rivals the correspondence between the Eastern theatre and his own.

Craig was very much aware of the fact that his *Ubermarionette* was a twentieth century concept. In differentiating himself from Conrad he attempts to move towards a more Modernist context, within which such an *Ubermarionette* could have actually been realized. One of the reasons this is never achieved is that he lacks the metalanguage to appropriate his Eastern influences. As long as the Eastern influence remains distant and exotic it can not be seen as a real and material creative process which can be analysed, understood and finally assimilated. Craig was very much aware of this dead-end situation he had reached with his *Ubermarionette*. By 1927, almost twenty years after the initial appearance of his essay, he seems less optimistic about the realisation of his schemes regarding the *Ubermarionette*:

> Nor you nor I will live to see whether 'The Actor and *The Ubermarionette*' is destined to affect the actor at all. It seems to have offended the English actor, though foreign actors, strange to say, can read it, without getting huffy.[14]

Dressing his *Ubermarionette* with a visionary prophetic quality, Craig manages to by-pass the accusation that his project was virtually unrealizable. His role is to conceive ideas, not to find a way of putting them into practice. The final product of art is what interests him and this product he fetishizes. The *Ubermarionette* itself can be read as an extreme form of a fetishized art. The creative process itself is of no interest. It is not worthy of a true artist's attention. In this way, claiming that his *Ubermarionette* is merely a vision for the future and not a specific project which he intends to carry out, he is safe and remains within the same idealistic framework.

Puppets and Theories on Acting

Craig's inability to see Oriental theatrical modes as particular techniques which he could analyse and then use for his own purposes was also spotted by Ananda K. Coomaraswamy in an article entitled 'The Human

---

[14] Ibid., p. 33.

Actor' published in *The Mask* in 1913. Coomaraswamy starts his argument with a quotation from Craig's 'The Actor and the *Ubermarionette*', stressing the fact that both Craig's notions on acting, and those of the theatres of the East, start from the same basic theoretical assumptions on the nature of art and man. He quotes from Craig's essay:

> The whole nature of man tends towards freedom; he therefore carries the proof in his own person that as material for the Theatre he is useless. In the modern theatre, owing to the use of the bodies of men and women as their material, all which is presented there is of an accidental nature. The actions of the actor's body, the expression of his face, all are at the mercy of the winds of his emotions...emotion possesses him; it seizes upon his limbs, moving whither it will... That then, which the actor gives us is not a work of art; it is a series of accidental confessions.[15]

This basic theoretical axiom of Craig's – that the human body is essentially not artificial enough to be creative – leads him to his concept of the *Ubermarionette*. An emotion-free, psychology-free creature, as pure artifice, could create pure art. The human form 'tends towards freedom' and lacks the rigid stylization of a ritualistic theatre. In its conception, this notion of the human actor is very Oriental indeed. The difference is that Craig goes one step further and obliterates the human form from the stage altogether. One possible explanation for such an extreme position could be his reading of Oriental acting techniques. Ignoring the idea of process from his study, he fails to learn from Oriental acting techniques in a real way. A more systematic/historical study could have helped him find a theatrical language that could create the stylization he was aiming at, using the body itself; something that other Modernist schools of performance would achieve. Within the framework that Craig was working in it seemed much more plausible to capture the final product – the *Ubermarionette* – and not to worry too much about how this would come about. Coomaraswamy criticizes Craig along the same lines:

> Had Mr. Craig been enabled to study the Indian actors, and not merely those of the modern theatre, he might not have thought it so necessary to reject the bodies of men and women as the material of dramatic art. For those principles which have with great consistency governed arts until recently have also governed dramatic technique.[16]

Coomaraswamy continues his article, exposing a very sophisticated and ancient Indian system for training actors, utilizing the human form as a

---

[15] EGC, 'The Actor and the Ubermarionette', first printed in *The Mask* (1908), Vol. 1, No. 1, pp. 3b–15b, quoted in Vol. 6, 1913, p. 120.
[16] Coomaraswamy, 'The Human Actor', *The Mask*, Vol. 6, 1913, pp. 120–8, p. 123.

material for art. 'The great consistency' that governed arts 'until recently' is, of course, stylization, ritual and abstraction, which were challenged with the arrival of European naturalism. Traditional Indian dramatic technique sees the potential for abstraction even in the human form. For Craig this was inconceivable.

Coomaraswamy knew Craig and almost certainly discussed such matters with him. Craig, true to his normal unreadiness to work with others and take advice, probably ignored him. Yet Coomaraswamy appears as quite a prominent figure throughout the pages of *The Mask*. Craig reviews all his books very favourably, but when he deals with matters in which Craig considers himself to be the authority the problems begin. Coomaraswamy ends the above article with:

> I have only one objection to meet. When I told Mr. Craig of this conventional Indian art of acting, he said he thought it was wrong for human beings to submit to such severe discipline. But apart from their acting these Indian actors are as human as any others. That their acting should be so severely disciplined, is not more painful than the observance of Form in any other art. The musician at least requires an equally arduous training. The truth's that the modern theatre has so accustomed us to a form of acting that is not an art, that we begin to think it is too much to demand of the actor that he should become once more an artist.[17]

This could easily have been said by Craig himself. For a man who believed in strict discipline and actually had students leave his school because they could not stand the rigidity of the programme, his objection sounds very strange indeed. In view of the fact, though, that one of Craig's main concerns was to establish his own identity as the 'Artist of the Theatre' who had complete control of every aspect of theatrical praxis, his blind spot is more understandable. The artistic quality of the human actor had to be got rid of. Formulating a theory for acting was not his chief concern. He believed that he had already done that with his *Übermarionette* – an artifice with no artistic character of its own unless it is 'animated' by the 'Artist of the Theatre'.

Sexism, Feminism and the Case of Sadda Yakko

Another aspect of Oriental theatre which coincided with one of Craig's favourite pet aversions was the banning of women from the stage. Again in the theatres of the East he found the justification he was looking for. Art for Craig was mainly a man's job. Women were themselves seen as

---

[17] Ibid., pp. 127–128.

11. Sambaso Dancer, Vol. 3, Nos. 4–6, p. 76c, 1910.

an artifice, expressing the classical notions of beauty and form. In a way women were a creation of man, so by definition they were unable to create art. Craig's antipathy to women actresses runs throughout *The Mask*, and it is one of his main weapons in his attack against naturalism in the theatre. On a more general level, Craig's strictly patriarchal notions are seen as yet another way of preserving the traditional past and protecting it from modern movements like feminism. Philosophically Craig shared the idealist Romantic view about women, as it is cogently expressed by Schopenhauer. A fourteen-page article by Schopenhauer is reprinted in *The Mask* entitled 'On Women'. The existence of such an article in a periodical on the art of the theatre seems odd in itself. In view of the fact, though, that Craig had appointed himself as a high priest figure of traditional cultural values it can be further understood. Quoting from Schopenhauer in *The Mask*, he theoretically exposes his position:

> Nature has made it the calling of the young, strong and handsome men to look after the propagation of the human race; so that the species may not degenerate.[18]

Craig saw himself as being all of these: he was young, strong, handsome and he was, most importantly, a man. He fulfilled all the ontological qualifications necessary for a true artist. Schopenhauer's article continues:

> It is only the man whose intellect is clouded by his sexual instinct that could give that stunted, narrow-shouldered, broad-hipped, and short-legged race the name of the fair sex; for the entire beauty of the sex is based on this instinct. One would be more justified in calling them the unaesthetic sex than the beautiful sex. Neither for music, nor for fine art have they any real or true sense and susceptibility and it is mere mockery on their part, in their desire to please, if they affect any such thing.[19]

The above was published with a foreword by John Semar (i.e. Craig) 'believing that a serious article by an eminent writer would be welcome at this time upon what is known as the "Feminist Movement"'.

Craig's determination to keep women off the stage seems particularly interesting considering the admiration he had for his actress mother Ellen Terry and the fascination he had developed for Isadora Duncan. It seemed, though, that he was decided to have his 'Theatre of

---

[18] Schopenhauer, 'On Women', *The Mask*, Vol. 7, 1914, pp. 1–14.
[19] Ibid., pp. 7–8.

the Future' without women actresses. Again he found his models in the theatre of the East and particularly in the theatrical arts of Japan. In the Japanese *onnagata* he found correlations with the Elizabethan theatre. Craig's ideas on the role of women in art are definitely patriarchal. He does not approach the gender issue in the theatre as later Modernists will. The trans-sexual, androgynous quality of Oriental actors, seen in a Modernist light, problematizes the issue of gender altogether. Modernist schools of performance will use the Oriental representation of the human form to move towards a genderless actor. Craig's *Ubermarionette*, lacking biological gender, still has ideological gender; he is most definitely a man.

An event which caused much confusion at the time was the discovery of Sada Yakko. Sada Yakko was Europe's first encounter with Japanese acting in 1900, at the International Exposition in Paris. Despite the Japanese tradition, here was a female actress playing female parts. On her arrival in England she performed before Queen Victoria and Ellen Terry herself was reported to have declared that the whole experience had been 'a great lesson in dramatic art'.[20] Even Henry Irving, Craig's artistic godfather, was reported as saying, 'I never had an idea of such an acting'.[21]

The truth is that Sada Yakko had never performed in Japan. She only started acting with her husband Kawakami once they had left Japan. She had been trained as a geisha, which meant she had mastered traditional Japanese arts like dance and song. The company had initially left Japan in order to study western drama. As a result their productions were anything but classical. There were only traces of Kabuki left. Instead they presented highly Romantic and slightly stylized melo-dramas. Yet she was hailed by the critics of the period as a Japanese Sarah Bernhardt. Craig is aware of the impression created by Sada Yakko but also of the misconception. So he does not fall into the same trap as his mother and godfather. He has too broad a knowledge of traditional Japanese theatre to accept Sada Yakko as an example of it. In *The Mask* he comments on Sada Yakko's reception in the West:

> Madame Sada Yakko was the first lady to go upon the stage in Japan. The innovation was a pity. She then went to Europe to study the modern theatres there, and more especially the Opera House in Paris, intending to introduce such a theatre into Japan, . . . it is to be presumed with the idea of advancing the art of the Japanese theatre. There can be no hesitation in saying that she is doing both the country and its theatre a grievous wrong. Art can never find a new way of creating better than the primitive way which the nation learned as children from nature.[22]

---

[20] Ellen Terry, quoted in L. C. Pronko, *Theatre East and West* (London, 1967), p. 120.

[21] Irving, *Le Theatre*, (Sept. 1900), quoted in L. C. Pronko, *Theatre East and West*, p. 120.

[22] Tao, 'Women in the Theatre', *The Mask*, Vol. 3, No. 2 (Florence, 1910), p. 96.

The main accusation against Sada Yakko derives from the fact that she is a woman. For Craig she becomes a symbol of what may happen if women were allowed artistic status in the theatre. He goes so far as to consider the presence of women in the theatre as the reason for the decline of the art:

> The introduction of women upon the stage is held by some to have caused the downfall of the European theatre and it's to be feared that it is destined to bring the same disaster to Japan since it is announced that Madame Yakko intends not only to use actresses for the female roles but to introduce other occidental customs upon her new stage.[23]

Craig seems hostile to any notion of synthesizing the artistic modes of east and west, especially if changes are introduced by a woman. The theatre of the East has to remain static and distant for him to call upon when he wants to justify his own theories. Again women are seen as being too modern. They do not acknowledge the great traditions of the past. Craig writes in an article entitled 'Japanese Players':

> The men were better than the women. They seemed better to under-stand and do more honour to the centuries behind them; they suggested art, . . . if they did not perpetrate it. The ladies, on the other hand, kicked over the centuries.[24]

For Craig women do not have a subject status, they are only understood in relation to and as creations of men. The last place they have a right to thrive in is the theatre. In using the theatres of the Orient to back his case against women he overlooks one main aspect that was to be taken on by other schools of drama – the potentially genderless masked Oriental actors. His overzealous accusations against women in the theatre do not only appear to be highly sexist, but also misinformed, as he fails to acknowledge the fact that early Kabuki theatre *did* use women actors, probably in an attempt to popularize and break the conventions of the very conservative and aristocratic Noh. Craig's reading of the androgynous character of the Eastern theatre was a traditional patri-archal one. He fails to see how this abstract representation can be used to de-naturalize gender altogether. This interpretation, which was ap-plied by Meyerhold and others, was almost inconceivable for Craig, who shamelessly claimed 'that women must withdraw from the stage and leave it finally and exclusively to men if the theatre is to be saved'.[25]

---

[23] Ibid., p. 97.
[24] EGC, 'Japanese Players', *The Mask*, Vol. 3, 1910, p. 143.
[25] EGC, 'The History of Japanese Colour Prints' (rev), *The Mask*, Vol. 4, 1911, p. 64.

Great Pasts and Fascist Presents

In the general theoretical context of the East 'regenerating the West', Craig includes sketchy studies of the overall historical and religious background of Oriental theatre. The assumption is that, by studying the great societies of the past that gave rise to such art forms, the twentieth century could possibly create the right environment for such art to flourish once more. In taking on such a task Craig utilizes one of the classic Orientalist themes (or myths), according to which the 'once great and all powerful Orient is now in total decline'. The greatness of the past is what will create the regeneration of Europe, but the decline of the present is what will justify its Imperialism. From an article entitled 'The Sacred Drama of Cambodia' Craig's elegy on Khmer dance-drama has a decidedly paternalistic tinge:

> Despite its so reduced power this fallen Cambodian people remains the Khmer race that once was the wonder of Asia, in its mysticism and in its pomp; we know too that it has never lost the hope of recovering its old capital, buried for ages in the forests of Siam,... and it is always the Ramayana, that old and indefinite epic that continues to arouse its imagination and to guide its dreams.
>
> May France, protectress of this land, understand that the ballet of the Kings Pnom-Penh is a legacy, an ancient marvel that must not be destroyed.[26]

The past of the Orient can only be of use to Europe in this process of regeneration if it is first protected, re-written, re-presented, by Europe itself. In its own right, as an actual historical process, it is of no interest. The real past of the Orient is of as much interest to Europe as is its real present. Craig truly believes the naive Romantic vision of Europe approaching the Holy East with the innocence of a child and the desire to learn. He writes, as Semar, in a note on 'Japanese Artists in the West':

> How strange! We of the West who in life are only children, and quite unable to cope with any but the simplest of matters, find it so touching to be 'studied and imitated' especially in our Arts! How happy we must feel in our kind of shy way to see the descendant and pupil of Hokusai studying at the feet of Alma Tadema or Matisse![27]

Craig makes it very clear here that this regeneration process is definitely a one-way road. Anything else would be an attempt to break down the

---

[26] Coomaraswamy, 'The Sacred Drama of Cambodia', *The Mask*, Vol. 5, 1911, p. 208.

[27] John Semar (Craig pseudonym), 'Japanese Artists in the West', *The Mask*, Vol. 6, 1913, pp. 89–91, p. 90.

opposition between Occident and Orient; the very opposition which provides Craig with the theoretical framework that allows him to fossilize what he terms 'the glorious past' of the Orient and remain oblivious to its historical present. He continues in the same article:

> What is great in you is what remains over in spite of your attempt to rid yourself of the influence of the Past. You are great only in so far as you venerate and keep alive that Past...and remember that the Store Monkey in spite of all his magic and his travels wasn't as clever as he supposed.[28]

The Orient in the decline of the present is somehow seen as being unable to acknowledge the treasure of its past. That past has to be preserved by Europe if it is to survive and in its term add to the regeneration of Europe. It is in this context that Craig urges his readers to study not only the arts of the East but the conditions that bred them. He writes in his 1913 review of *Plays of Old Japan: The Noh*, a set of translations by Marie Stopes:

> But it should be clearly remembered by those who examine these, or other ancient forms of dramatic ceremonial that, although they may afford an interesting study for archeologists (sic), may afford a particular kind of enjoyment to those who have the opportunity of witnessing their performance, the only real value of either the study or the spectacle in relation to the Living Theatre towards which our hopes turn is that which lies in tracing the peculiar conditions among which such drama arose, the peculiar spirit which gave it life. We see back in those days a great National spirit is glowing... The King is a god...and the nobles are astir and noble.[29]

The 'peculiar conditions' Craig speaks of are in most cases (certainly in the case of Noh) very conservative feudal ones. Craig was aware of this. Hence what he terms the grand past of the Orient can fuel and serve as justification for his fascist tendencies. As he saw it, fascism was to provide the grand, epic context within which the theatre of the future would thrive. In his review of Arthur Waley's *The Noh Plays of Japan*, in *The Mask*, Craig writes:

> These great plays, this great way of playing for a great audience! There is nothing to be said in a brief review about this sort of thing so good it is.

---

[28] Ibid., p. 91.

[29] EGC, Marie Stokes, *Plays of Old Japan. The Noh* (rev), *The Mask*, Vol. 6, 1913, p. 265.

> What the No can be to us except something sad, I, after many years
> knowing of it and knowing what it stood for, dare not trust myself
> to say.
> In Italy, they will perhaps, make, one day, something heroic from the
> coming of Mussolini.[30]

Using the Oriental tradition in the theatre as a vehicle for his conserva-
tism, Craig sets up yet another barricade against Modernity. Mussolini
was to create the great empire that would inspire a grand theatre. Craig,
as the Artist of the Theatre, would certainly play a decisive role in such
an empire. He would act as intermediary between the world of politics
and the world of art. These two, according to Craig, should be distinctly
separate. If anything it is the world of art that should influence and
aestheticize the other realms. It is within this context that Mussolini
appealed to Craig. Aesthetically he fulfilled all the requirements Craig
had envisaged for the heroic figure that would act as mentor for his art.
Such a view, innocent and naive as it may sound, is itself an expression
of fascism. The aesthetization of politics and history is certainly a
manifestation of fascism. Craig attempted to explain his vision to
Mussolini himself. He writes in 1934:

> Soon I shall be able to thank this great person for an act which shall
> bring every blessing on the Theatre for which I have lived.[31]

After a very disappointing brief meeting during which Mussolini forgot
Craig's name, he reported:

> Next day I report result of meeting to Orestano. He shakes his head
> about the delay of 1 hour and 10 min., and he says after I describe the
> interview 'He was not there'.[32]

This failure of reality to comply with vision, only resulted in further
idealization of Craigian thought. The present was all the more disappointing so he turned with a greater conviction to the past. The Orient
was a paradigm of the exact model Craig was formulating theoretically:
a glorious past that had deteriorated into an insignificant present.

Yeats, Noh Drama and the Contribution of *The Mask*

The Noh drama of Japan, as we have seen, played a significant role in
this scheme of things and occupied a privileged position in the pages of

---

[30] Arthur Waley, *The No Plays of Japan* (rev), *The Mask*, Vol. 9, 1919, p. 34.
[31] EGC, in letter of 1934, Humanities Research Centre, University of Texas at Austin.
[32] Ibid.

12. 'Shunzan': dance of four geishas, two disguised as monkeys, Vol. 4, No. 2, p. 96a, 1911.

The Mask. Craig's journal, together with Pound's highly personal completion of the first major translation of Noh plays into English, constituted the first substantial attempts to initiate western audiences to this highly abstract and ritualistic theatrical practice.

The contribution of *The Mask* in spreading the Noh cult among the more literary Modernists is very important. Yeats and Pound were working on a translation of Noh plays between the years 1913–15. This was based on the Fenollosa manuscript. Ernest Fenollosa was an American scholar and diplomat who played a vital role in the introduction of Noh to western audiences. After his death (1908) his wife asked Pound to edit his manuscript of Noh plays. In 1916 *'Noh' or Accomplishment, A Study of the Classical Stage in Japan* was published in London with an introduction by Pound. This book is not referred to in *The Mask*. The omission appears to be rather deliberate as *The Mask* appears to have dealt with Noh from its first issues (1908, 1909) and views with suspicion similar endeavours, especially if they are undertaken by poets and not artists of the stage. Indeed *The Mask* could claim to have influenced Pound when editing the translation, as he worked closely with Yeats who in turn, at that time, was enjoying a creative partnership with Craig.

Between 1909 and 1912 Craig had collaborated with Yeats at the Abbey Theatre, where he first had the opportunity to experiment with his screens: the scenic device that was to substitute for every form of scenery. This collaboration proved very fruitful for Yeats who, as Karen Dorn claims in her book *Players and Painted Stage*,[33] was influenced by Craig in writing and revising his plays (notably *The Hour Glass*, which was published in *The Mask*[34] and *The Player Queen*). Yeats wrote to Craig in 1913:

> Your work is always a great inspiration to me. Indeed I cannot imagine myself writing any play for the stage now, which I did not write for your screens.[35]

Craig repays the honour through the pages of *The Mask*:

> I have myself acted as a most willing aid in the interpretation of the drama of Yeats and it has been one of the special happinesses of my life

---

[33] For a further investigation of Craig's creative encounter with Yeats see Karen Dorn, *Players and Painted Stage, The Theatre of W. B. Yeats* (Brighton, 1984), chapter entitled 'Dialogue into Movement: W. B. Yeats's Theatre Collaboration with Gordon Craig', pp. 13–33.

[34] W. B. Yeats, *The Hour Glass*, in *The Mask*, Vol. 5, 1910, pp. 327–46.

[35] From a letter from Yeats to Craig, 29 July 1913, in the Gordon Craig Collection, Bibliotheque de l'Arsenal, Paris, quoted in Denis Bablet, *Edward Gordon Craig* (Paris, 1962), trans. Daphne Woodward (London, 1966), p. 130.

to have been connected with his poetic dramas in Dublin . . . but only as a servant . . . seeing his as a 'brother art'.[36]

It was during the same years that he was providing a context for Pound to work on the Fenollosa manuscript that Yeats wrote his first dance play, *At the Hawk's Well*. In the Noh drama he found the combination of poetry, music and dance that he was striving for. As Pound wrote of the Noh, he saw in it 'a complete service of life. We do not find, as we find in *Hamlet*, a certain situation or problem set out and analyzed. The Noh service presents, or symbolizes, a complete diagram of life and recurrence'.[37]

Over the same period 1913–15 Yeats was a regular contributor to *The Mask*[38] and, one also assumes, a devoted reader. Indeed in 1913 he was planning to visit Craig in Florence as a literary advisor 'for a big scheme on poetic drama'.[39] So it is very likely that Yeats, in approaching the Fenollosa manuscript, was not approaching the Noh for the first time. He had already been exposed to its charms, probably with Pound, through the pages of *The Mask*.

The material available in English on Noh drama at the turn of the century amounted to a few published books and the prints at the British Museum. The most important publications were: M. A. Hink's *The Art of Japanese Dancing* of 1906 and Marie Stopes's *Plays of Old Japan* of 1910. These are reviewed and quoted in *The Mask*. But, as we have seen, Pound's book is interestingly ignored. In addition to the above *The Mask* introduces quite a few more books on the Noh, adding to the growing scholarship in the field. The most important of these are: Frederick Perzynski's *Japanesche Masken: No und Kyogen*, Isawaki and Hughes, translators, *Three Modern Japanese Plays* and a presentation of a book on the Bunraku writer Chikamatsu by Asataro Miyamori entitled *Masterpieces of Chikamatsu, the Japanese Shakespeare*.[40] These, together with

---

[36] In *The Letters of W. B. Yeats*, ed. Allan Wade (New York, 1955), p. 577, or *The Mask*, Vol. 5, 12–13, p. 291. This volume includes two articles by Jack B. Yeats on producing plays for miniature stages, which Craig revives as part of his crusade to revive the miniature stage. See chapter 7.

[37] Ernest Fenollosa and Ezra Pound, *'Noh' or Accomplishment, A Study of the Classical Stage in Japan* (London, 1916), p. 17.

[38] Yeats appears as a regular contributor to *The Mask*: he is referred to in the following issues: Vol. 2, p. 148; Vol. 4, p. 61, p. 161; Vol. 5, p. 2; Vol. 7, p. 139, p. 174; Vol. 9, p. 50; Vol. 10, p. 66; His contributions appear in the following issues: *The Hour Glass* (play and preface printed), Vol. 5, pp. 327–46; 'The Tragic Theatre' (article), Vol. 3, p. 77; The following are reviewed: *Per Amica Silentia Lunae*, Vol. 8, p. 39; *Plays and Controversies*, Vol. 10, p. 90; *Plays for an Irish Theatre*, Vol. 9, pp. 342–43.

[39] In *The Letters of W. B. Yeats*, ed. Allan Wade (New York, 1955), p. 577.

[40] See *The Mask*, Frederich Perzynski, *Japanesche Masken: No und Kyogen* (rev), Vol. 12, pp. 162–63; Isawaki and Hughes, *Three Modern Japanese Plays* (rev), Vol. 10, p. 91; Asataro Miyamori, *Masterpieces of Chikamatsu, the Japanese Shakespeare*, Vol. 8, p. 33.

numerous articles analysing Noh technique and philosophy, mainly by Craig, make *The Mask* a very useful handbook for anyone at the time wanting to study the Noh.

Yeats's admiration of the Noh drama resulted in his *Four Plays for Dancers*. In writing these plays, some of them adaptations of original Noh plays, Yeats was of course as much influenced by the Fenollosa manuscript as by the material in *The Mask*. For Yeats, as was the case for Craig, the Noh presented a set of theatrical conventions both men could use and adapt. In true Orientalist manner, it is doubtful whether Yeats had actually seen any Noh drama performed, but relied on the Fenollosa translation and, one infers, on Craig's interpretations. In his introduction to *Certain Noble Plays of Japan* Yeats mentions that 'my play is made possible by a Japanese dancer whom I have seen dance in a studio and in a drawing-room and on a very small stage lit by an excellent stage-light'.[41] What Yeats describes here is not a traditional Noh per-formance, as the Japanese dancer Michio Ito, as was the case with Sadda Yakko, had come to the West to study European dance, but was urged to remain Oriental for the sake of intellectual and poetic speculation by figures like Pound and Yeats.

It was not only theatrical technique that attracted Yeats and Craig to the Noh. It came as part and parcel with an ideology that was grand, total and highly conservative. Shamelessly aristocratic in its origins, it is not surprising that the Noh was favoured over the more popular Kabuki theatre. In the Noh Yeats could find parallels for a traditional and nationalistic Irish theatre, and Craig and Pound could find historical precedents for their present attraction to fascism.

Contrasting Appropriations and the Case of Mei Lan-Fang

Historicity (or perhaps pseudo-historicity) of this sort, and indeed a more general fascination with the past, particularly characterizes the

---

[41] W. B. Yeats, introduction to *Certain Noble Plays of Japan*, in Essays and Introductions (London, 1961), p. 224. Also see Liam Miller, *The Noble Drama of W. B. Yeats* (Dublin, 1977), pp. 223–225, where the influence of Michio Ito is analysed. 'Mitchio Ito (1893–1961) came from a wealthy Japanese family and ʾafter a period spent in the study of the traditional dance forms of his native country at the Mizuki Dancing School, where he graduated in 1911, he travelled to Europe to study European forms of dance and spent the following three years in Paris at the Dalcroze School. From Paris he went to London where he became a protege of Ezra Pound's, and assisted Pound with his work of deciphering and editing the Fenollosa papers. Ito's study of Japanese dance forms was not related to the forms used in the Noh theatre, but he became interested in Noh forms when he came into contact with Pound in 1915, and in October of that year gave some performances of Noh dancing for Pound and a group of friends in a costume specially reconstructed by Dulac and Charles Ricketts', p. 224.

later volumes of *The Mask*. This might seem rather inconsistent in the work of someone who has since been celebrated as the prophet of a new movement in the theatre. But then Craig's concept of the new does not wholly coincide with his age's concept of the 'modern'. His reference to and application of Oriental theatrical modes is one example of this; for, while Craig was using the Orient as a means to re-discover and maintain his idea of a glorious past, other, more Modernist schools of performance applied Oriental theatrical modes to a redefining of their art, dissociating it from the past and enlisting it in the creation of a new future.

Meyerhold, Brecht and Artaud could stand as Craig's Modernist counterparts in their reference to the theatre of the Orient. All three theoreticians use Oriental theatre to redefine their art form and contextualise it within a broader world theory. It is their ideology which will provide the framework that will eventually de-exoticize the Orient and use it as a purely theatrical reference. Meyerhold and Brecht occupy one side of the spectrum, which conceives of the appropriation of Oriental modes as a materialistic process, and Artaud occupies the extreme opposite, viewing the Orient as the epitome of idealism. Both sides express the two main trends in Modernism. Meyerhold views theatre as a materialistic creative process which has to bear a direct relationship with the historical moment, whereas Artaud sees theatre as a ritual that transcends history, as an idealistic process of catharsis and sacrifice. In trying to bridge the two and realize the unrealizable, Artaud was perhaps inevitably led to madness. He lacked the metalanguage that could have provided the distance and at the same time articulated his visions. Artaud used himself as his language, and according to his own theories, literally (and by the end of his life no longer metaphorically) sacrificed himself. He became the holy actor. He tried to explain the 'magic of the Orient through magic', as Grotowski says. In a sense Artaud became the Orient. Meyerhold and Brecht followed quite a different process. In applying a very clear and material methodology, they distanced themselves as far as possible from the idealization of the Orient. The theatre of the Orient was used as a theatrical reference, not a philosophical one. In terms of theatricality, the theatre of the Orient would provide Meyerhold and later Brecht with techniques that would help them formulate the self-conscious and at the same time revolutionary theatre that they were striving for. Craig, in relation to the Orient stands somewhere in between the radically different trends. Like Artaud he sees the Orient in idealistic awe, but unlike him Craig is too conscious of himself, his identity and history, to take the risks that Artaud took. Extremities were never his style anyway. The notion of common sense was deeply rooted within him. Like Meyerhold and Brecht he tried to find ways of appropriating his knowledge of the Orient towards the formulation of his own theory. Unlike them, though, he lacked the ideology that could provide him with a metalanguage to undertake such a task.

A comparison of Craig's *Ubermarionette* with Meyerhold's theory of acting and how they both relate to Oriental notions of theatricality will serve to expose the differences between the two stage masters. For both artists re-defining the role of the actor was a goal directly related to establishing their own roles as directors. In the theatre of the future, according to Craig's vision, the actor as flesh and blood would have to be sacrificed if the art is 'to be saved'. A theatre of ritual had no room for anything 'natural' on its stage. Meyerhold, on the other hand, was concerned with human form as a material. This did not make his theatre more naturalist. On the contrary, it served to de-naturalize the human body so it could be used as a raw material for a theatre that was just as ritualistic and spectacular as Craig's.

Both Craig and Meyerhold found in Japanese and Chinese methods of acting not only an inspiration, but most importantly an example of the type of actor they were theorizing about. Craig saw a rigid stylization that substituted psychological acting for rhythmic motion and dance, changing the human body into a scenically flexible material. He writes in his review of M. A. Hink's *The Art of Japanese Dancing*:

> The fact that the body itself is never seen and that Japanese dancing is yet so fine a thing as it is and was dispels once and for all the illusion that it is necessary...for the movement of the natural body to be seen. ...The Japanese (style) with its strict ritual, its noble conservatism which still preserves traditional posture without change, or modification, its obedience to a fine tradition, its perfect control of its material,...that is the human body, approaches more nearly to the stately and splendid ceremonies of the past, of which, among us, some trace yet lingers in the symbolic gestures of the priests celebrating mass, and it thus partakes more nearly of the nature of an art.[42]

Craig is impressed by this style in acting not only because it seems to do away with the natural body, but also because it is reminiscent of a glorious past. Meyerhold, on his behalf, saw in Eastern acting styles a particular method that he could utilize for his revolutionary theatre that would do away with the past altogether. Meyerhold was under the influence of the 'cult of the new' – a new art form for a new revolutionary world. Their very different attitudes determined the way they assimilated their influences.

Craig is a Romantic idealist, an artist of dreams and visions, not in the least interested in methods and technologies for the realization of

---

[42] EGC, M. A. Hink, *The Art of Japanese Dancing* (rev), *The Mask*, Vol. 3, 1910, pp. 90–1.

his concepts. He sees in Oriental acting a final result, helping him reach the absolutist notion of the *Ubermarionette*. Meyerhold, functioning within the theoretical framework of Marxism, is interested in nothing but processes. For him and for the Russian Constructivists in general, the idea of art as a materialistic process de-fetishizes the artifice and places it in an historical context. What he saw in Oriental acting in particular was a methodology. The deliberate theatricality of Eastern acting styles helped him establish the self-conscious method of acting that Brecht was later to call 'double showing'. In much the same manner as a Kabuki actor might announce to the audience what he is about to portray and then proceed to enact it, the actor of Meyerhold has this dual function. This dialectic between the character, and character as re-enacted by the actor, is the centre of Meyerhold's theory for acting. Alpers writes:

> The splitting up of the art of acting into character and its commentary did not contain anything mystical. It was altogether a rationalistic art; it laid open before the outsider the very mechanics of the creation of a scenic image.[43]

Biomechanics was the shamelessly modern name that Meyerhold was to call his system of training actors. In developing his system, like Craig, Meyerhold used the puppet as a metaphor. Unlike Craig, though, it was not the puppet that would substitute for the human form, but the human form would model itself on the puppet. Meyerhold followed Craigian thought inside-out, as it were. Rather than ban the body from the stage, and for the same reasons as Craig's, Meyerhold strove to turn it into an *Ubermarionette*, but one of a decidedly uncraigian complexion. According to him such a task was possible for a materialistic actor. Through his very rigid *biomechanics* the human body would transform into a purely mechanized material object that could be manipulated as such on the stage.

Meyerhold was certainly aware of Craig's work as early as 1908 when he himself wrote a small biographical sketch on Craig for a Russian journal.[44] The two men were almost contemporaries and admired each other's work. By 1912, when Meyerhold started to develop his own theories, he probably had read Craig's essay on the *Ubermarionette*. Most importantly though, he had translated in 1909, from the German, the Japanese Kabuki tragedy *Terakoya*. As we can see both artists, at

---

[43] Boris Alpers, *The Theatre of the Social Mask*, trans. Mark Schmidt (New York: Group Theatre, 1934), pp. 36–37.

[44] Meyerhold's articles on Craig appeared in *Zhurnal Literaturno – khudozhestvennogo obshchestva*, No. 9 (Petersburg, 1909–10), also see Meyerhold's *O Teatre*, (Petersburg, 1913), pp. 90–93. Also see Edward Braun ed., *Meyerhold on Theatre* (London, 1969), p. 112, note 1.

approximately the same periods were influenced by similar sources in the formulation of their very different theories. An example of how the two were moving in the same direction, but on very different tracks is the case of Mei Lan-Fang, the Chinese actor who took Moscow by storm in 1935. Meyerhold, Brecht, Tretiakov and Eisenstein were all enchanted by his performances, and each bore marks of the strong influence of this experience. Mei Lan-Fang's acting style helped Brecht formulate his famous *Verfremdungseffekt*, which could already be seen in the work of Meyerhold. Meyerhold himself was so impressed by the performance that he dedicated his next production, Griboedov's *Woe to Wit* to Mei Lan-Fang, and included aspects of Chinese theatrical folklore.[45] A. C. Scott records that after the performances, at a public meeeting, Meyerhold spoke of the technique of Mei Lan-Fang's art.[46]

Mei Lan-Fang appears in *The Mask* as early as 1927, probably before he even visited the west. Under the pseudonym C. G. Smith, Craig writes:

> A writer living in Pekin reports to an American periodical that there is a remarkable Chinese actor called Mei Lan-Fang who performs, as did the Elizabethan, the principal female roles. He writes of this young actor that he deserves all his fame, and proceeds to tell us something (by now quite familiar to us); i.e. that the conventions of the Chinese Theatre are much like the Elizabethan, -scenes, make-believe and all. 'It is necessary only to walk about a little and to go out by the left hand door and reappear immediately afterwards through the right hand door to make it clear to the spectators that the scene is changed.'[47]

After correcting the 'writer living in Pekin' by giving another name for the actor ('Mri-Ran-Fan according to Miss Zoe Kincaid), Craig uses the example of Mei Lan-Fang to attack western actors. He claims that all the other arts of the stage have developed to make up for the inability of actors. For Craig acting in itself for the western actor is no longer an art. He continues:

> Let him but show us that he is able to do this – to act a scene into existence, and will not Appia, will not Roerich, will not Stern and the shade of Bakst rejoice, and go into the stalls and forget all their old non-sense and enjoy the immense spectacle – the actor alive again.[48]

---

[45] Meyerhold, *Stat'i, pis'ma, rechi, besedy*, Vol. 2 (Moscow, 1917–39), p. 322, quoted in Katherine Bliss Eaton, *The Theatre of Meyerhold and Brecht* (London, 1986), p. 23.

[46] A. C. Scott, *Mei Lan-fang: Leader of the Pear Garden* (Hong Kong, 1959), pp. 117–18.

[47] C. G. Smith (Craig pseudonym), 'Only – A Note by C. G. Smith', *The Mask*, Vol. 12 bis, 1927, p. 73.

[48] Ibid., p. 74.

It is interesting that Craig does not mention himself here. This is because he does not consider himself to be merely a stage designer. As the 'Artist of the Theatre' he fulfils the role of both designer and actor, through his *Ubermarionette*. The main conclusion he wants to arrive at is that 'the actor is more or less dead'. As such he can be substituted by a marionette.

The example of Mei Lan-Fang is not used to inspire or explore the possibility of new expressive modes. There is no analysis of the actual acting style. He is used by Craig as something static, as a glorious Eastern figure out of a grand tradition with whom Craig can once again criticize the western actor. He ends his article:

> Let these artists but leave him, and unpropped he will fall to the ground; for he has no longer the knowledge of what it means to act. Perhaps the Chinese stage can instruct and convince him where he lacks knowledge and faith. Who is there who will not be ready to welcome the true actors the day they appear strong at all points.[49]

Craig seems well informed, but is still unable to utilize his exposure to Oriental theatrical modes systematically towards the formulation of his own theory. Craig once called Meyerhold 'a technical artist of immense ability'. The term 'technical' used by Craig always has a modern, hence derogatory ring to it. He wrote in an article in 1930:

> London may expect to be told through the press how all theatre ideas came streaming from Russia, and that Moscow is the very cradle of ideas. Believe me, London need not bother to believe this... The talent of the Russian is great, but it is the talent for annexation of ideas... to which he then applies his technique.[50]

Application of technique, assimilation, are not according to Craig part of the creative process. Had he been able to show a 'talent for annexation' towards the theatre of the Orient his *Ubermarionette*, at least, might have taken a more concrete shape. Lacking a *technology* for his art he does not have the tools with which to do this. Like Mary Shelley's Romantic creation, Craig's *Ubermarionette* risks the danger of turning into a monster or a ghost.

Although *The Mask* is very much aware of Orientalism as a distinct movement of the period in the visual and performing arts,

---

[49] Ibid., p. 74.
[50] EGC, 'New book and Old Memories', (rev. of Rene Fulop-Miller's and Paul Gregor's, *The Russian Theatre with Special Reference to the Revolution*), The Boston Transcript, Nos. 4–6 (Boston, 1930).

Craig's own Orientalism is of a more theoretical nature, helping him form his own views on the art of the theatre. He does not produce clearly Orientalist works like Diaghilev's *Scheherazade* or Reinhardts's *Sumurun*. Indeed European Orientalism as a modern style, as a trend is severely criticized in *The Mask*. The Orient for Craig is something that is too sacred to set the new style, as happened in areas ranging from fine art to popular fashion.

Craig's Orientalism is very different from Diaghilev's in *Scheherazade* and Reinhardts's *Sumurun*. Both these productions rely on Western reconstructions of the Orient. The Orient appears as a theme, as a style in general, not as a theatrical reference. *Scheherazade* and *Sumurun* utilize the Oriental myth of despotism, hedonism and decadence, projecting an image of the Orient as Europe's *other*, but rely very little on Oriental theatrical modes as such. Craig understands this as imitation, which is his main criticism against the Russian Ballets:

> Imitating to perfection is certainly a talent and it is this special talent which is possessed by the Russians. They derive it from the far East. And in the Russian theatre this talent has been so cleverly employed that it has thoroughly dazzled Europeans and Americans.[51]

Against Reinhardt Craig launches his usual attack:

> Everyone here is speaking of 'Sumurun', the Pantomime brought over by Professor Reinhardt from Berlin.
> Of course the production is as Mr Paul Konody, writing in the Daily Mail, rightly points out, 'merely the latest development of the stage reform initiated by Mr Gordon Craig'.[52]

In 1914 a production of a mock Chinese play, *The Yellow Jacket*, appeared in London. This was exactly the type of Orientalism that outraged Craig. He thought it to be ridiculing a grand style. Besides he knew his facts well enough to realize that the common understanding of Oriental theatrical modes was completely mistaken:

> London has recently been interested in a chinese play, The Yellow Jacket, in which the leading actor takes the part of the property man in a trice, follows the actors and relieves them of their properties, and throughout the play assumes an air of unconcern and indifference, as

---

[51] Jan Klaassen (Craig pseudonym – a Netherlands folk puppet character), 'Imitation – A Note by Jan Klaassen', *The Mask*, Vol. 11, 1925, p. 40.
[52] John Semar (Craig pseudonym), in column entitled 'Foreign Notes', *The Mask*, Vol. 3, 1910–11, p. 189.

though he were not part and parcel of the performance and had no interest in the character.

But this English property man is quite contrary to ideas held regarding him in China or Japan. He has been the central figure of the play and has quite eclipsed the real actors who interpreted the story. Thus he has produced an effect which is quite opposite to that intended on the stages of the East.[53]

It is interesting to note that Craig corrects the London production with reference to the property man. It is on a theoretical level that it is important to him that the west has a true picture of Oriental theatre, since it is this he uses to justify his own role as 'Artist of the Theatre'.

The Mask, earlier than other Modernist theatrical projects, approaches oriental forms of theatre with the intention to study, analyse, learn and to hopefully integrate this experience into its 'new theatre'. It doesn't always fulfill all these aspirations. Yet again, it sets a tone, an attitude towards the 'orient', mainly highly Romantic and Orientalist, that later generations of theatre makers and schools would follow. Craig's fascination, idealisation and, in some cases, fetishisation of oriental theatre – quasi-historical and partly imaginary – acts as a type of springboard for the varied east/west relationships in the theatre that would form an integral part of most twentieth century schools of performance.

---

[53] From unsigned article probably by EGC, 'Puppets in Japan', *The Mask*, Vol. 6, 1914, p. 217.

13. Cover of, Vol. 3, Nos. 7–9, 1911.

5

A MASK FOR THE COMMEDIA DELL'ARTE

The Commedia dell'Arte as Inspiration

Just as the Arts and Crafts background provided *The Mask* with the ideal aesthetic setting, placing it in the tradition of the Book Beautiful, the Commedia dell'Arte, possibly more than any other feature of the periodical, gives shape to its performative quality. The Italian theatre of the sixteenth, seventeenth and eighteenth century acts as the perfect historical reference for Craigian notions of theatricality. At the same time, the chameleon-like quality of the Commedia provides *The Mask* with a paradigm for narration. Craig's use of pseudonyms and his creation of fixed 'characters' for each one, his own discourse which fuses the historical with the whimsical, his suspicion of ideas of authenticity[1] can be read as a Commedia-type outlook desperately trying to take shape on the pages of a magazine. The title of the periodical itself simultaneously comments on the Commedia as a distinct theatrical mode and also uses it as a mode of presentation. Commedia notions of theatricality help the magazine to present itself, to act as a stage for the various Craigian *masks*.

Like his Modernist contemporaries (Meyerhold, Copeau, Diaghilev), Craig saw in the Commedia an ultimate remedy to the damage done to the theatre through naturalism. With its ambivalent relationship to the written text, its emphasis on improvisation, its *lazzi*, and its apotheosis of the notion of performance, the Commedia helped re-shape Modernist ideas of theatricality. The Commedia presented one more instance of an oral and popular tradition which provided ready-made forms that could accommodate much of Modernist theatrical experimentation. Either elevating this oral tradition, turning it into 'high art', or discovering in it the locus of the ever-popular – hence revolution-ary – the Modernist schools of theatre practice found in the Commedia yet another mode they could appropriate. For *The Mask*, the Commedia offered a language of theatricality that, combined with Craigain theories, could generate the desired renaissance of the stage. Craig writes in

---

[1] See chapter 3 for a further discussion of Craig's scepticism about 'the shock of the new' in modern movements like Cubism and Futurism.

The Mask in an article entitled 'The Commedia dell'Arte Ascending', seeing, as early as 1912, a possible model for his theatre:

> How much has been written about this wonderful attempt to raise Theatricals to a higher state...to lift them from interpretative into creative realms. And how much more will have to be written, and that before long on this plucky attempt. No one fails to understand that in the Commedia dell'Arte the Italians of the late 16th century gave to future generations a hint as to the possibilities of the Art of the Theatre. The hint was never taken by those of the subsequent centuries.[2]

The Mask definitely takes the hint and presents itself as the continuation of the Commedia tradition, both in its content and in its form.

For Craig, unlike his Modernist colleagues, the Commedia not only presented a point of historical and theatrical reference but, more importantly, a clear set of historical facts. For most Modernist theoreticians of the theatre the Commedia was fundamentally an oral tradition and as such very difficult to codify and register. As a result it became a reference, an allusion, at most used to recall the defiant and anarchic nature of carnivalesque, popular performance modes. It became a type of raw material that, like Oriental theatre, could be remoulded and appropriated according to one's views on theatre and the world in general. Schoenberg's *Pierrot Lunaire* acts as a fine example of a Commedia-based or a Commediaesque piece where the relationship is one of influence and reference – even between genres – with most of the appropriations remaining of a highly Romantic/Symbolist order. For *The Mask* the relationship with the Commedia is of a very different order. For Craig, living and working in Italy, the Commedia was a very real fact, not merely a reconstructed one. He probably had more access to authentic, unpublished material on the Commedia than any other European director of the period. Indeed, *The Mask*, from the very early issues, promises to provide its readers with rich material on the Commedia and never fails to do so throughout all of its issues. 'John Semar' writes in an editorial of 1910:

> Until now *The Mask* has had only a few words to say about the Commedia dell'Arte, that powerful development of the theatrical art which has done more credit to the stage than any later development, yet which was unable to survive Molière's friendship; but now we publish all we can collect upon this subject...and in trying, to collect together all that is to be said about this vivid renaissance of the theatrical art, we do so, not for its value from an antiquarian point of

---

[2] *The Mask*, Vol. 5, 1912, pp. 104–8, p. 104.

view, considerable though that may be, but for its value to the sincere student of the future.[3]

With missionary zeal *The Mask* sets out to rediscover the Commedia and exclusively present it to its readers. The material covered is indeed impressive as Craig and his secretary Dorothy Nevile Lees roam through libraries in Florence, Venice and Rome discovering old manuscripts and reference books on the Commedia. Many of the articles constitute the first English translations. In this, the role of Dorothy Nevile Lees in *The Mask's* Commedia project is vital, as she was herself an Italian scholar who did most, if not all, of the translations and whose expertise Craig badly needed. As usual though, he pays her little or no acknowledgement. It is significant that most of the articles translated from seventeenth and eighteenth century manuscripts appear unsigned. At the same time Craig congratulates himself in a letter to the editor Semar:

> My dear Semar,
> How well you are doing to print in *The Mask* for the younger generation the facts about the Commedia dell'Arte; your translations from the Italian are great blessings. I feel sure that the few students for whom they are published will not fail to express their gratitude. Signor Scherillo's articles have given me great pleasure and the Biographical Notes are very valuable.[4]

Whether acknowledging the role of Dorothy Nevile Lees or not, *The Mask* is full of her translations and introductions. At a time when scholarship on the Commedia in English was limited, *The Mask* proves to be a vital source book for the Italian improvised theatre. It is Craig's most comprehensive study of any aspect of theatre history. *The Mask* also presents reviews of most books on the Commedia of the period. Its main sources, though, remain the manuscripts and leaflets that Craig discovered, and in this field most of the work is pioneering. The Signor Scherillo mentioned above is only one of the Italian scholars whose work on the

---

[3] *The Mask*, Vol. 3, 1910, p. 50.

[4] *The Mask*, Vol. 3, 1911, p. 147. Dorothy Nevile Lees was Craig's chief collaborator on the whole of *The Mask* project, sharing many of Craig's pseudonyms (including that of the editor John Semar — Pierre Rames backwards). For more information on Dorothy Nevile Lees's role in *The Mask* and why this remained invisible see Lorelei Guidry, *The Mask: Introduction and Index* (New York, 1968).

Using her own name Dorothy Nevile Lees appears in *The Mask* in the following issues: Vol. 1, p. 85, p. 103, p. 106, p. 200, p. 226; Vol. 2, p. 28, p. 52, pp. 95–96, p. 134, p. 174; Vol. 4, p. 137, p. 219, p. 322; Vol. 5, p. 72, p. 290; Vol. 6, p. 188, p. 286; Vol. 10, p. 42, p. 187; Vol. 11, p. 55; Vol. 12, p. 3, p. 78; Vol. 14, p. 162; Vol. 15, p. 13, pp. 27–30, p. 48, p. 121, p. 137.

Commedia appears in *The Mask*. It is not only Italian academics but, editors of Italian magazines that contribute to *The Mask's* Commedia campaign. Craig had access to a whole aspect of the Commedia which remained essentially 'other' for the rest of European Modernism. For him the Commedia was more than a convenient metaphor of theatricality; it was something which presented itself as historically concrete and knowable. As such he set out to master it through the pages of *The Mask*.

In shaping the actual physical appearance of *The Mask*, the Commedia is the form that gives it its highly performative quality. Unlike the magazines of the Arts and Crafts Movement or the late aestheticist 1890s, *The Mask* does not use the Commedia in the late Romantic mode, filtered mostly through French interpretations. Although *The Mask* springs from the same tradition in the production of the magazine beautiful, it nevertheless chooses to use the Commedia in quite a different way. *The Savoy, The Dial, The Studio*, and mostly *The Yellow Book* all employ Commedia-type illustrations, that refer mainly to the late Romantic and chiefly French readings of particular Commedia characters – characters that have become almost independent from their Italian roots (see Beardsley's illustrations for *The Yellow Book* and more especially for *The Pierrot of the Minute*). Craig is less interested in the Romantic or decadent Symbolist appropriations of particular Commedia characters. For him the Commedia constitutes a theatrical tradition with a very specific set of theatrical conventions, ones he applies in not only shaping his notion of the 'Art of the Theatre', but in writing, editing and printing a periodical. Gone are the moonstruck Commediaesque figures that appeared in the 1890s journals. *The Mask* is full of reproductions of original prints, showing Commedia characters, performances, costume design etc. (An example of this is the frontispiece: 'A Grotesque Arlecchino's Mask' printed in *The Mask* in 1910.) And Craig is indeed proud when he announces to his readers information such as: 'reproduced from an old engraving hitherto unpublished in the possession of Signor Villoressi of Florence'.[5] He finds printed Commedia scenarios and publishes them in their first English translation in *The Mask*. (The first of these appears as early as 1911 and the last in 1914.) In terms of content, no other contemporary arts periodical can boast such a rich coverage of Commedia history and bibliography. Few scholarly works of the period compare with the very comprehensive study *The Mask* offers its readers. None though has appropriated the spirit of the Commedia so creatively in its very narrative and discourse. The Commedia provides Craig with the ultimate mask behind which he can edit, write and direct possibly his most successful and certainly his longest running performance: *The Mask*.

---

[5] See frontispiece, 'A grotesque Arlecchino's mask', *The Mask*, Vol. 3, Nos. 7–9, 1911.

The Mask as a Source of Commedia Scholarship

With a wealth of primary and secondary sources available to him, Craig set out to codify what was no less than a comprehensive study of the history of the Commedia dell'Arte. He writes in 1912:

> In my spare moments of the last year I filled a little book with a mass of *facts* relating to the Commedia dell'Arte which I hope shortly to publish. I felt such a book had to be made if one wished to get a clearer idea of this amazing Drama, because the theatrical historians carried away by their enthusiasm for the subject have been too liberal...
> 'Perhaps' and 'In my opinion' and 'It is likely that' is charming, but not history.[6]

Such a book was never, of course, written. Instead he gathered all the information he found in *The Mask*. His main sources can be divided into three broad categories: (a) studies on the Commedia, mainly in Italian and French from the seventeenth, eighteenth and nineteenth centuries; (b) contemporary studies on the Commedia, which are reviewed thoroughly; and (c) manuscrpits and prints he discovered in Italian libraries. Most of the material presented appears in its first English translation (apart from a few contemporary studies originally in English), as few source books on the Commedia existed in English before the beginning of the twentieth century.

One of the studies which proved most useful to *The Mask's* Commedia presentation was Andrea Perrucci's *Dell'Arte Rappresentativa, Premeditata ed All'improvviso*. Written in 1699 in Naples it is one of the earliest printed documents on the Commedia. From Perrucci he chooses the extract on the roles of the *Corago*, the *Director* and the *Manager*. The translation reads:

> The *Corago*, manager or most experienced of the company, should plan out the subject before it is acted, so that one may know the contents of the Comedy, understand where the speeches are to end and diligently study the addition of some new quips and Lazzi The *Director* then goes on pointing out and explaining the Lazzi and the plot.
> Let all the actors he gathered to listen, and let them not trust to knowing by heart, or having previously acted, that Comedy; because it might happen that different *Managers* would arrange the plot differently and that the names and places might be different.[7]

---

[6] *The Mask*, Vol. 5, 1912, p. 105.
[7] *The Mask*, Vol. 4, 1911, pp. 113–5. From Andrea Perrucci, *Dell'Arte Rappresentativa, Premeditata ed All'improvviso* (Naples, 1699), trans. by Dorothy Nevile Lees.

14. Four 'Moods of Arlecchino' by Claude Gillot, Vol. 3, Nos. 7–9, p. 107b, 1911.

With its emphasis on improvisation and virtuoso acting, the Commedia can be understood as a quintessentially *actor's theatre*. Craig very quickly corrects that notion by asserting his own role as 'Artist of the Theatre', one that combines the qualities of the *Corago*, the *Director* and the *Manager*.

From another vital source book *L'Histoire du Theatre Italien* (1728) written by Luigi Riccoboni, who was initially a Commedia actor, *The Mask* explains what the lazzi of the Commedia are:

> We call *Lazzi* that which Harlequins or the other masked actors do in the middle of a scene to interrupt it either by expressing fear or by making jokes which have no connection with the subject of the play and to which they are constantly obliged to resort. So it is these superfluities suggested to the actor by his own genius on the spur of the moment which the Italian comic actors call *Lazzi*.[8]

Riccoboni is vital for Craig: he refers to him often and publishes a bibliography of his works in *The Mask*.[9] Two other studies which are referred to in *The Mask* are: Evaristo Gherardi's *Le Theatre Italien* (1714), and Luigi Rasi's *I Comici Italiani. Biografia, Bibliografia, Iconografia* (1897–1905). These texts, different in their historical orientation and academic approach, nevertheless comprise for *The Mask* key source books for information on the Commedia. *The Mask* publishes Dorothy Nevile Lees's translation of Gherardi's introduction to his book, and Craig comments on it:

> Among the most delightful as well as the most useful books for the student of the Italian Improvised Commedia dell'Arte is undoubtedly *Le Theatre Italien* by Evaristo Gherardi. Indeed (according to Professor Rasi) it is, with the exception of the Scenarios of Flaminio Scala, the most important of all for the history of the Italian actors.[10]

---

[8] Ibid.

[9] The study Craig uses as a source book is Luigi Riccoboni, *Histoire du Theatre Italien*, 2 vols. (Paris, 1730–31). Ending an article entitled 'Experiment in Literary Drama', written by Pierre Rames (Lees's Commedia pseudonym) the readership is presented with a comprehensive bibliography of Riccoboni's works:

L'Histoire du Theatre Italien, illus. by Joullain (Paris, 1728).

Nuovo Teatro Italiano (Paris, 1733).

Observations sur la Comedie et sur la Genie de Moliere (Paris, 1736).

Reflexions Historiques et Critiques sur les differents Theatres de l'Europe, avec les Pensees sur la Declamation (Paris, 1738).

Dell'Arte Rappresentativa (London, 1728).

Reformation du Theatre (Paris, 1767).

[10] *The Mask*, Vol. 3, 1911, p. 164, from Evaristo Gherardi, *Le Theatre Italien*, 8 vols. (London, 1714).

Professor Rasi's book is almost contemporary with *The Mask*. A contributor and advisor to Craig, he forms part of a group of Italian scholars who write in *The Mask* on the Commedia, or whose work (with their permission) Craig reprints there. Of *I Comici Italiani* Craig writes:

> We are glad to have been the first to introduce this remarkable work to English readers, grateful for the information it has given us, happy to seize the opportunity of publicly expressing to Professor Rasi our appreciation of and gratitude for several little services which he, so rich in knowledge of, as well as in objects of historical value relating to the Commedia dell'Arte has rendered to *The Mask* in its preparation of the numbers which it has especially devoted to that most interesting phase of the Italian Theatre.[11]

Dr. Michele Scherillo is another Italian scholar to appear in the pages of *The Mask*. Not only did *La Commedia dell'Arte in Italia* (1884) prove useful but he also wrote regular contributions on the Commedia especially for *The Mask*.[12] Cesare Levi, the author of *Rivista Teatrale Italiana*, published in 1912, also wrote Commedia articles for the periodical. His major contribution, though, was his translation of a scenario published for the first time in English in *The Mask*.[13]

---

[11] *The Mask*, Vol. 3, Nos.10–12 (Florence, 1911), p. 187, from Luigi Rasi, *I Comici Italiani. Biografia, Bibliografia, Iconografia*, 2 vols. (Florence, 1897–1905). Professor Rasi contributes to *The Mask* in the following issues: Vol. 3, p. 181; Vol. 4, p. 340; Vol. 5, p. 146; Vol. 14, p. 132.

[12] Michele Scherillo, *La Commedia dell'Arte in Italia* (Torino, 1884). Dr. Scherillo appears in the following issues of *The Mask*: Vol. 3, p. 22, p. 108, p. 149; Vol. 6, p. 146; Vol. 7, p. 33. Of these contributions perhaps the most extensive is a ten-page article entitled 'The Genealogy of Pulcinella' written for Vol. 3 of *The Mask*.

[13] Cesare Levi, *Rivista Teatrale Italiana*, 1912. Dr. Levi appears in *The Mask* in the following issues: Vol. 5, p. 20; Vol. 11, p. 71, p. 151; His most valuable contribution was as translator of the (unpublished in English) Commedia scenario *The Roguish Tricks of Coviello* (*Gli Intrighi di Coviello per la Moglie*) in Vol. 6, pp. 353–56.

Dr. Levi's collection of scenarios in *Rivista Teatrale Italiana*, based on the manuscripts in the National Library of Naples, proved very useful for Craig. Dorothy Nevile Lees translates another scenario from that collection entitled *The Betrayed* (*Il Tradito*) in Vol. 7, pp. 53–57 of *The Mask*. The collection complied by Dr. Levi was published in three instalments: in 1911, 1912 and 1914. Altogether it comprises an overwhelming 15 volumes. The appearence of the scenarios in the pages of *The Mask* in Volumes 6 and 7 (1913 and 1914) is almost simultaneous with their Italian publication. An English translation of these has not as yet been published. Two more Commedia scenarios feature in *The Mask*. These are *The Three Princes of Salerno* (*Li Tre Principi di Salerno*) in Vol. 4, pp. 335–39, and *The Four Lunatics* (*I Quattro Pazzi*) in Vol. 4, pp. 116–21. These are translated from Adolfo Bartoli's *Scenari Inediti della Commedia dell'Arte* (Florence, 1880). Craig was familiar with the collection as he refers to it elsewhere in *The Mask* (while compiling a list of Commedia characters he writes 'I can find no such list either in Bartoli – *Scenari inediti della commedia dell'arte* – or elswhere'. See last note 43.) All four scenarios can be found in Volume 5 of Vito Pandolfli's *La Commedia dell'Arte, Storia e Testo* (Florence, 1959). They do not appear in Henry F. Salerno,

As part of his research into the history of the Commedia, Craig presents readers of *The Mask* with four Commedia scenarios. Two of these – *The Three Princes of Salerno* and *The Four Lunatics* – he found in Adolfo Bartoli's *Scenari Inediti Della Commedia Dell'Arte Contributo Alla Storia Del Teatro Popolare Italiano* (1880). (Although Craig does not acknowledge the source we know he was aware of the Bartoli collection as he refers to it elsewhere in *The Mask*. It was also conveniently published in Florence.[14]) The translation of these scenarios is probably Dorothy Nevile Lees's but this is unfortunately not stated. Two more scenarios Craig reprints from C. Levi's *Rivista Teatrale Italiana*: *The Betrayed* and *The Roguish Tricks of Coviello*. The *Coviello* scenario is translated for *The Mask* by Dr. Levi himself.

To this team of experts Craig adds Umberto Fracchia,[15] himself an editor of a periodical called *Comoedia*, and the picture is complete. No other project undertaken by *The Mask* was ever so democratically distributed among experts other than Craig. If we add to this quite impressive endeavour Craig's own Commedia studies we have a mass of material, whether original, re-printed or translated, that makes *The Mask* a formidable authority on the Commedia dell'Arte for its period.

Though for Craig the Commedia presented the perfect paradigm for his own theories on the 'Art of the Theatre', it had another level of appeal: it was a field in which he could excel at the expense of his English colleagues. Having abandoned England to live and work in Italy he nevertheless strongly felt the need to constantly teach his countrymen a lesson for having ignored his creative abilities. This love/hate relationship finds fruitful ground in the study of the Commedia. Most of it is

---

trans. *Scenarios of the Commedia dell'Arte: Flaminio Scala's Il teatro delle favole rappresentative* (New York, 1967), which is the only comprehensive collection translated in English to date.
[14] *Scenari Inediti della Commedia dell'Arte*. See note 13.
[15] Umberto Fracchia was the editor of a journal called *Comoedia* published in Milan in the same period as *The Mask*. His article 'English Actors and Italian Actors' appears in Vol. 11, p. 161 of *The Mask*. Apart from editing amagazine and contributing to *The Mask* Umberto Fracchia was an accomplished novelist. His *La Stella del Nord* was published in 1930 and the study *Vincenzo Monti* in 1927 in Milan. *Robino and Other Stories*, translated by Sir. H. Scott, was published in London in 1932. Under the title 'Book Notes in *The Mask*', Vol. 11, No.1, 1925, p. 49. Craig writes on the collaboration of *The Mask* and *Comoedia*: 'Here in Italy much Theatre literature is continually published. An interesting article on the work of Gordon Craig by Henry Furst appeared in *Il Piccolo* lately. Another appeared on the same subject in *Comoedia* for November 10th, which is issued in Milano. The article was written by A. Nasalli Rocca, who contributed an article on the old Theatres of Piacenza to the October number of *The Mask*. *Comoedia* often contains interesting items. It is published by Mondadori (Galleria Vittorio Emanuele 74), Milano, and edited by Umberto Fracchia, a young writer of talent and experience'.

virgin ground to the English audience, and Craig can present himself as the new apostle who has brought to light a wonderful remedy that can revive the theatre. He takes particular pleasure in correcting English scholars on facts about the Commedia. In a review of Enid Welsford's *The Court Masque* he writes, in one of the last issues of *The Mask* (1928):

> Were I an influence in Oxford or Cambridge (this book comes from Cambridge) I would counsel young men and women always to avoid attempting a big work on a subject covering several nations, thousands of persons and a couple of centuries. I would suggest that to take the life's work of a Laniere or a family like the Parigi or a group like the Gelosi was quite sufficiently difficult, and really valuable to their fellow-students and even to the wisest professors. I feel students who have learned so much from these big men should dedicate a year or two of their time to at least one small subject such as I have indicated, as a return for all things received from these masters... But I am always saying this. I wonder if anyone is listening.[16]

Educating the English audience in particular about the Commedia is one of the roles assigned to *The Mask*. Craig is interested in drawing parallels between the Commedia and the Shakespearean stage. He treats his audience as if they believed that theatre began with Shakespeare. Whether this was the prevailing attitude of the English stage at the time or not is of little consequence, as it triggers one of Craig's most extensive studies in *The Mask*. In an article/leaflet entitled 'The Pre-Shakespearean Stage' he maps out the most important happenings regarding the Commedia of the sixteenth century together with the most important aspects of the English stage of the same period. 'John Semar' introduces his study:

> We have not found any such list as this elsewhere. Probably no one has considered it worth while to compile one. We, however, think differently, and in subsequent pages we shall give some of our reasons for so thinking, and shall explain why we wish to draw the serious attention of students of the theatre to that great Pre-Shakespearean period which the historians, for the most part, skim lightly over in their eagerness to arrive at Shakespeare himself, and the Elizabethan stage.[17]

In a detailed account that follows, Craig traces the history of the famous Commedia companies *I Gelosi* and *I Confidenti*; the most important Italian plays of the sixteenth century; and the most important events of the

---

[16] *The Mask*, Vol. 14, 1928, p. 40.
[17] *The Mask*, Vol. 6, 1913, p. 135.

English stage at the time. It is characteristic that Shakespeare is initially mentioned as 'adapting old plays'. Inigo Jones's travels throughout Italy are recorded. The emphasis, though, is on the lives and times of Commedia actors. In presenting this account of 'the century that gave Shakespeare birth', Craig mainly wants to:

> ...show that there were men at work in the Theatre long before Shakespeare; they show that that Shakespearean Theatre over which Mr. William Poel and Mr. Allbright and their confreres enthuse as the very apotheosis of the history of the theatre was, in truth, but the dying close of a glorious day and that it was more in its quality as the 'setting sun and music at its close' that it was 'writ in remembrance more than things long past' than for its own intrinsic glory: that it marked, in fact, already a period, not of development, but of decline.[18]

The Mask's ambivalent relationship with the work of Shakespeare running throughout the periodical is quite clear from the above.[19] Craig acknowledges Shakespeare as a great playwright, but that quality itself goes against his beliefs on the 'Art of the Theatre'. With the Commedia he did not have to face such problems. Virtually authorless, relying on improvisations based on set scenarios, it presents no threat for Craig and offers him a scheme that can artistically accomodate his 'Artist of the Theatre'. The playwright for Craig is seen as 'the sourse of all evil' in the theatre. Shakespeare, despite all his greatness, is somehow seen as the epitome of the written play tradition. What this particular study of Craig's sets out to prove is the there were 'men working in the theatre before Shakespeare' but they were not playwrights. In a neat and simplistic pattern that sees written drama springing directly from the oral tradition Craig explains:

> But we suspect that these written plays upon which the later actors depended were really at the outset composed by the actors themselves

---

[18] Ibid., p. 147.

[19] Craig expresses his interest in Shakespeare mainly in the form of a homage to his designer/architect father E. W. Godwin. From *The Architect* he reprints most of Godwin's designs for costumes and settings of Shakespeare plays; *All's Well That Ends Well*, Vol. 3, p. 19; *Antony and Cleopatra*, Vol. 2, pp. 127–30; *As You Like it*, Vol. 3, p. 18; *Coriolanus*, Vol. 1, pp. 112–15; Greek Plays, Shakespeare, Vol. 1, pp. 134–39, pp. 156–58, pp. 192–94, pp. 216–18; *Julius Caesar*, Vol. 2, pp. 77–80; *King Henry VIII*, Vol. 3, p. 73; *Love's Labour's Lost*, Vol. 3, pp. 20–21; *The Merchant of Venice*, Vol. 1, pp. 75–80, pp. 91–94; A *Midsummer Night's Dream*, pp. 134–39, pp. 156–58, pp. 192–94, pp. 216–18; *Othello*, Vol. 2, pp. 165–68; *Pericles*, see Greek plays. *Richard III*, Vol. 4, 191–96; *The Taming of the Shrew*, Vol. 5, pp. 199–203; *The Tempest*, Vol. 5, p. 204; *Timon of Athens*, pp. 134–39, pp. 56–58, pp. 192–94, pp. 216–18; *Troilus and Cressida*, pp. 134–39, pp. 156–58, pp. 192–94, pp. 216–18; *Twelfth Night*, Vol. 4, pp. 286–18; *Two Gentlemen of Verona*, Vol. 2, pp. 168–70; *The Winter's Tale*, pp. 134–39, pp. 156–58, pp. 192–94, pp. 216–18.

and only written down afterwards by scribes... not the whole but parts of them; so that by degrees a play, originally a living thing varying from night to night with the humour of the players, became stereotyped into one permanent form, and the living tree of the actors' invention slowly petrified into the fossil which future generations could discuss, study, and pass from hand to hand.[20]

In shaping a theory of performance for the theatre, the Commedia dell'Arte, possibly more than any other genre in theatre history, offers Craig a model that is authorless. At the same time though, it gives rise to the actor. Based on his/her abilities for improvisation and reworking of scenarios, the Commedia is arguably the ultimate actor's theatre. Most of the collections of scenarios were written by actors who, having acted in them for a number of years, later recorded them. Craig mentions such actors-cum-scenarists with brief biographical notes.[21] The most important collection of this type and the first to appear is Flaminio Scala's *Il Teatro delle Favole Rappresentative* (1611) which Craig had access to, and which was not published in English until 1967. These Commedia scenarios look more like a director's note-books on a performance, rather than conventionally written play-scripts. Craig quotes Riccoboni on Scala's collection: 'they only explain what the actor must do on the stage, and the actions of the play, and nothing more'. It is this 'nothing more' aspect of the Commedia scenario that Craig finds appealing. The fact that it also gives considerable creative power to the actor does not seem to bother him. He writes:

> Whether the inventors were peasants or actors or both is immaterial. The point has not been decided; but it has been very clearly decided and recorded that they were not play-writers. Is it possible? Can a Drama which holds the stage for two centuries be created without the assistance of the literary man? It can. Then if it can be created once it can be created twice? It can.[22]

It is chiefly this aspect of the Commedia, as a model for an authorless performance, that Craig appropriates in his scheme of the 'Art of the Theatre'. He is also aware, though, of the influence the Commedia had on the written drama of Europe. Molière is seen as an intruder who borrows shamelessly from the Commedia. Craig quotes from Tiraboschi's

---

[20] See note 17, p. 147.
[21] *The Mask* Vol. 6, 1913, pp. 147–156. A list of Commedia actors/playwrights follows with detailed biographical notes.
[22] *The Mask*, Vol. 3, 1911, p. 99a.

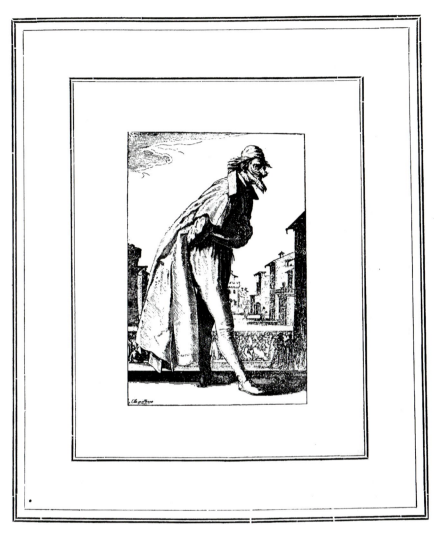

15. 'Pantalone' by Giacomo Callot, Vol. 3, Nos. 7–9, p. 118b, 1911.

Storia della Literatura Italiana:

> Molière has made so much use of the Italian comic writers, that, were
> we to take from him all that he has taken from others, the volumes of
> his comedies would be very much reduced in bulk.[23]

Craig's presentation of Molière[24] is not as flippant as the above quotation may read. Cesare Levi, the Italian Commedia scholar, also writes in
The Mask on the influence of Commedia masks on Molière characters.[25]
Nevertheless when he has to make a point Craig is definitely biased
towards the oral Commedia tradition in performance. His rhetoric,
contradictory in places, seems to polarize themes and issues that coexist
harmoniously in other parts of the periodical. In the Commedia Craig
finds one of his few allies. It is a type of theatre that he can totally accept
without compromising his own beliefs. As such, he feels he must defend
it against the literary drama.

The Commedia Actor and the *Ubermarionette*

The Commedia dell'Arte was chiefly an actors' theatre. It took particular
delight in highlighting the ingenuity, the skill and the grace of improvisation. Based on virtuoso acting, the Commedia allowed the actors to
indulge in the mechanics of their technique, the whole process of acting
itself was part of the performance; the audience was asked not only to
follow the story being told but also to admire the actors' skills. This meta-
theatrical quality of the Commedia actor is what appealed to Modernist
stage directors like Meyerhold. Craig's understanding and use of the
Commedia actor, like other ideas he re-works, is not as straightforward.

On one level it may seem totally incongruous with Craig's
general theories on the 'Art of the Theatre'. Craig theoretically accommo-
dates the role of the actor with his concept of the *Ubermarionette*; a
mechanical device that would be the sole interpreter of the director's
'genius'. Apart from a few notes on monodrama written while he was
working on the Moscow *Hamlet* project, his theories have little space for
ideas and formulations on acting as a creative process. Fighting certain

---

[23] *The Mask*, Vol. 3, 1910, p. 100.
[24] Molière is referred to in *The Mask* in the following issues: Vol. 8, p. 7; Vol. 10, p. 26,
p. 66; Vol. 11, pp. 71–79; Vol. 13, p. 48; Vol. 15, p. 8, pp. 35–36; *Augusta*, Lady Gregory,
translation, Vol. 3, p. 132; *Le Mariage Force*, Vol. 6, pp. 277–78; plays, Vol. 13, p. 35; as
playwright, Vol. 12, p. 123; studies in, Vol. 11, p. 70; theatre ground plan, Vol. 8, p. 7.
[25] Cesare Levi, 'How Doctors Were Satirized in the Ancient Theatre' in *The Mask*, Vol. 11,
No. 2 (Florence, 1925), pp. 71–79. This essay, which traces the Commedia influences in
Molière, is reprinted from Cesare Levy's *Studii Molieriani*, ed. Sandron, Palerno.

aspects of the old actor-manager system and defining his own role as the all-powerful director left no room for theories on acting. For Craig the actor/star, as a creative entity, bore almost as much responsibility for the decline in the theatre as the playwright. In this scheme of things it appears highly unlikely that Craig would find in the Commedia actor a prototype of any sort; least of all for his *Ubermarionette*.

Yet for Craig the Commedia actor appeared as the perfect example of a highly disciplined, well trained actor. The Commedia's emphasis on non-psychological, stereotypical portrayal gave rise to the notion of technique as part of the creative process. Indeed technique was fetishized as it became one of the main sources of pleasure for the audience. It is this non-psychological, stylized acting with its emphasis on the physical that Craig saw as analogous to his *Ubermarionette*. In the Commedia actor Craig saw a type of primitive *Ubermarionette*. Free from the constraints of a written text, technically trained to perfection and assisted by the fixed face of the mask, all the Commedia actor *really* needed to turn into its modern equivalent the *Ubermarionette* was the 'genius' of the 'Artist of the Theatre' to provide coherence and inspire creative force into the otherwise highly trained body/form.

Throughout *The Mask* Craig prints considerable material on the Commedia actor. Again Dorothy Nevile Lees is the main translator of most of the original material. This consists of biographies of major Commedia actors, lists of the performances and essays on acting. Craig's main argument for praising the Commedia actors is that he believes that the Commedia actor was a 'creative actor'. He writes introducing a rare book by Barbieri:

> The reproduction of this rare leaf has been put here so that any actors or critics curious to have proof of the truth of what we have been asserting since 1908, can have it here.
>   Between 1500–1900 it was the custom for all good actors to create.... But I will give you two extracts, and also the names of a few of the most famous actors in Italy, who most assuredly created their plays, inventing the dialogue and the action of the plays, led by acapo-comico, or head-actor.[26]

---

[26] *The* Mask, Vol. 9, 1923, pp. 12–14. The title of this leaflet by Barbieri (1576–1641) in Craig's possession reads *La Schiava Comedia Nuova e Ridicolosa Nuovamente Posta in Luce, ad Instantia D'Ogni Spiriti Gentile. Colophon in Pavia, per Pietro Bartoli. 1602 con Licenza de'Superiori.*
He introduces it saying: 'I give you here for your eyes to see and for your common sense to reason about, a page from an Italian book of about 8 pages in my possession. You will find a translation in the side of the column'. This is followed by a list of head actors. Scarpetta, the last name on the list was still working at his theatre in Naples while Craig lived in Italy. His theatre attracted artists as diverse as Stravinsky, Picasso, Massine and

The extracts themselves are from Evaristo Gherardi and Riccoboni[27] and stress the importance of improvisation. Improvisation itself seems to contradict Craig's *Ubermarionette* theory. The fixed gesture of a mechanized object on the one hand, and the total fluidity of the human form on the other appear to be utterly conflicting. However, what Craig discerned behind the principle of improvisation was a very strict and rigorous training procedure, which theoretically could render the actor free from psychology and interpretation. The philosophy of the actual Commedia masks which gave them the power to not only hide identity but, to also create a new theatrical one also contributed to a form of improvised theatre that was, at the same time, highly structured and fixed. Having in this sense 'broken' or 'freed' the human form it could in turn transform into an *Ubermarionette*. On another level, raising the principle of improvisation to artistic heights gave Craig yet another chance to attack the English star-system. He writes:

> Still something must be said for these antagonists of improvisation who dwell in England. They are frightened; they fear to encourage the principle lest a mere imitation be offered the public and accepted as the real article. They dread that something 'artistic' might be let loose and they prefer the 'theatrical'. So do we all. But what a strange place is England where the good words 'artistic' and 'theatrical' have become terms of derision used by artists and theatrical people.[28]

Improvisation becomes yet another key term in Craig's attack on the English theatrical tradition. For him it was the ultimate safety-valve that protected theatre from the menacing powers of the playwright. As long as virtuoso acting could help create the final performance, the authority of the playwright seemed to be limited. Craig's fascination with Irving

---

Diaghilev. Craig and Dorothy Nevile Lees would visit Scarpetta's theatre in Naples and write articles about it in *The Mask*. See note 41.

[27] The extract from Evaristo Gherardi reads: 'To be a good Italian actor means to be a man who possesses a rich store of knowledge, who plays more from fancy than from memory, who invents all he says, who seconds his colleague on the stage, that is matches his actions and words so well with those of his comrade, that he enters at once on all the movements to which the other invites him, and in such a way as to make everybody believe that all has been settled beforehand'. The extract is from *Le Theatre Italien* (1714), and is reprinted in *The Mask*, Vol. 9, 1923, pp. 12–4.

The extract from Riccoboni reads: 'To an actor who depends on improvisation, it is not sufficient to have face, memory, voice, even sentiment, if he is to distinguish himself, he must possess a lively and fertile imagination, a great facility of expression, he must master all the subtleties of language, possess all the knowledge which is required for the different situations in which his part places him'. This extract is reprinted from *L'Histoire du Theatre Italien* (1728) in the above issue of *The Mask*.

[28] *The Mask*, Vol. 3, 1911, p. 101.

seems understandable in this context. For him, Irving was an example of a highly skilled actor, who, combined with his quality as a manager, stood against the power of the playwright. Irving's mannered and stylized acting was seen by Craig as a form of improvisation. Improvisation itself is seen as the sometimes 'raw', but always effective corrective to the literary theatre. He writes:

> I hope that no one will commence *writing plays* for Pierrot and Columbine and Puncinella for a written play is an absurd thing and a dead thing into the bargain.
>   One dreads to think what sweet stuff a minor or even a major poet would fashion out of these masked giants that strode across the centuries for a while, helping Shakespeare, suckling Molière, creating Goldoni and being driven away from the haunts of man by the ungrateful children they had reared.[29]

What Craig rightly sees is that the Commedia was essentially an *acting* tradition with improvisation as its main theatrical convention. In this context, possibly the only one in *The Mask* that allows for it, he concerns himself with actors and acting. The Commedia actor becomes an idealized figure, graced with a mixture of ingenuity and innocence. What the Commedia actor represents for Craig is chiefly the embodiment of the notion of skill and technique; both qualities that could be filtered and used by his 'Artist of the Theatre'. What Irving represented for the theatre of the present, the Commedia actor represented for the theatre of the past. Craig's aim was to somehow fuse these very different traditions through the creation of his *Ubermarionette*.

It is not surprising, therefore, to find much material in *The Mask* devoted to the Commedia actor. Biographies of actors translated by Dorothy Nevile Lees appear throughout its issues. The history of the famous companies *I Gelosi* and *I Confidenti* is meticulously presented. Craig himself searches libraries in Italy for rare documents referring to Commedia actors. Such a document is one entitled *An Actor's Petition* signed by the company of the *Comici Confidenti*.[30] It is a plea dated June 25th 1574, asking 'his Catholic Majesty' to drop charges of theft, that had been made against one of the actors. Craig identifies the writer of the petition as one Battista da Rimino, with the help of Luigi Rasi's *Comici Italiani*. His main interest lies in the fact that through the discovery of such documents he can trace the history of the Commedia companies. He ends the article by stating that 'the famous Company of the *Confidenti*

---

[29] Ibid., p. 100.
[30] *An Actor's Petition*, rpt. in *The Mask*, Vol. 14, 1928, pp. 132–33. The petition is in Dorothy Nevile Lees's translation.

16. Characters from the *Balli di Sfessania* (1622) by G. Callot, Vol. 3, Nos. 10–12, p. 156b, 1911.

would be shown by this letter to have been during that year in Cremona, Pavia and Milano'.[31]

In the same spirit *The Mask* publishes Riccoboni's *Advice to Actors*, translated and introduced, with a biographical note, by 'Pierre Rames'. The article summarizes the main ideas in Riccoboni's essay:

> The author gives his advice in metrical form, using that same 'Terza Rima' as Dante used for the 'Divina Commedia', and dividing the aurgument into six cantos:
>
> • The need for the study of nature
> • Physical qualifications
> • Gesture
> • The trivial to be avoided
> • Facial expression
> • The voice
> • Silence[32]

Together with a bibliography of the work of Riccoboni[33] the article 'contains much which is well worth the serious consideration of the actor today'.

In general, when referring to the Commedia actor Craig has nothing less than words of praise. He goes to great lengths to find documentation to support his views; something not very typical of Craigian discourse.

The history of the Commedia is mainly the history of the lives of the great actors and their companies. Craig is very much aware of this fact and apart from presenting his readers with accounts of the famous Commedia companies (*I Gelosi, I Confidenti*) he also sketches out the lives and times of renowned Commedia actors, that helped shape the improvised theatre of the late sixteenth century.[34] What Craig does not seem to be interested in are the transformations the Commedia underwent as it was filtered through the various European stages, mainly the French. Craig's concerns are with the Italian life of the Commedia. The role of the Commedia as a chief influence on the European literary drama of the late-seventeenth and mid-eighteenth century is seen by Craig as yet another invasion of the sophisticated, written tradition upon the somehow raw, naive but, authentic oral tradition in the theatre. In a scheme that simplifies and polarizes an otherwise very complicated and

---

[31] Ibid., p. 133.

[32] Luigi Riccoboni, *Advice to Actors*, rpt. in *The Mask*, Vol. 3, 1911, p. 175.

[33] For bibliography on Luigi Riccoboni see note 9.

[34] See note 21.

interesting process of re-writing and appropriation, Craig speaks of Molière and Goldoni as 'intruders':

> We have not the same veneration for the great masters of the written drama that we ought to have, but we know too much about their methods of obtaining renown to be very enthusiastic about them. When the true theatre receives the acknowledgment due to it, when actors shall have come to their senses after learning that they have been bought by these same methods of the dramatic writers, when theatres shall be erected to harbour the true theatrical expression, then we shall not be unmindful of the value of these writers of drama have been to us; but till then we look upon them one and all as intruders, who have proved dangerous to the very life of the stage and who have brought it to the lowest level of dependence that independence dare ever sink to.[35]

Here Craig is not just mounting one of his general attacks against the playwrights' theatre but he is specifically talking about Molière and Goldoni. This sheds some light on the fact that he is not at all interested in any ramifications of the role of the actor apart from the model of the Commedia actor. For Craig, Molière and Goldoni are responsible for somehow depriving the actor of his/her creative powers. Goldoni and Molière are seen as betraying the Commedia tradition mainly by depriving their actors of masks, and, in doing so, starting the process of three-dimentionalising and psychologising them. Substituting the literary script for the mask is seen by Craig as possibly the greatest betrayal of all. He says that they 'have been bought by these same methods'. In re-writing Commedia characters, three-dimentionalising them and placing them in a more classical literary tradition, Molière and Goldoni are seen as distorting the true spirit of the Commedia; in the process the role of the actor, according to Craig, changes from artistic creator to mere interpreter.

In this context it is not surprising that the European transformations of the Commedia leave Craig totally indifferent. The one bright exception is *The Mask's* account of the great actor-mime Jean-Gaspard Debureau. Debureau's reshaping of Pierrot was the aspect of the Commedia that enraptured the Romantic imagination of the mid-nineteenth century. As Robert F. Storey writes:

> This actor has often and justly been acknowledged as the godparent of the multifarious, moonstruck Pierrots who gradually found their way into Romantic, and Symbolist literature; but Debureau's real role in the transmission of the type from the popular to the literary world – and

---

[35] *The Mask*, Vol. 5, 1910, p. 100.

17. 'The Commedia dell'Arte', Vol. 3, Nos. 10–12, p. 172b, 1911.

in its transformation from the naïf to neurasthenic pariah – has been only imperfectly understood, when it has been understood at all. To chart the development of Pierrot's character in the nineteenth century, we must, therefore, follow the career of this actor quite closely.[36]

Craig does not present his readers with such an account mainly because his project is of a very different nature. He is not interested in the literary and metaphorical dimension of the Commedia. His main goal is to chart a history of the Commedia as a *theatrical mode*, through the lives and times of Commedia actors. In the 1914 issue of *The Mask* he prints an abstract from the little known, to English readers, *Souvenirs des Funambules* by Jules Champfleury. This is translated and introduced by Dorothy Nevile Lees (as Pierre Rames). The article itself deals with the life of Debureau. For Craig the various transformations of the Commedia outside its Italian context remain interesting and useful as long as they are 'of the theatre', and Debureau is seen as such a pure child of the theatre. Quoting from Champfleury the aricle in *The Mask* ends with the epitaph:

> The costume of Pierrot was white.
> His shroud is white.
>
> Debureau passed his life on the boards.
> He rests peacefully between the boards.[37]

Nowhere else in *The Mask* or indeed in Craigian thought in general (apart from his homage to Irving, who he sees as more than an actor) is there so much space devoted to the actor. Incongruous as this may seem in view of Craig's theories of the *Ubermarionette* and the all-powerful director, the Commedia actor – masked, highly skilled and almost mechanized – is the one model of acting which he totally adheres to, studies meticulously and presents to his readers with an all consuming reverence.

The Commedia: Another Point of Conflict and Connection with Modernist Contemporaries/Another Model

Like most of Craig's schemes, his Commedia project remained an ideal. The Commedia masks were for him the perfect model of the actor of the past and the *Ubermarionette* the *ideal* actor of the future. The intervening

---

[36] Robert F. Storey, *Pierrot. A Critical History of a Mask*, (Princeton, 1978), p. 94. For Commedia influences on Romanticism and Symbolism see chapter entitled 'Romantic Adolescence', pp. 93–138.
[37] *The Mask*, Vol. 7, 1914, p. 74.

process that would have connected the two extremes of this spectrum was of no interest to him. The whole notion of 'process' as a creative act was foreign to Craig; in many ways it was too *modern*. Process implies reconstruction and appropriation, the application of a *technology* and finally *praxis*. As long as the Commedia mask and the *Ubermarionette* were fixed and polarized, the theoretical gap between the two could not have been bridged. No matter how studiously he studied the Commedia, it remained an *idealistic* abstraction; one that he could not apply to his own theories of acting. Lacking the *materialistic* notion of process, the lessons learnt from the Commedia theoretically could never have been put into practice. By the same token and almost by definition the *Ubermarionette* was *unrealizable*. What Craig's few designs of his *Ubermarionette* show is that it was really never meant to be realized; it was mainly an abstraction. Draped figures in stylized Romantic settings fixed in highly expressionist gestures are not what we would associate with a *Modernist* and anti-humanist marionette replacing the human form on the stage. His citing of Irving as the ultimate *Ubermarionette* only reinforces this view. Despite his careful and almost life-long study of the Commedia, Craig never made the leap necessary to render the Commedia dynamic and applicable to his own theories. As a method of training actors and channelling their creative activity on the stage, the Commedia could have taught the *Ubermarionette* a few lessons. The way the *Ubermarionette* was conceived though, as a closed and fixed system allowed little room for appropriation and adaptation.[38]

Meyerhold, in many ways Craig's Modernist contemporary, saw in the Commedia a system of training actors that he adapted to his own system of *biomechanics*. Rather than conceive of an abstract mechanized device he set out to *mechanize* the human body. The Commedia actor for Meyerhold was the perfect example of what he termed the *dialectic actor*; an actor who, while portraying, also enunciated the process of acting. This was later to be used effectively by Brecht, carrying it a step further with his alienation devices. Unlike Craig though, Meyerhold did not study the Commedia as comprehensively. For him it was a useful mode which he neatly adjusted to his own theoretical and practical needs. For Craig the Commedia was something which he loved, admired and researched. Having outgrown the Romantic and literary metaphors of the Commedia, popular in England at the turn of the century, but not quite *modern* enough to re-write it according to his own needs the Commedia acts as yet another example of the conflicts and tensions in Craigian thought. This is only obvious in *The Mask*, as it provides a platform for many of the problematic areas in Craig's work, which in his books seem neatly resolved.

---

[38] See chapter VII on puppets, where this is further developed.

18. Menu design by Albert Rothenstein for the Banquet given in honour of Gordon Craig in London, 16 July 1911. Vol. 4, No. 2, p. 81a, 1911.

Most of all the Commedia was *The Mask's* quintessentially *Italian experience*. Unlike his study of Oriental theatre which had to be filtered through reconstructions and re-readings of others, Craig was *there*, The Mask was *there*. This places the periodical in a unique position regarding the English and indeed the European stage of the period. The Commedia for Craig was something very concrete which he could research and register, and not something which was necessarily mythicized or exoticized. If anything, his account of the Commedia is an historical and scholarly one. This diminishing of the *otherness* of the Commedia may have limited its metaphorical quality which so entranced the decadent 1890s. At the same time, the lack of a *Modernist technology* that would see the Commedia as a theatrical convention/device constrained its metonymical potential, so well applied by Modernist stagecraft. What becomes very clear is that *The Mask* is free of *Commedia-ism*[39] in any form. Craig wears his most humble and respectful mask in his study of the Commedia; that of the eager and almost naive student who is bewildered with the discoveries he is making. He becomes very supportive of Italy and the Italian theatre against attitudes of the English press he considers patronising:

> To judge from some recent articles in *The Manchester Guardian* and *The Daily Telegraph* people do not seem to realize in England that Italy is not a Museum or a Theatre, and that its Cities however superb, have no wish to crumble just to oblige the tourists and the archaeologists.
>
> It is because we somehow believe Venezia to belong to us,... to be our *honeymoon spot*, our playground. And what are we? A nation of people more forward than any in praising speed, electricity, cinema, listening-in,...and we quickly produce a million pounds if promised a safe investment in something up-to-date and a curse to everyone. When Manchester can save one Theatre, and a grand old place like the Theatre Royal, it will be quite time enough for Manchester to lecture Venezia.[40]

If anything, the Commedia as part of Craig's Italian experience presented a safety-valve *against* the modern world and Modernism and not something which could actually help shape it. This is why historical documentation became vital. This was a case of the theatre of the past recreating the theatre of the future – the Modernist idea of the present destroying and reconstructing the past according to its own needs turned inside out. The Commedia, for Craig, was an example of the 'great

---

[39] Commedia-ism, like Orientalism, can be defined as that process of appropriation that relies on constant 'othering', rather than historical–political–geographical reality.
[40] *The Mask*, Vol. 11, 1925, p. 52.

19. Masked Actors from *Il Carnevale Italiano Mascherato*, Vol. 6, No. 2, p. 156b, 1913.

tradition of the past', which could rejuvenate the present. In Italy he could still find examples of the glorious tradition. In an article entitled 'The Theatres in Italy, Naples and Pompei', he writes:

> I was last night at Scarpetta's theatre; that *simpatico* theatre in Naples where all that is to be laughed at in and out of existence without a thought too much to oppress us. All the difference between this breed who give birth to laughter and the breed on the London stages whose cacklings even miscarry.
>
> Scarpetta exists and we know he is of flesh and blood. Shaw to me does not live, and is something other than flesh and blood. By the way, I ought to tell you who Scarpetta is. He is the author-actor of Naples... that is to say one of our few real dramatists. His Drama came into being by the grace of Improvisation, and as we know by now, this is the only way real drama can be born. All other dramas are made... patchworks,... not good woven stuffs.[41]

Despite his praise of this Neapolitan actor-author Craig does not really follow his example. (Stravinsky and Picasso, on the other hand used their visit to Scarpetta's theatre – at about the same time – as an influence on *Pulcinella* which they were creating for Diaghilev.) Borrowing the conventions of the Commedia could have loosened much of the tension in his own work and opened new roads for him. Ideas such as the total lack of text and author that he advocates are never realized and remain problematic. In a true Modernist tradition the relationship of text and performance is problematised but, never resolved. The Commedia scenario shaped by improvisation could have provided Craig with a scheme, which did not require a playwright as such but, relied on the power of the director to reconstruct and interpret it.

The Commedia as a language of performance remains almost useless for Craig. Meta-theatrically, it presents yet another lost chance. Had he appropriated Commedia conventions in acting and staging, his *Ubermarionette* may just have been realized. The Commedia is part of the 'glorious' tradition of the theatre of the past. The basic difference, though, compared with the way Craig approaches other such total theatres, is that his stance is not floating in a cloud of nostalgia and awe. Regarding the Commedia dell'Arte Craig is a scholar. With the precision of a historian he maps a history of the Italian theatre of the sixteenth and seventeenth centuries.

Although the Commedia offered Craig very little in terms of the scenic stage, it definitely offered him a language for that other main stage he was working on: *The Mask*. If *The Mask* is to be seen as a

---

[41] *The Mask*, Vol. 6, 1914, p. 357.

G.ᵐ Mitelli .F.

COMICO	MORTE
Io uò uendendo altrui frottole, e fole Pur non contratto mai senza bolletta; E per più far la mercantia perfetta, Accresco il capital di capriole.	Dal Tarlo mio tù per sottrarti, i salì Inuan di tua comedia usi, ò faceto, E salti inuan, ch'io farti far decreto Nella Tragedia mia salti Mortali.

20. 'Arlecchino' by G. M. Mitelli (1634–1718), Vol. 9, No. 1, p. 1a, 1923.

performance, then it has to be one without an author. Craig would have never approved of his one permanent stage being inhabited by a playwright. As a paradigm for writing a periodical/performance the Commedia helps Craig dispense with his author status. With the use of masks/pseudonyms he manages to make himself invisible as the playwright of this performance. At the same time the ideology of the Commedia with its playfulness and scorn of notions of authenticity and authority is something Craig includes in his rhetoric. Even though his readers are very much aware of who is hiding behind the masks, he nevertheless continues to keep up the act for the 20 years of the periodical's publication.[42] Just like the Commedia actor who portrays a character and at the same time takes particular delight in exposing the process of deception to the audience, Craig shamelessly continues to 'pretend', to hide behind his numerous masks. Indeed, possibly more than any other aspect of the Commedia, it is the masks that interest him.[43] There Craig not only finds a metaphor for the staging of *The Mask* but, a paradigm which manages to three-dimensionalized the pages of his journal and almost literally transform it into a stage.

---

[42] The following quotation from *The Marionette* acts as a perfect example of the transparency of Craig's disguise:

And if I may express a second wish, it is that you do not start your letter with 'Dear Horace... I know you are Gordon Craig in another mask ... and so I will begin by saying 'Look here, Craig, my first quarrel is with you... why the deuce, etc. etc.' Don't, I beg, begin in that gracious tone. For even if I am not Gordon Craig, I have been working a good deal longer at this craft than you, and to be a whipper-snapper (if only on manner) does not become you any the better just because you hail from America. *The Marionette*, Vol. 1, (Florence, 1918).

[43] Craig's extensive study of Commedia masks, *The Characters of the Commedia dell'Arte* appears in *The Mask*, Vol. 4 (Florence, 1912), p. 199–201. This study is cited in Laura Falavolti, *Commedie dei Comici dell'Arte* (Torino, 1982), and in Giacomo Oreglia *The Commedia dell'Arte* (London, 1968). In general, studies on the Commedia dell'Arte published since the publication of *The Mask* mainly refer to this article and not to the rest of the Commedia material in *The Mask*.

6

'GENTLEMEN, THE MARIONETTE'

If *The Mask* borrows its narrative strategies from Commedia-like notions of presentation and theatricality, in a scheme that creates a stage-like quality throughout its pages, then those pages are inhabited by equally theatrical and elusive 'characters': puppets. *The Mask* is literally peopled by puppets in all forms and from all possible backgrounds. Javanese and middle-eastern shadow puppets, Burattini, Bunraku, Punch and Judy and fully-mechanised marionettes all feature. Their presentation is at the same time historical – which, like the studies in the Commedia dell'Arte, is a case of scholarly pioneering – and aesthetic. Puppets appear both as part of a glorious theatrical tradition and as a proposal for the theatre of the future. Like most Craigian obsessions, puppetry is presented in extremis. The puppet is not only seen as the perfect substitute for the living form on stage, contributing to a theory of acting, but it is presented as the ultimate art form itself. If theatre was to be the total art form, then the puppet would represent the total and absolute artifice. Indeed in the meta-theatrical drama which is being enacted throughout the pages of *The Mask* the puppet definitely surfaces as the visible *protagonist*. (Craig himself, of course, is the invisible *Überprotagonist*). To the idealized Romantic legacy on puppets that Craig inherits from Kleist, Maeterlinck and Oscar Wilde, he adds his very meticulous and pragmatic study conducted through *The Mask*. From using puppets as a metaphor of the artifice he shifts to presenting very detailed accounts of their origins and history. Like most of the projects undertaken by Craig a process of Romantic 'othering' is constantly undermined by an equally strong process of Modernist 'demythicizing'.

The study of puppets in *The Mask*, like that of the Commedia dell'Arte, is the most systematic and comprehensive to appear in any magazine of the period. It is present and consistent throughout all its issues and indeed surpasses most of the scholarship of the period on the subject in English. Craig, together with a team of academics and zealots, in general sets out to furnish both a history and a eulogy of puppets. The work of Walter Pater and Arthur Symons provides the aesthetic setting for the presentation of academic studies by Italian scholars like Ferrigni, Carlo Gozzi, Cesare Levi and Dorothy Nevile Lees.

In general the presentation of puppets in *The Mask*, both as theatrical mode and as historical fact, can fall under three main categories, through works that are presented in its pages; these works, in many ways, determine Craig's understanding of puppetry. The historical aspect is focused in a series of articles entitled 'History of Puppets', which ran through Volumes 3 to 9. These were by P. Ferrigni who, following Craig's example, writes under a pseudonym: Yorick. In addition Craig himself writes historical articles. As for the aspect of theatrical theory, this appears mainly through Craig's own formulations on the nature and the role of puppets. His essay on 'The Actor and the *Ubermarionette*' presents his testimony on the modern and modernist use of puppets for the stage and is re-echoed in all his writings on puppets. However, there is an essay which helped shape Craig's and which sheds light on his Romantic roots, an essay which Craig published in translation. This is Kleist's 'On the Marionette Theatre', which in German (*Uber Das Marionettentheater*) even has audible pre-echoes of Craig's *Ubermarionette*. It places Craig's essay in a historical context and helps explain much of the contradiction embedded in Craig's formulations of the *Ubermarionette*.

Kleist's work is printed in a special magazine-interlude which was published in 1918–19 – *The Marionette*, though Craig was probably aware of Kleist's thesis on marionettes as early as 1908, when he formulated his own ideas on acting in his *Ubermarionette* essay. 1918–19 was a hard time for *The Mask*. The Arena Goldoni was requisitioned by the Italian government, and the address for both journals was reduced to a post-box in Florence. Yet Craig took the chance to issue a periodical wholly devoted to puppets. The tone is much lighter than *The Mask*: the editor appears as one Tom Fool! The publication itself validates the hypothesis of this book with regard to its big sister by announcing itself as a magazine/performance: phrases like 'the curtain rises' or 'the curtain falls' appear between articles and issues. *The Marionette* presents itself as a Commedia-type interlude of lazzi between the more serious 'acts' of *The Mask*. It is a temporary carnival mask for *The Mask*. Or perhaps a more appropriate metaphor would envisage *The Marionette* as the puppet and *The Mask* as the puppet-master in a play that deals with the history and significance of marionettes.

The turn of the century had enjoyed a celebration of the role of puppets in the theatre. In the aestheticist context this contributed to the overall *man or marionette* debate that was to be one of the main concerns of later Modernist stagecraft. Although the final articulation of the argument is a Modernist one, the role of the human actor is problematised from Romanticism onwards. The marionette is viewed as the perfect artifice, the perfect expression of the almighty *aesthetic will*. Arthur Symons, Walter Pater and Oscar Wilde all write on the role of the marionette and are frequently quoted on the subject in *The Mask*. And a passage from the letters of Joseph Conrad

21. Javanese marionette from the collection of the Gordon Craig studio, Vol. 6, No. 4, p. 284b, 1914.

(see chapter V, note 10)[1] also quoted in *The Mask* (1928), shows that one did not have to be a person of the theatre to share the interest and the fascination of the period with the puppet. There, Conrad analyses main faults of the human actor – he or she is mortal and hence not very good material for art. It is life itself that is seen as poor and vulgar. In a scheme that substitutes aesthetic life for real/historical existence, there can be no space for the human form. Conrad's references to murder and suicide are not entirely inappropriate as he, together with many of his contemporaries, is (however whimsically and paradoxically) propagating the total banishment of actors from the stage. (It is interesting that in the process he should involve the *Ubermensch* to describe the puppet. The *Uberpuppet* cannot be far away).

The high priest of aestheticism, Walter Pater, quoted frequently in *The Mask*, also expresses one of the main theoretical issues in this actor–puppet conflict. In an essay entitled 'Another Estimate of the Actor's Character', he touches upon a point to be further elaborated by Craig; namely the ancient criticism of actors as being somehow corrupted through the process of mimesis itself. This argument is at least as old as Plato: the acting process is seen as something that can ultimately corrupt the human actor. Consequently, in his corrupted, degenerate form the human actor can no longer act as the proper medium of art. Walter Pater is quoted in Volume 3 of *The Mask*:

> The stage in these volumes presents itself indeed not merely as a mirror of life, but as an illustration of the utmost intensity of life, in the fortunes and characters of the players. Ups and downs, generosity, dark fates, the most delicate goodness, have nowhere been more prominent than in the private existence of those devoted to the public mimicry of men and women. Contact with the stage, almost throughout its history presents itself as a kind of touchstone, to bring out the *bizzarrerie*, the theatrical tricks and contrasts of the actual world.[2]

The main Platonic[3] idea inherent in this concept is that mimicry is potentially dangerous and consequently not a task to be undertaken by

---

[1] Quoted in *The Mask*, Vol. 14 (Florence, 1928), p. 76. From a letter Joseph Conrad sent to R. B. Cunnunghame Graham, 6th December, 1897, in Jean Aubry, *Joseph Conrad: Life and Letters*, p. 213.

[2] Walter Pater, 'Another Estimate of the Actor's Character', in *The Mask*, Vol. 3, Nos. 10–12 (Florence, 1911), p. 174.

[3] For Plato's attack on mimesis see his dialogue *Ion* where the process of enacting by imitation is seen as potentially corrupting for both the actor or the rhapsode and his audience. See D. A. Russell and M. Winterbottom (eds), *Classical Literary Criticism, Ion,* (Oxford, 1972), pp. 1–13. In the *Repubulic* he further elaborates, he writes that the imitative artist 'rouses and feeds this part of the mind [the non-rational] and by strengthening it destroys the rational part'. See *Classical Literary Criticism, Republic,* p. 47. Plato scornfully calls actors and rhapodes 'interpreters of interpreters', *Ion,* p. 6. Aristole's famous notion of *catharisis* is a reaction to Plato, proposing theatre as the ultimate therapeutic rather corrupting art.

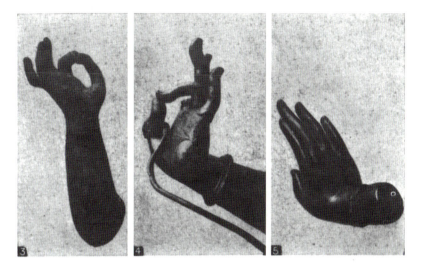

Argument or Discussion   " Do not fear ! "

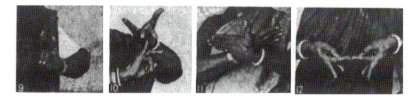

Hands of a Dancing girl

THE MASK.
January 1914.

9. A Deer.
10. Krishna's ra'sing Mount Govardhan.
11. Vishnu's Garuda.
12. A Bed.

22. "Four positions of the hands photographed from a bayadère of Tangore", Vol. 6, No. 3, p. 272b, 1914.

humans. Craig develops this view further in his essay on the *Uber-marionette*. Generally, though, the notion that the human actor is deficient, corrupted, egotistical and simply not good enough material for art is the spring-board for much Craigian theorizing about acting. It sheds light on his idealistic–Romantic roots and separates him from other modernist theorists on the subject. In negating the human actor and complimenting him with the puppet, Craig is by no means introducing a new idea; instead he is borrowing from the spirit of the 1890s. In 1892 in an article in the *Daily Telegraph* Oscar Wilde expresses his views on the matter:

> There are many advantages in puppets. They never argue. They have no crude views about art. They have no private lives. We are never bothered by accounts of their virtues, or bored by recitals of their vices; and when they are out of an engagement they never do good in public or save people from drowning; nor do they speak more than is set down for them. They recognise the presiding intellect of the dramatist, and have never been known to ask for their parts to be written up. They are admirably docile, and have no personalities at all.[4]

If we substitute Wilde's 'intellect of the dramatist' with 'genius of the artist of the theatre', all of the above could have been written by Craig himself. Further on in his letter Wilde describes a performance he saw in Paris which exclusively used puppets. The theatre was the Petit Theatre des Marionettes run by Maurice Bouchor at the Galerie Vivienne from 1889 to 1894.

> I saw lately, in Paris, a performance by certain puppets of Shakespeare's *Tempest*, in M. Maurice Bouchor's translation. Miranda was the image of Miranda, because an artist had so fashioned her; and Ariel was true Ariel, because so had she been made. Their gestures were quite sufficient, and the words that seemed to come from their lips were spoken by poets who had beautiful voices. It was a delightful performance, and I remember it still with delight, though Miranda took no notice of the flowers I sent her after the curtain fell.[5]

The English intelligenstia at the turn of the century was fascinated with the possibility of a wholly puppet theatre. European puppet theatres were highly praised and attendance was considered compulsory if one were present in a city with such a theatre. Puppet theatres in Europe

---

[4] Rubert Hart-Davis (ed), *The Letters of Oscar Wilde* (London, 1962), p. 311, from a letter to the editor of *The Daily Telegraph*, 19 February, 1892.
[5] Ibid., *The Letters of Oscar Wilde*.

acquired an almost cult status. In a passage from his *Apology for Puppets*, which appears in *The Mask* in 1912, Arthur Symons writes:

> After seeing a ballet, a farce, and the fragment of an opera performed by the marionettes at the Costanzi Theatre in Rome I am inclined to ask myself why we require the intervention of any less perfect medium between the meaning of a piece, as the author conceived it, and that other meaning which it derives from our reception of it.[6]

In the same issue of *The Mask* Anatole France, another keen apologist for puppets, and one also quoted in *The Marionette*, writes of his visits to the Petit Theatre des Marionettes:

> In the meantime I have twice seen the marionettes of the rue Vivienne and have taken great pleasure in them. I am infinitely pleased for them to replace the living actors... A truly artistic idea, a graceful and noble thought, ought to enter more easily into the head of a marionette than into the brain of a fashionable actress.[7]

In propagating the substitution of the living actor by the marionette *The Mask* is not alone. However, it shifts the whole *man or marionette* debate into a more Modernist context. Craig seems fully aware of the historical framework of this debate as he introduces Volume 5 of *The Mask*, wholly devoted to the marionette, under the banner of 'Gentlemen, the Marionette':

> This number of *The Mask*, being dedicated principally to the Marionette, we have asked Mr. Gordon Craig, who has studied him so closely and knows him so well, to act as Master of Ceremonies and make the Introduction; and so together with Mr. Anatole France, 'Yorick', Mr. Arthur Symons and others of those who believe in 'the majesty of marionettes', make better known to many who have long been estranged from them these wonderful little beings which, with centuries of life behind them and centuries before, have 'in them something of the divine' and 'live with the life of the immortal gods'.[8]

---

[6] *Arthur Symons, 'Apology for Puppets', The Mask*, Vol. 5, No. 2 (Florence, 1912), p. 103. Arthur Symons, a regular contributor to *The Mask*, especially with material relating to marionettes, also appears in Vol. 4, p. 188, 1912 with the article 'Pantomime and the Poetic Drama', taken from his *Studies in Seven Arts*. In Vol. 3, p. 173, 1911 *The Mask* reprints an essay entitled 'On Actors and Actresses', from a translation of Count Gozzi's memoirs by Arthur Symons.

[7] Anatole France, 'The Marionettes of M. Signoret', *The Mask*, Vol. 5, No. 2 (Florence, 1912), pp. 98–103.

[8] EGC, *The Mask*, Vol. 5, No. 2 (Florence, 1912), p. 1. In the same issue Craig announces the founding of the 'Society of the Marionette', 'We intend to form a Society of the Marionette. Mr. Gordon Craig has consented to act as president of the Society', p. 144.

23. Indian stencil figure, Vol. 1, No. 2, p. 114a, 1913.

In this context Craig's essay on the *Ubermarionette* does not seen so extreme or new. It already had not only continental, but native precedents. Like most of these, the *Ubermarionette* never really left the stage of rhetoric. The fact that Craig practically avoided experimenting with his own ideas, and simply reiterated them over and over again, could be due to the particular background they sprang from; one that ultimately saw the marionette as a metaphor of the perfect artifice. However, the impact that this essay had on the whole man-marionette debate in Modernist theatre practice is crucial. What is important to establish here is that *The Mask*, because of its on-going nature, provides insight into much of Craigian contradiction concerning marionettes. His other works present us with, more or less, the finished product with little or no reference to its historical framework. In this way *The Mask*, despite its layers and layers of masking and disguising, proves more revealing and explanatory than Craig's other works.

While *The Mask* presents its readers with a theoretical context for understanding Craigian ideas on marionettes and their use, at the same time it publishes much material on the history of puppets. Most of this is new for the English speaking public, and again Craig shows quite a surprising spirit of cooperation and understanding in allowing *The Mask* to present and promote studies of other scholars in the field. The most comprehensive study is a series of articles entitled 'History of Puppets',[9] written by one Yorick. Following the overall presentative strategy of *The Mask*, its author, P. C. Ferrigni, appears under a pseudonym. The articles are taken from his work *La Storia dei Burattini* and are published in its first and only English translation, especially for *The Mask*. Ferrigni's work is largely based on *Histoire des marionettes en Europe* (1852)[10] by Charles Magnin, with much additional information on Italian puppets. He deals with puppetry of the East, of ancient Greece and Rome, and of the Commedia dell'Arte. The study of puppets as presented by Yorick fits in quite neatly with Craig's perception of puppets and their role. Yorick's history is concerned with puppetry, not only as a particular theatrical mode, but also as a general statement on art and life itself. His introduction to the article 'Ancient Puppets in the Temple' reads:

> We will therefore content ourselves with a simple excursion into the
> field of venerable antiquity; with the swiftest of journeys through the

---

[9] P. C. Ferrigni (Yorick), 'History of Puppets', *The Mask*, Vol. 5, p. 95, p. 111, p. 248, p. 303; Vol. 6, p. 129, p. 297; Vol. 7, p. 17, p. 26, p. 116; Vol. 9, p. 301.

[10] P. C. Ferrigni (Yorick), *La Storia dei Burattini* (Florence, 1902), based on Magnin, *Histoire des marionettes en Europe* (Paris, 1852). Charles Magnin (1793–1862), french historian, drama critic and also critic author of *Les origines du theatre en Europe* (Paris, 1838), translated into French the plays of Saxon nun Hrostwitha (c. 930–1000) some of which were performed at M. Signoret's 'Petit Theatre' and seen by Anatole France, see note no. 7.

stately temples once inhabited by the gods who have departed from them; with a hurried excursion through the sacred woods, where the initiated by the mysteries of the old religions, now passed out of fashion, celebrated the mysterious rites, and the solemn feasts and the sacrifices and the processions and the pomps,... at times obscene as at others awful, but always poetic,... of the pagan liturgy.[11]

Ferrigni is probably referring to the mysteries at Eleusis of ancient Greece, where marionettes called *neurospasta* were said to take part in the rituals. The general atmosphere of the passage is one of awe and wonder. Throughout his studies puppetry is almost always connected with the divine and the mysterious. For Yorick, as for Craig in many respects, puppets represented the lost thread that would re-connect theatre with its past religious and ritualistic roots. This turning of the stage into a temple belongs to the trend set by Nietzsche's *The Birth of Tragedy*. The marionette as that representative of the holy theatres of the past; one that could possibly help revive the theatre of the present.

Craig's interest, however, is not limited to a Romantic fascination. He filters this with practical and historical knowledge. He sets up a collection of puppets at the Arena Goldoni, one of the most impressive of the period, and begins to experiment in matters of construction, manipulation and overall performance practice. *The Mask* is full of designs and instructions on how to construct and use puppets. He writes in Volume 6:

> The two figures represented in the accompanying illustrations are taken from the collection of Javanese Marionettes in the Gordon Craig School at Florence, some of which have been lately exhibited at Zurich. Some account of these wonderful shadow figures known as 'Wayang' figures and of the great Javanese drama in which they play their part will appear in a future number of *The Mask* but meantime we give you the accompanying notes on the construction of the figures...[12]

Indeed Craig presents his readers with a history of the Wayang shadow theatre mainly in the pages of his other publication *The Marionette*.[13] Out of the whole puppet/marionette family, the Javanese shadow puppets in

---

[11] P. C. Ferrigni (Yorick), 'Ancient Puppets in the Temple', *The Mask*, Vol. 5, No. 2 (Florence, 1912), pp. 112–114.

[12] EGC, *The Mask*. Vol. 6, No. 4 (Florence, 1914), pp. 283–5.

[13] This history he probably got from the 'Dutch couple' who helped with *The Mask* and were researching Javanese Shadow Theatre at the time. We do not have more information about them. They are mentioned in Edward Craig, *Gordon Craig* and in Lorelei Guidry *Index and Introduction to The Mask*, p. 9. The history of the Wayang puppet theatre appears in *The Marionette* (Florence, 1918).

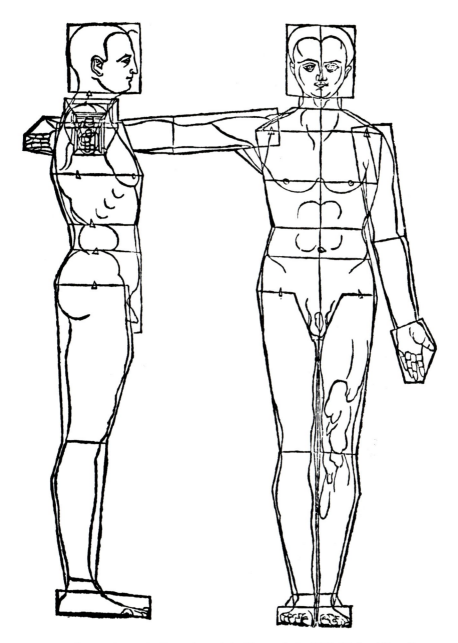

24. From *The Treatise on the Proportions of the Human Body* (1500–23) by Albert Durer. Vol. 6, No. 1, p. 72b, 1913.

25. A Venetian marionette, Vol. 6, No. 1, p. 1a, 1913.

general are Craig's 'pets'. He studies them extensively, collects them and even derives his main pseudonym from their cast. Semar, the guise of the editor of *The Mask*, is a character from the Wayang shadow drama. Nowhere in *The Mask* or *The Marionette* does he actually reveal this, as most of his studies avoid listing or naming the characters of this shadow theatre.[14]

Craig's collection and study did not limit itself to Wayang puppets. He gathered every sort of puppet he could discover. Japanese Bunraku puppets were amongst his favourites and, with Orientalist undertones, he presents notes on them in *The Mask*. The designs he publishes in 1914 are tracings sent to him by one Mr. Porter Garnett. He explains his reasons for studying these:

> I still feel this. My judgement has had time to ripen, and if not convinced of the immediate advent of a world of super-marionettes to rescue a special branch of the art of acting from decay, I am persuaded that the marionette is the basis for a revival of that particular branch... But by studying the nature of this creation of artists (and marionettes have been made by artists of all nations since the earliest recorded times), by careful and serious and protracted study of the Idea in the Idol, in the Puppet, in the Doll, in Images of all kinds, we shall widen and not narrow our vision.[15]

Here Craig exposes his attitude towards the study of puppets and provides some insight into the problems that his specific stance created for him and his *Ubermarionette*. In approaching the great puppet theatres of the past he is chiefly concerned in what he calls the 'Idea in the Idol'. The general ideological/religious background to puppets was mainly

---

[14] Craig's collection forms part of the greater one at the Kunstgewerbemuseum at Zurich. It has proved vital for the work of other scholars and theatre practitioners working with puppets. Lotte Reiniger, for example, refers to it and uses it to illustrate her book *Shadow Theatres and Shadow Films* (London, 1970). Madame Reiniger, almost a contemporary of Craig's, was one of the main advocates of shadow puppets in Europe. She went on with her husband Carl Koch to experiment with the application of shadow puppet techniques to the then newly formed art of the cinema.

[15] EGC, *The Mask*, Vol. 7, No. 2 (Florence, 1914), pp. 104–7. Craig adds a note to this article where he warns his contemporaries that, although he is willing to share his knowledge of puppets, he will not accept mimicry and 'theft':

Experts Browne, Smythe and de Jones, who are bad at finding out anything but what Appia, Bakst, Fortuny, Brazicolli or I have discovered, will not be in the game or share any of the fun (except by stealth) because they have not observed the 'rules' of the game.

I have to mention this, for it is these experts who so often write to the press or chatter at tea-tables in a wrythe or fury, that we are forgetting them, are not acknowledging that their art of theft is the art of creation, and are therefore setting it down as valueless to the theatre. p. 106.

what he wanted to restore in the theatre. The puppet was to be the agent of this project. Through it he could communicate with the great artists of the past. Therefore, Craig was more interested in the puppet as an *idea* rather than as an agent of a specific technique in theatre practice. Although he systematically studied puppet construction and manipulation, any application of puppetry and its methods to acting or even to his own *Ubermarionette* aroused in him that dreaded fear of imitation. He concludes in the same article:

> Neither will it do to copy the Japanese and put on it a European or Russian costume. That short cut can be left to Messrs Browne, Smythe and de Jones. They *will* take it, rest assured. Impotence detests creation for obvious reasons.[16]

Craig's obsession with originality and his loathing of copying did not allow space for notions of borrowing, influence, reference, appropriation and in general intertextuality.[17] This fear did not allow him to take advantage of the wealth of material he had at his disposal. Unlike most of his contemporaries, and especially the Russians, he could only see a 'force', an ideological framework, in the tradition of puppets and not necessarily a methodological one.

Despite its limited application Craig's historical account of puppets continued to fill the pages of *The Mask*. Another related mission the periodical undertook was to re-establish the reputation of the Toy Theatres (or 'Juvenile Drama' as it was known). *The Mask* contributed to the rediscovery of this aspect of popular culture. For Craig the Toy Theatres were one expression of the English stage that he could accept. It was part of the privileged and almost mystically endowed oral tradition: it relied on the puppet-master and not the playwright, and it used puppets as its protagonists. More part of a popular tradition than the established, institutionalised theatre, it remained non-threatening for Craig. He could, therefore, patronize it, displaying it as yet another model for the ideal theatre. He writes in *The Mask*:

> In England we possess the best Toy Theatre and the worst of grown-up Theatres. We consider that Pollock's Theatre is the best Toy Theatre in the world, and that Beerbohm Tree's Theatre is the worst grown-up Theatre in the world.[18]

---

[16] Ibid., p. 107.
[17] Here the term is used as it is defined by Mikhail Bakhtin and Julia Kristeva. Intertextuality places a work in history, in relation to its medium and understands its very existence as forming and formed by that relationship.
[18] EGC, *The Mask*, Vol. 5, No. 1 (Florence, 1912–13), p. 1.

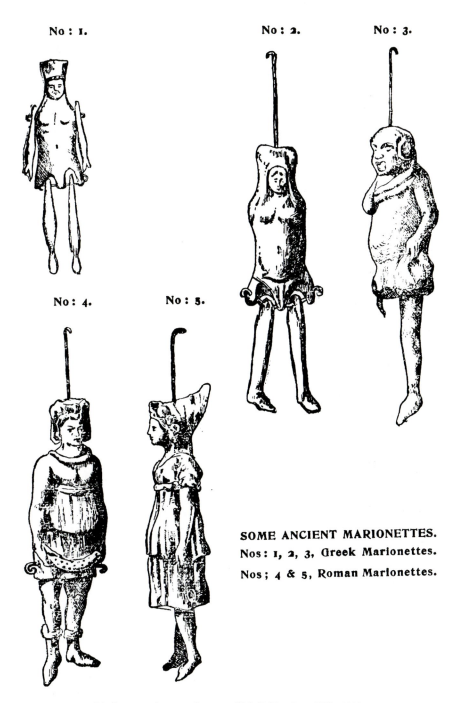

No : 1.

No : 2.

No : 3.

No : 4.

No : 5.

SOME ANCIENT MARIONETTES.
Nos : 1, 2, 3, Greek Marionettes.
Nos ; 4 & 5, Roman Marionettes.

26. Some ancient marionettes, Vol. 5, No. 4, p. 302b, 1913.

Pollock's theatre was and probably still is synonymous with Toy Theatres.[19] Founded by Benjamin Pollock (1856–1937), it dealt mainly with publishing sheets of characters for the miniature stages. Apart from the 'penny plain, twopence coloured'[20] sheets it also manufactured and sold new stages and plays, puppets, toys and much seasonal material for Christmas and Easter. Clearly this was not going to be the school of drama that would change the course of the European stage. Still, Craig exhibited that Modernist tendency of heralding the oral and the popular as the last remaining traces of real theatrical art, the last bastions against what was considered academic, over-refined and Establishment theatrical practice.

Another Toy Theatre boosted by Craig was that of Jack B. Yeats – W. B.'s painter brother – who even wrote an article for *The Mask* explaining how he produced his plays for the miniature stage. Of Jack B. Yeats Craig writes:

> His toy theatre is the most natural Europe possesses. His Dramas are filled with all the winds of heaven. They are short,...yet no one who reads them, but feels they are as long as life. *The Scourge of the Gulph* is without exception quite the first drama of the century. You may think, Reader, that I exaggerate, that I am carried away by these pirates,...or that I am mad.[21]

Using a common Craigian technique of disarming his audience by anticipating its response, Craig manages to shroud an otherwise outrageous claim. It is not Ibsen, Chekhov or Strindberg who herald the new writing in drama but, this puppeteer of the miniature stage. The model

---

[19] The Toy Theatre, founded by Benjamin Pollock (1856–1937), was located in Hoxton Street, London. After being damaged by air-raids during WWII, it continued for a time run by Pollock's daughters (until 1944) when it was taken over by a company of Toy Theatre enthusiasts and re-opened in John Adam Street, Adelphi. In the late sixties it had premises at 44 Monmouth Street, where Pollock's Toy Museum was established as well, with a permanent exhibition of miniature stages and original sheets by West, Green, Redington, and an interesting collection of toys, games, dolls, dolls'-houses, gollywog book, magic lanters and coloured slides, and 3-D peepshows.

[20] *The Mask* also quotes from Robert Louis Stevenson on Toy Theatres. In an article entitled 'Robert Louis Stevenson and the Drama of Skelt', which includes information taken from his *Memoirs and Politics*, Dorothy Nevile Lees presents Stevenson's views on Toy Theatres. The article in Vol. 5, No. 1 (Florence, 1912), pp. 72–76, concludes:

There, in the Hoxton shop you may still buy them; there if you go pence in hand, you may yet purchase your entry into a world, Plain or Coloured according to your capacity to pay, but in any case flooded through with the Gold sunlight of romance; a little gay world into which no realism can enter, no actor's personality protrude, since the ghost of Skelt, that 'stagey and piratic' figure, stands like an angel with a flaming sword at the entrance to that cardboard Eden where the poplar, palm and potato tree flourish and the all-pervasive hollyhock runs wild.

[21] EGC, *The Mask*, Vol. 5, No. 1 (Florence, 1912), p. 44.

27. Designs from *The Blue Jackets*, Vol. 5, No. 1, p. 1a, 1912.

of the puppet-master/playwright is one that can easily be accommodated within Craig's scheme for the 'Theatre of the Future'. A few pages further in the same issue, again referring to Pollock's shop, he calls it 'the best theatre in London'. This particular article was signed by one Edward Edwardovitch, Craig's Moscow pseudonym, who was corresponding as a foreigner from London.[22] *The Blue Jacket* is published in the pages that follow from Mr. Pollock's collection plus a comprehensive list of his plays.[23] To complete the picture the Book Review section of that issue praises the recently published *Jack B. Yeats: His Pictorial Dramatic Art* by Ernest Marriott.

In the art of Clunn Lewis, an Irish puppeteer who toured mainly in Kent and Sussex and was contemporary with Craig, he found another

---

[22] Edward Edwardovitch was to be the main exposer of the Craig-Stanislavsky working relationship on the Moscow production of Hamlet.

[23] This list in *The Mask*, Vol. 5, No. 1 (Florence, 1912), p. 57, reads:

	Plain		Coloured	
	s	d	s	d
Aladdin or The Wonderful Lamp	1	3	2	4
Blue Jackets	0	6	0	10
Brigand	0	10	1	6
Charles the Second	0	6	0	10
Children in the Wood	0	10	1	6
Cinderella	0	11	1	8
Corsican Brothers	0	8	1	2
Don Quixote	0	8	1	2
Daughter of the Regiment	0	5	0	8
Douglas	0	7	1	0
Forty Thieves	1	6	2	10
King Henry	0	7	1	0
Lord Darnley	0	9	1	4
Lord Mayor's Fool	0	6	1	10
Mistletoe Bough	0	9	1	4
Miller and his Men	1	0	1	10
Oliver Twist	1	1	2	0
Paul Clifford	1	1	2	0
Silver Palace	0	8	1	2
Timour the Tarter	0	11	1	8
Waterman	0	5	0	8
Woodman's Hut	0	10	1	6
Blind Boy	0	10	1	6
Maid and the Magpie	0	8	1	2

PANTOMIMES

	Plain		Coloured	
Baron Munchausen	1	4	2	6
Jack the Giant Killer	1	4	2	6
Whittington and his Cat	1	4	2	6
Sleeping Beauty	1	3	2	4

These prices are with Book of Words, Scenes, Figures and Directions Complete.

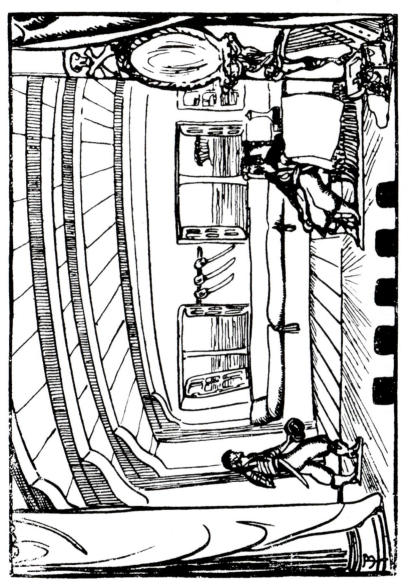

28. A Scene for *The Scourge of the Gulph* by Jack B. Yeats, Vol. 5, Nos. 7–9, p. 46b, 1911.

representative of a dying tradition. Under the name John Bull, Craig writes:

> Mr. Clunn Lewis is the remaining link in England with Bartholomew Fair, and he now wanders through England, supported at times by the church and at times by the public... Here is the case of a man who has been giving performances for the last fifty years whenever he can find an audience of forty to sixty, and yet the English public do not support him.[24]

This statement is only partly true: Lewis was supported by quite a few eminent figures of the time, among them G. B. Shaw and Chesterton.[25] A production by Clunn Lewis is recorded in a later issue of *The Mask*. This took place at the 'Children's Welfare Exhibition' in 1912. The performances themselves were said to have attracted an audience of 2,500. 'Many of these evinced the keenest interest in the marionettes and Mr. Lewis's much-travelled puppets received an applause which might easily have turned the heads of any actors less severe.'[26] Craig does not miss the chance to express another attraction of the Lewis theatre. Not only is it in keeping with the finest of English popular traditions but, it also provides an object lesson for the contemporary actor.

Recording contemporary English puppet performances is a project keenly undertaken by *The Mask* and elaborated by *The Marionette*, as we shall later see. Ernest Marriott, the author of *Jack B. Yeats: His Pictorial Dramatic Art*, comments on a production at Liverpool organised by the Sandon Studios Club. Marriott writes:

> From the point of view of *The Mask*, perhaps the happiest sign of the Club's activities was the puppet-play organised and carried out by certain of its members, for it wrought exceedingly well when it endeavoured to establish a dwelling place in the cold north for the Marionette, who was born in the East so many centuries ago.[27]

In the same 1912 issue *The Mask* presents its readers with a history of yet another pioneer in the long life of this Toy stage. William George Webb, born in Surrey in 1819, appears in an article by H. E. Francis Eagle as 'the only member of the trade who combined these capacities, as artist-etcher, printer and publisher of his own Theatrical Portraits and

---

[24] EGC, *The Mask*, Vol. 5, No. 3 (Florence, 1912), pp. 220–22.
[25] Clunn Lewis and his work appear in George Speaight, *The History of the English Puppet Theatre* (London, 1955). Chesterton quoted from 'In Praise of Puppets' from an unidentified magazine in *The World's Fair*, August 31, 1940.
[26] *The Mask*, in 'Foreign Notes', Vol. 5, No. 3 (Florence, 1912), p. 381.
[27] Ibid., pp. 234–6, p. 234.

characters and scenes for the Miniature plays'.[28] This article is followed by a list of the plays published by Webb.

Craig's fascination with the Toy Theatre obviously stems from his vision of it as the perfect model of an institution that can accommodate his directorial extremism. At the same time, forming part of an oral tradition makes it less theoretically suspect. It is neat, clear, even though slightly naive. This touches upon one of Craig's other keen interests, namely designing toys for children. His *Book of Penny Toys* is a fine example of Arts and Crafts aesthetic in the design and production of toys. Indeed his whole interest in Toy Theatres has Arts and Crafts undertones: these theatres were also fine realizations of Arts and Crafts principles. They were run by single individuals who designed, produced and performed every aspect of a performance single-handed. Simultaneously they appeared to have an organic and healthy relationship with tradition, which was also a vital concern of the movement. Craig's book on toys was published in 1899, and a few months later he was to publish the magazine that acted as a dress rehearsal for *The Mask*. This was *The Page*, published in the finest of Arts and Crafts traditions.[29]

---

[28] Ibid., p. 347.

[29] *The Page* (London, 1899), was in the finest of Arts and Crafts traditions. Its contents reveal its particular background:

'*The Page* is a publication in which one finds original Poems, Music, Prose, Woodcuts, Posters, Portraits, Bookplates, and other curious things.'

The table of contents for the Xmas edition of 1900 reads as follows:

January	EGC
King Henry	EGC
Robert Burns	J. W. Simpson
A Design for a Poster	EGC
'I Had No Thoughts of a Blue Gauze Veil'	Oliver Bath
The Understudy	EGC
Miss Queenie Tarvin as 'Dick'	EGC
A Page for Children	Oliver Bath
Roses in the Night	A. Lowther
The Palaquin Bearers	M. F. Shaw
Sir Frederick Leighton	J. W. Simpson
A Scandal in Paradise	A Legend
The Sorceress	EGC
Irving in 'The Secrets of London'	EGC
Perfidious Albion	W. Challinger
Cave	EGC
Henry Purcell	Sir Kneller
An ABC for Children	EGC
Seven Verses and Another	E. F. Howard
A Post Card Design	EGC
Four Bookplates	EGC
Head and Tail Pieces	Wesley & Bath
Supplement – Irving as 'Dubosc'	EGC

It is with *The Marionette* that Craig combines the playfulness, naivety, designer-conscious aesthetic of *The Page* with the more theoretically-slanted *Mask*. Published in 1918, as an interval between issues 8 and 9 of *The Mask*, it deals exclusively with the lives and times of marionettes. This allows Craig to indulge with no hesitation or shame whatsoever in all the narrative techniques he was hinting at in *The Mask*. The theme of the periodical allows it to metaphorically function as a marionette for *The Mask* itself. The puppet-master, of course, of this magazine-within-a magazine, is none other than Craig, under the appropriate name Tom Fool. The launching or 'opening night' of the journal is heralded as follows, introduced by a reproduction of a design of a Javanese shadow puppet:

Before The Curtain.

Ladies, Gentlemen, and Egoists.

Having lost our offices owing to an unforeseen burst of enthusiasm on the part of nobody, we are reduced to a box: a private box; Box 444. Easy to remember...and they still say artists are unpractical... Being reduced to a Box for an office, after the luxury of the tumbledown Arena Goldoni (the coldest place in the world) it only remains to thank nobody for his burst of enthusiasm which caused us to skedaddle. This pleasant duty executed, the Curtain may go up for all we care.

The Curtain Rises.[30]

The character of *The Marionette* as comic lazzo allows it to fire comments, often abusive, against its audience. This tone is continued throughout its 12 issues and touches most of the themes covered. *The Marionette* too, like *The Mask*, presents us with a history of puppets. The author here, though, is not a renowned academic but Craig himself. A series of articles under the general title 'History of Puppets'[31] is presented in its pages. Craig, using his own name this time, takes the role of Yorick, the author of the series in the "mother" magazine under the same title. Craig's account is much more impressionable, much more personal and less historical and scholarly. The nature of the publication calls for this attitude as he is himself doubling the Yorick of *The Mask*, acting as his more flamboyant, opinionated counterpart. It is characteristic that all the pseudonyms used by Craig in *The Marionette* are totally transparent, and the audience is almost told that Craig is the man behind the various guises. It is possible that Craig himself felt more comfortable in this mode of writing, that it was closer to his individual discourse. In general, the history presented in

---

[30] *The Marionette*, Vol. 1, April (Florence, 1918), p. 1.
[31] EGC, 'History of Puppets', in *The Marionette*, pp. 20–23, 54–57, 152–54, 171–75.

its pages contrasts sharply with the equivalent series in *The Mask*:

> We are here on earth to live, not to die. We happen to die, but it doesn't
> make it any less certain that we are here to live; to create, not to kill.
> Now the historian has always done his very best to kill us. Oh, I know
> how fascinating a book of facts and dates can be. But a clerk can do that
> work. What I object to is all the *evidence* of the historian; that's what kills.[32]

Following such an introduction we are prepared for a highly impressionable, not necessarily historical – in other words typically Craigian –
account of puppets. The fact remains, however, that Craig *did* conduct
an extensive study of puppets and their history. The series continues
with more accounts of Wayang puppets, Burattini and eastern shadow
puppets. Craig categorizes puppets according to their performative
features, proposing such categories as Flat Puppets, Round Puppets,
Marionettes suspended from above and Burattini and Shadow Figures
held from below. The important aspect of this process is that they are
treated in the context of performative practice rather than in terms of
their religious background. There is quite an extensive account of
matters of handling, articulation and materials of puppets.

Despite his disregard for historical research he, nonetheless, is
quite meticulous when presenting the history of puppets. The scholarly
aspect of this history he leaves to other authors. The Italian academic
Corrado Ricci presents an article entitled 'The Burattini of Bologna',[33]
which is published for 'the first time in English by permission of the
author'. Craig urges his readers to read other books written by Corrado
Ricci. Their books 'everyone in the New Movement should possess'.[34]
Many more translations of essays by European scholars feature in *The
Marionette*. Some of these are 'Japanese Marionette plays and the Modern
Stage' by Oskar Munsterberg (sic); 'The Marionettes of the Ancients' by
Father Mariantonio. All of these works appear in their first English
translations and do not appear again until 1936 when Bruce Inverarity's
Manual of Puppetry is published containing both.[35]

---

[32] *The Marionette*, p. 21.

[33] Corrado Ricci, 'The Burattini of Bologna', in *The Marionette*, No. 5 (Florence, 1918),
pp. 131–163, taken from *I Teatri di Bologna* (Bologna, 1888).

[34] From the above source book Craig mentions *I Bibiena... Architetti Teatrali 1625–1780*
(Milano, 1915).

[35] These essays were to play an important role in later scholarly studies. They would be
published in English by the American puppeteer and director of the University Of
Washington Puppeteers R. Bruce Inverarity in his *Manual of Puppetry* (Binfords Mort, 1936).
Oskar Munsterberg's essay (whose name Craig spells Mansterberg) appears in this volume.
Father Mariantonio (1695–1737) whose surname, Lupi, is omitted is a very important figure
in the history of puppetry. He was an Italian Jesuit priest whose studies of puppets in
classical Greek and Roman literature is probably one of the first attempts to chart a history
of puppets. In his *Sopra i burattini degli antichi*, in Vol. 2 of *Dissertazioni lettere ed altre operette*

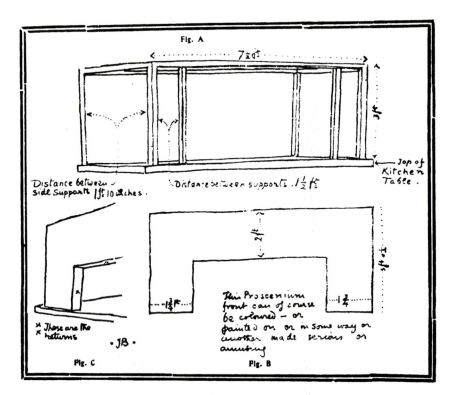

29. Plans for a marionette theatre, Vol. 5, No. 2, p. 146b, 1912.

The accounts themselves are interspersed with witticisms by Craig. Although they may have an apologetic tone, they ironically still draw the audience's attention to the all-powerful puppet-master, who remains in control throughout every aspect of this performance/publication:

> Do not grow cross until you see how ill I do it; and when you have glanced through and thrown away my compilation do not laugh at me for having gone to such lengths to show off my ignorance.[36]

The Marionette acts as a stage for Craig's actual plays for puppets or 'motions' as he called them, borrowing the Elizabethan term. These are: *Mr. Fish and Mrs Bones*, *The Tune the Old Cow Died of*, *The Gordian Knot*, and *The Men of Gotham*.[37] They are all signed by Tom Fool and are not reprinted in any other publication. Apart from the above four motions Craig also wrote another 'sketch for a little farce for Marionettes' entitled *Blue Sky*. This was written after the publication of *The Marionette* had ceased in 1920 and appeared in *The English Review*.[38]

Keeping the balance between the amusing and the serious, *The Marionette* constantly reflects, refers to and doubles *The Mask*, albeit in its own differing mode. It presents its readers with a full bibliography of material printed in *The Mask* relating to marionettes. Its rhetoric allows it to be more outrageous and personal but this does not stop it from taking its task very earnestly indeed. Laughter, disguise and trickery are simply used as devices to attract attention. Craig writes:

> are you going to find it merely laughable because of this admirable quality? Must we drop the names puppet and call it merely the *Moving Form*, before it can command serious attention? Probably. Good, then; call it the Moving Figure. The Theatre of Moving Figures...is in existence not to exalt egoism but to damn it.[39]

On a theoretical level, *The Marionette* is just as serious as *The Mask* and makes just as many claims, probably more in fact. Due to its specific

---

(Zaccaria, c. 1720), he cites Herodotus, Xenophon, Aristotle, Apuleius, Horace, Petronius Arbiter, Antonius, Favorinus, Aulus Gellus. This work provided the chapter in Magnin *Histoire des marionettes en Europe* (1852), which in turn provided the model for Yorick's 'History of Puppets'. A French translation of Lupi appeared in *Journal étranger* (Jan., 1757). In English the first translation appears in *The Marionette* (June, 1918) and the second in *Manual of Puppetry*.

[36] EGC, *The Marionette*, No. 5, (June, 1918), p. 152.
[37] EGC (Tom Fool), *The Men of Gotham*, p. 1; *Mr. Fish and Mrs. Bones*, p. 12; *The Tune the Old Cow Died of*, p. 48; *The Gordian Knot*, p. 82 in *The Marionette*, (Florence, 1918).
[38] EGC, *The Blue Sky*, (1920), Humanities Research Centre, University of Texas at Austin.
[39] EGC, *The Marionette*, No. 1 (Florence, 1918), p. 9.

character, it sheds more light on Craigian formulations on puppets and their relation to the living actor.

For instance (and crucially), it is in *The Marionette* that Craig publishes a translation, the first in English, of Heinrich von Kleist's *Uber Das Marionettentheater*.[40] Although this essay appears in 1918, and Craig had already formulated his *Ubermarionette* theory as early as 1908 in *The Mask*,[41] it is very probable indeed that Craig was aware of Kleist's work before that. One piece of evidence is Otto Brahm's book on Kleist which was published in 1911 and mentions Kleist's *Marionettes*. Craig was familiar with the work of Otto Brahm and even before 1911 had had meetings with him to discuss the possibilities of a collaboration.[42] Whether directly or in more subtle ways, the work of Kleist was a definite influence on Craig; their intertextual relationship cannot be doubted.

The concerns of both men are essentially the same and derive from a common ideological framework. Both essays start on the assumption that the human form is not the proper material for art. If theatre was to be the new 'secularlized' art form of the future, the human actor had to be replaced by the idol. Marionettes were conceived in their quasi-religious facets. Craig writes:

> Acting is not an art. It is therefore incorrect to speak of the actor as an artist. For accident is an enemy of the artistic. Art is the exact antithesis of Pandimonium [sic], and Pandimonium is created by the tumbling together of many accidents; Art arrives only by design. Therefore in order to make any work of art it is clear we may work in those materials with which we can calculate. Man is not one of these materials.[43]

The main problem Craig poses is the parameter of chance. As he mentions further on, 'man tends towards freedom' and consequently 'as material for the theatre he is useless'. Kleist expresses more or less the

---

[40] Heinrich von Kleist, *Uber Das Marionettentheater, Berliner Abendblatter* (c. 1810). Craig presents his readers with the first English translation of Kleist's essay by Amadeo Foresti in *The Marionette*, No. 4 (Florence, 1918). Subsequent English translations of this essay appear in McCollester, *Theatre Arts* (New York, 1928); Jelas, *Vertical* (New York, 1941); Beryl de Zoete, *Ballet* (London, 1946) rpt in *Puppet Master* (B.P.M.T.G. Oct., 1946). Kleist's essay has featured in numerous German publications since its first appearance in serial form in the Berlin newspaper. For the impact of the essay in its German context, and on the work of Kleist in general see, Walter Silz, *Heinrich von Kleist: Studies in his Works and Literary Character* (Connecticut, 1961).

[41] EGC, 'The Actor and the Ubermarionette', *The Mask*, Vols. 1 and 2 (Florence, 1908). The essay was incorporated in Craig's book, *On the Art of the Theatre* (London, 1911). (Paperback edition, Mercury Books, 1962).

[42] See Christopher Innes, *Edward Gordon Craig: Directors in Perspective* (Cambridge, 1983), pp. 100–111.

[43] EGC, *The Mask*, Vol. 1, No. 2 (Florence, 1908), p. 3.

same argument in his support of marionettes:

> I said that however clear his paradox might be he would never persuade me that there could be more grace in a mechanical doll than in the structure of the human body. He replied that a human being was simply incapable of rivalling the marionette in this respect. Only a God could measure himself against matter... and this was the point, he said, where both ends of the world's circle fit into each other.[44]

In a form of polemic very much used by Craig as well[45] – the dialogue – Kleist too talks of the minimising of the factors of chance and chaos with his notion of the *asymptote* of marionettes. The main limitations of the human form are imposed by its very nature, by its materiality. The constant need to de-materialize the body of the actor is present in the works of both. Kleist writes:

> Another advantage of the puppets is that they are not subject to the law of gravity. They know nothing of that worst enemy of the dancer, the inertia of matter; for the force which lifts them into the air is greater than that which binds them to earth... We use the earth to rest on, to recover from the exertions of the dance, a moment which is clearly not in itself dance, and with which there is nothing to be done to make it disappear as quickly as possible.[46]

If we were to substitute Kleist's idea of 'dance theatre', as the perfect mode for puppets with Craig's term of puppet plays as motions, we arrive at two very similar views indeed. This highly idealized puppet has to somehow expiate for its earthly existence. The earth is only used 'to rest on' and any aspect of it is certainly not suitable material for art. In yet another expression of that aestheticist notion that life itself is somehow merely a 'nuisance', that can only hinder the creative process, Kleist's words echo a very Craigian ring. Craig takes the argument even further:

> If you can find in nature a new material, one which has never been used by man to give form to his thoughts, then you can say that you are on the high road towards creating a new art. For you have found that by which you can create it.[47]

---

[44] See Kleist, note 40.

[45] Most of Craig's instructive/propagandistic essays are in dialogue form, between an actor–manager/actor and the 'Artist of the Theatre'. See his dialogues, *The Art of the Theatre* (1905), 'Proposals Old and New' (1910), 'The Perishable Theatre' (1921). This form of teaching, essentially Platonic, using inductive guidance should not be considered as exhibiting any notion of a dialectic narrative. This strategy of argumentation (*maueutike*) imposes a very authoritative narrative voice.

[46] See Kleist, note 40.

[47] EGC, 'The Actor and the *Übermarionette*' in *The Mask*, Vol. 1, p. 8.

If for Kleist such a feat could only be undertaken by 'a God', for Craig it seems less fantastic. Both men see the role of the puppet-master as crucial. He represents that totalising power of the artistic genius. For Craig, though, this was no longer a rhetorical device. The metaphor materialized in the shape of the dominant director. His appearance is heralded by Kleist:

> Now since the puppeteer can only have control over this center of gravity through the medium of his wires or strings, all the other limbs are, as they should be, inert, mere pendulums, obeying only the law of gravity.[48]

For Kleist, as is the case with Craig, the main obstacle impeding the human actor from creation is his nature, his personality; the fact that he is endowed with experience. Craig formulates the *Ubermarionette* as the actor minus 'personality'. Kleist states that it is impossible for the human actor to create 'since we have eaten from the tree of knowledge'.

Kleist and Craig both derive a 'grand theory' from the theatre and in particular from the marionette. In as much as it represents the perfect artifice, it becomes not only a statement about the theatre but about art in general. Taking this logic to its extreme, and since life only counts as 'artistic life', the marionette is seen as the new idol of this quasi-religious art form, endowed not only with artistic qualities but also with metaphysical ones. It comes to represent a total, eschatological theory that may redeem, not only the art of the theatre but life itself. Kleist ends his essay in an apocalyptic manner:

> 'Well, then, my friend,' said Herr C., 'you have all that you need to enable you to understand me. In an organic world we see that grace has greater power and brilliance in proportion as the reasoning powers are dimmer and less active. But as one line, when it crosses another, suddenly appears on the other side of the intersecting point after its passage through infinity; or as the image in a concave mirror, after retreating into infinity, suddenly reappears close before our eyes, so, too, when knowledge has likewise passed through infinity, grace will reappear. So that we shall find it at its purest in a body which is entirely devoid of consciousness or which possesses it in an infinite degree; that is, in the marionette or the god.'
> 'You mean,' I said rather tentatively, 'that we must eat again of the tree of knowledge in order to relapse into the state of Innocence?'
> 'Certainly,' he replied. 'That is the last chapter of the history of the world.'[49]

---

[48] See Kleist, note 40.
[49] Ibid.

Kleist proposes the marionette as the divine image that will somehow re-connect man with his divine creator and restore truth and order in the universe. His elevation of grace over the 'dimmer powers of reason' and his reference to the notion of the 'concave mirror' have a distinctly Platonic ring to them. This only highlights Kleist's idealistic roots and also clarifies similar formulations by Craig:

> I pray earnestly for the return of the Image, the *Ubermarionette*, to the Theatre; and when he comes again and is but seen, he will be loved so well that once more will it be possible for people to return to their ancient...homage rendered to existence...and divine and happy intercession made to Death.[50]

The two closing paragraphs could have been written by either writer. Both have a messianic tone to them and exhibit the idealistic–Platonic background of both Kleist and Craig.

The essay *Uber Das Marionettentheater* creates a historic context for Craigian formulations on the role of the actor and the marionette, and, at the same time, defines his relationship with corresponding modernist schools of acting. Craig is much closer to the Romanticism of Kleist than he is to the Modernism of his contemporaries. The 'man or marionette' debate was one which determined many Modernist schools of performance. Parallel to Craig's *Ubermarionette*, and in many ways inspired by it, similar theories were being experimented with all over Europe and the Soviet Union. The Russian and Italian Futurists and the Bauhaus theatres all saw in the puppet a possible model for the actor. Still, Craig has quite an ambivalent relationship with his younger contemporaries. Although his essay on the *Ubermarionette* seemed radical at the time and was essentially the work that placed him among the chief theoreticians of European theatre, it was left to other schools of performance actually to undertake and realize these highly innovative Craigian views. The acting theories of Meyerhold, for example, which admittedly[51] owe much to Craig, couldn't be more removed ideologically and practically.

Again Kleist can help solve the seeming contradiction that is evident throughout most of Craig's work. Despite the newness and boldness of Craigian thought, very little of it actually became reality. The *Ubermarionette* theory and all the repercussions it caused can act as a distinct paradigm of Craig's ideological background. Had this essay been written almost a century earlier, as was its predecessor, it would

---

[50] EGC, 'The Actor and the *Ubermarionette*', in *The Mask*, Vol. 1, p. 156.
[51] Meyerhold acknowledges his theoretical debt to Craig. He was the first to translate Craig's work into Russian. For Meyerhold's views on Craig see, Edward Braun (ed), *Meyerhold on Theatre* (London, 1969), p. 61, p. 93, p. 112, p. 154, p. 172, p. 176.

have been received as an instance of excessive Romanticism, not ever meant to be realized. As it happened, however, Craig wrote in the 1910s and everyone, both fans and critics, expected to see results.

Craig's *Ubermarionette* is called to replace the human actor through a process that negates, discharges the human form completely. Other schools of performance followed quite the opposite trail. The Russian Constructivists and the Bauhaus theatre, for example, also propose the puppet as the paradigmatic actor. This conclusion, however, is reached through a very different process. Where Craig and Kleist negate the human form, they celebrate it. Craig's negation contrasts with their total affirmation of the human form. Instead of de-materialising, their position was to re-materialize the human actor. If Craig's *Ubermarionette* was to connect the puppet with the divine, Meyerhold's *biomechanics* were to establish a historical connection, to place the human form in history. For the idealistic relation of puppet-idol with God is substituted the materialistic relation of puppet-machine with history. Instead of replacing the human actor by the puppet-idol the goal was to *puppetize* the human form itself. Its materiality was no longer an obstacle but the very substance of creative art. It was this materiality that would place the human form in history and help it find a language of expression for the theatre. The actor was no longer seen as degenerate, corrupt, but was now considered to be the primal material for theatre. 'Above all drama is the art of the actor', wrote Meyerhold.[52] Oskar Schlemmer expressed similar views in his famous definition of the theatre as 'the history of the transfiguration of the human form'.[53] The material of the human form was the very substance that was to create the new dialectic actor as Meyerhold put it. Rather than work in abstraction on the *Ubermarionette*, as with Craig, his Modernist counterparts chose to work on the human form itself. Meyerhold explains this process of shifting from the inanimate/immaterial to the living and human. The director, he says:

> quickly realized that as soon as he tried to improve the puppet's mechanism it lost part of its charm. It was as though the puppet were resisting such barbarous improvements with all its being. The director came to his senses when he realized that there is a limit beyond which there is no alternative but to replace the puppet with a man. But how could he part with the puppet which had created a world of enchantment with its incomparable movements, its expressive gestures achieved by some magic known to it alone, its angularity which reaches the heights of true plasticity?[54]

---

[52] See *Meyerhold on Theatre*, note 51, p. 53.
[53] Oskar Schlemmer, 'Man and Art Figure', in Walter Gropius, ed., *The Theatre of the Bauhaus*, trans. Arthur S. Wesinger (Connecticut, 1961), pp. 17–48.
[54] See *Meyerhold on Theatre*, p. 128.

For Meyerhold, in many ways an admirer of Craig, the whole 'man or marionette' debate had come full circle. Replacing the human actor by the puppet was a process not without its merits: it left Meyerhold with a particular technique, with a method of training that could in turn puppetize the human actor. Meyerhold follows Craigian thought but goes beyond it. Rather than conceiving of an abstract idea and posing it as the final result, i.e. the *Ubermarionette*, he is interested in the process, in the method of training, hence his *biomechanics*.

For Craig, as with Kleist, the marionette did not offer a language for training actors, a system that could be reproduced and developed. It presented an ideal, not necessarily one that was meant to be realized. Certainly on a practical level this was impossible. Despite all his collections of puppets, his designs and reproductions for his journals Craig never actually worked on designing and making an *Ubermarionette* that was in line with all his theoretical claims. The very fact that he conceived of Irving as the perfect marionette shows that there must have been much misunderstanding going on. Craig's ideas, as they were interpreted by theatre practitioners like Meyerhold, may not have been at all what he had in mind. When criticising his contemporaries, Craig fails to see the threads that connect them with his work. One such account of a Futurist marionette performance in *The Marionette* reads:

> Just got back from the *Teatro dei Piccolo*, ... Diavoli. It is quite as bad as you guessed. The music had just about as much form and structure, the colours true futurism, and as ugly as the music, which as usual contained not one sound not displeasing to the ear... Their announcements in the paper spoke of studies in light and rhythm, etc...to me the whole thing is like a young girl proposing to play her scales, not well, in public... and talking all the while about the 'beauty of diatonic sequences' and 'harmonic simplicity'. That would be funny if anyone else were fooled... but perhaps not, since there is never a lack of gulls.[55]

The fact that the above account has no reference whatsoever to the marionettes used is in itself characteristic. Craig, had to say something, and something critical at that. He could not, however, be critical of the marionettes, as he himself had nothing to show apart from ideas and schemes. He is very articulate when talking about puppets of the past but becomes very vague and general when criticising marionette productions of his time. On the other hand, Craig shows no hesitation when proposing Irving as the perfect actor/marionette:

> I consider him to have been the greatest actor I have ever seen, and I have seen the best in Italy, France, Russia, Germany, Holland and

---

[55] EGC, 'Futuristic Marionettes', *The Marionette*, Vol. 1, No. 4 (Florence, 1918).

America. They were all imitable, and yet he was unique. By Irving the *Mask* and the *Marionette* were better understood than by all other actors... and it is because of his trust in these two ancient traditions... the two unshakeable traditions...that he stood unique. Some of you know this... I need hardly remind you of it. But you who are younger, and who never saw Irving, will see him now...a figure solemn and beautiful like an immense thought in motion... If you will be an Actor in such a day as this, and if you are an English man, take but one model,...the masked marionette.[56]

In suggesting Irving as the 'masked marionette', we are led to believe that the whole affair of masks, marionettes and *Ubermarionettes* may have been nothing more than a rhetorical device. The *Ubermarionette* could merely be a metaphor for a type of stylized, highly Romantic and expressionist acting. It is possible that Craig had had very different ideas in mind when originally formulating his theories of marionettes. The impact which these had, however, was something he could not foresee or control. His essay on 'The Actor and the *Ubermarionette*' – whether he meant it literally or not – was certainly taken literally and aroused much controversy. Having helped to trigger the man/marionette debate, Craig could not continue his innovations in practice. Theoretically he was covered but practically Irving could not be accepted by other Modernist theatre experimenters, as the prototypical *Ubermarionette*. There was something very incongruous in Craig's combination of Modernist rhetoric with Romantic idealisation.

Kleist's essay helps resolve this seeming contradiction. The work of Craig on the theory of theatre in general, and on marionettes in particular, may be seen as springing from the idealistic Romantic tradition. As expressed by Kleist this is a tradition that conceives of marionettes in their quasi-religious context, that negates the human actor and in general proposes an idealised abstraction in its place. The tensions that such a view encompasses remain subdued as long as one is not involved in theatrical praxis. From the moment the theory has to take shape and form another step has to be taken; one taken by other modernists, that creates a technique, a system of training, a performative language that bridges the gap between theory and practice.

The fact that Craig chose to feature Kleist in *The Marionette* and not in *The Mask* only adds to the periodical's performative quality. *The Marionette*, acting as a magazine-within-a-magazine, functions on a meta-level, revealing Craig's sources, placing his work within a historical context and, at times, presenting possible solutions to areas of Craigian thought that appear problematic.

---

[56] EGC, *The Marionette*, Vol. 1, No. 6, p. 170.

THE

MASK

THE MASK
WHY THE MASK

o

BECAUSE THE THEATRE
IS STILL FAST
ASLEEP
AND IN LOVE WITH
WELL ORGANIZED
SHORT HOURS
AND LAZY DREAMS,
EASY AND QUICK
RETURNS AND
INTRIGUE.

NOTICE.
WITH THE NEW YEAR BEGINS A NEW VOLUME

o

VOLUME X.

ITS FOUR PARTS
WILL BE ISSUED
IN
JANUARY
APRIL, OCTOBER
AND JULY OF 1924.

NEEDED ONCE

1 9 0 8

1 9 2 3

AND STILL NEEDED

TODAY THE STAGE
PUFFS & BLOWS
ATTEMPTING TO
ORGANIZE THE
OVER-ORGANIZED.

o

STOP ORGANIZING

o

SACK THE ORGANIZERS

o

FOLLOW THE ARTISTS
AND LEND A HAND
WHILE THEY
CREATE

ONLY A POSITIVE
NEED FOR THE MASK
HAS CALLED IT
AGAIN
INTO EXISTENCE.

o

THE STAGE IS
ORGANIZING ITSELF
OUT OF
EXISTENCE

o

STOP ORGANIZING
THE THEATRE

o

CREATE FIRST.

30. Advertising notice in *The Mask*, Vol. 9, No. 1, 1923.

7

MASKS! MASKS! MASKS!: AUTHORSHIP AND NARRATIVE IN THE PERIODICAL

Were we to look for a slogan or epigraph for Craig's work the above phrase would serve quite aptly. Re-writing Shakespeare's 'words, words, words', the work of Craig proposes a non-literary view of theatre with the mask as both its medium and its emblem. Craig's notion of the *Ubermarionette*, his formulations of the role of the director, his underlining of the concept of performance at the expense of the literary text, are all ideas which can be read as embodying, extending, ramifying the concept of the mask. The periodical that was to carry all this Craigiana could have the same name: *The Mask*. The title of the publication not only acts as an indicator of its content, but also provides a paradigm of its procedures. For *The Mask* symbolizes Craigian notions of theatricality through its very physicality and the way it 'narrates' these notions. The title of Craig's periodical is not merely a transference of meaning but a generator of meaning as well. In this way Craig, as the voice behind *The Mask*, both shapes and is shaped by it. It provides Craig with an arena where his ideas can be analyzed, exemplified and eventually enacted. In its turn, this arena is not merely a neutral medium carrying and transferring meaning. It sets up its own parameters. The author of such a project has to assume the guise of the mask himself. Eventually this guise overtakes its subject and the author becomes a mask. Craig as the author of the periodical turns himself or is turned into a mask.

In writing *The Mask* Craig employs narrative strategies that give form to its performative stance. As a masked writer, his use of pseudonyms only seems natural: a consequence of his struggle to turn himself into the only pure form of *theatrical writing* he acknowledged: the mask. This constant shifting of the identity of the author launches *The Mask* on some exciting narratological adventures. Editors, contributors, foreign correspondents, all seem to fuse into one voice. What this strategy manages to do is to three-dimensionalize the two dimensional quality of a magazine. It allows us to visualize and enact in our minds the goings-on in its pages. What readers are seduced into doing in order to maintain their sense of who's who is to imagine the page of contents as a form of theatrical wings where the masked actor/writer waits until he is called upon to adopt or speak through a particular mask for the performance taking place. As a metaphor of performance, the mask provides the magazine and Craig with the most apt narratological strategies.

What Craig's various masks try to achieve is the gradual diffusion of his status as an author. In this project Craig is not alone. He manifests one of the main concerns of Modernism in general: that of the relationship of the author/creator to his creation/artifice. This problematizing of the role of the author led to much theorising by writers such as Ezra Pound and T. S. Eliot, who articulated a novel relationship of author to work, based on impersonality. This 'cult of impersonality' was much argued over, with consequences (according to more recent criticism) at times opposite to those initially suggested. Instead of doing away with the author's personality, it rather creates a certain 'theology of the author' that places him beyond history in a totally aestheticised realm. This is a useful context in which to examine Craig's experimentations with masks. As with the activities of many of his literary counterparts, Craig's seeming deconstruction of the author almost always reconstructs itself under the auspices of that grand theory so favoured by 'high' Modernism: fascism.[1] Craig's flirtations with fascism are not as systematic and articulate as Ezra Pound's. Yet his fascination with masks, his attempt to do away with the personal in favour of the 'artistic genius', can be theoretically justified and explained in a fascist framework.

'So that I wasn't always there'[2]

Asked about his use of pseudonyms in an interview in 1962, Craig stated that this process allowed him to hide his identity. He went on to explain, 'you see *The Mask* could do anything'.[3] The result, of course, was quite the opposite. It made its author ever-present and all-powerful. Assumimg some 65[4] pseudonyms, Craig was in control of almost every article, every commentary, every drawing, even of the correspondence in the pages of his journal. Rather than 'hide the identity of the man behind it', as Craig's son writes,[5] *The Mask* could not be a better promoter of that identity.

The pseudonyms themselves ranged from the sublime to the ridiculous. The most prominent one was John Semar, the name

---

[1] For a comprehensive analysis of the relationship between Modernism and fascism see, Cairns Craig, *Yeats, Eliot, Pound and the Politics of Poetry* (London, 1982).
[2] Quoted in Lorelei Guidry, *The Mask: Introduction and Index* (New York, 1968), p. 8.
[3] Ibid.
[4] See *The Mask: Introduction and Index*, pp. 10–12.
[5] See Edward Craig, *Gordon Craig* (London, 1968), p. 242.

attributed to the editor. Craig borrowed the name from the Javanese puppet Semar. This fact is not actually stated in *The Mask*, and in all his writings on Javanese puppets Craig avoids naming them (perhaps in an attempt to keep up the pretence and not give away his guise). Craig decided to assume the guise of Semar while he was still in the planning stages of *The Mask*. As Lorelei Guidry writes in her intro-duction to her index of *The Mask*,[6] and Craig's son in his *Gordon Craig*, a Dutch couple were hired by Craig to help with organizing the publication (and with the housework – in typical Craigian style). Their main contribution was in translation work. One of these translations was a presentation of Javanese shadow puppets which inspired Craig's editorial pseudonym. It is interesting to note that Semar, one of the most respected figures of the Javanese cast of shadow puppets, is him-self a figure in disguise. As a tramp or as a wrinkled old man, he symbolizes the all-knowing, wise figure whose superficial appearence is there to deceive and distract. Semar the puppet and Semar the editor assume here a meta-theatrical as well as a stage-like quality, one that in part stresses their artificiality and foregrounds the act of masking itself. The Craigian Semar voices his views mainly in the editorial section of the periodical. There he comments on matters of world theatre and world affairs in general from a Craigian stance. (Even when Craig was away from Florence, notably during the period he spent in Russia and Dorothy Nevile Lees took over *The Mask*, he could also use the guise of Semar without bothering to disturb his scheme of things.)

Craig went to great lengths to maintain his supposed cover. Numerous announcements in *The Mask* try to falsify rumours that Craig is the absolute agent behind it all. A typical one reads as follows:

> There have appeared lately more than once in the Press two erroneous statements in regard to *The Mask*: first, that it is edited by Mr. Gordon Craig at Rapallo; second, that its first eight volumes were written by him.
>
> Such reports are incorrect.
>
> *The Mask* remains in the same hands as heretofore. Its home is still in Florence, and it is edited, as it has been from the first, by Mr. John Semar.
>
> Mr. Craig continues to send as hitherto, his contributions. In regard to the second error...while Mr. Craig has contributed largely to them, and certainly has a capacity for work, they were not all written by him. Such a feat were surely an impossible one.[7]

---

6 See *The Mask: Introduction and Index*, pp. 8–9.
7 *The Mask*, Vol. 10, No. 1, editorial notes, 1924.

Craig could not expect even the most faithful of readers to believe such a statement, especially as he generously hands himself a compliment at the end of the announcement. What Craig is chiefly aiming for is a certain suspension of belief in his audience/readers. It is a theatrical strategy partly called for to add to the periodical's performative quality. With pseudonyms like Yoo-no-hoo, Britannicus, Edward Edwardovitch or X. Y. Z., the audience could not possibly believe that they were real and separate people. In a way, the more obvious the pseudonym, the more readers were compelled to apply theatrical ways of 'reading'. Such names could only be characters on a stage. In this case the stage was provided through the pages of a magazine. Craig's cunning and devious attempts to hide his identity and claim that he was merely one contributor to *The Mask* are paralleled by jaunty and fanciful attempts to make his cover transparent and charade-like.

Craig went to great lengths to establish personalities for the supposed characters behind the pseudonyms. In quite a Stanislavskian manner he creates biographies for the most important ones and sketches them out in his notebooks.[8] John Balance, as the name suggests is the voice of reconciliation and common sense in *The Mask*. He is not as outspoken as Semar, as befits the voice of objectivity. He signs at least 32 articles 2 engravings and 6 foreign notes. Lorelei Guidry writes:

> Of the 32 articles, one was a tribute to Sarah Bernhardt, one was rambling and whimsical, 10 were somewhat didactic, 12 combined reasoned teaching with fresh ideas or other useful material, and 8 gave useful information without noticeably expounding Craig's theories as such. Some of the best writing in *The Mask* – and some of the most profound – appeared under this pseudonym.[9]

Pierre Rames (Semar spelled backwards) deals with oriental theatre, as befits his exotic name. Craig shared both these pseudonyms with Dorothy Nevile Lees, whose main contribution to *The Mask* was the translation and publication of material on the Commedia dell'Arte, and who, following Craig's example, eventually took various disguises. The name Allen Carric appears in Craig's notes under the entry 'Portico. Fanciful. Rather humorous. Old engravings. Often in Paris'.[10] Carric was to be mainly

---

[8] These notebooks are part of the Craig Collection at the National Library, Paris. The notebook on the use of pseudonyms is Notebook No. 30.

[9] See *The Mask: Introduction and Index*, p. 10.

[10] See Allen Carric in *The Mask*: Vol. 1, p. 55, p. 140, p. 219, p. 226; Vol. 2, p. 52, p. 88, p. 95, p. 133, p. 161, p. 172; Vol. 3, p. 57, p. 181; Vol. 4, p. 19, pp. 132–34, p. 182, pp. 185–86, p. 197; Vol. 5, p. 2, p. 42, p. 196, p. 299, p. 367; Vol. 6, p. 225, p. 250; Vol. 7, p. 130, p. 167; Vol. 9, p. 20, p. 26; Vol. 10, p. 42; Vol. 11, p. 96; Vol. 12, p. 28, p. 139; Vol. 13, p. 9, p. 147; Vol. 14, p. 10, p. 57, p. 134.

concerned with historical matters, and hence signs articles like 'A Venice and a Rome for the Consideration of Young Scene Painters' in Volume 1 and Giuseppe Bibiena in Volume 12. (It is interesting to note that Craig's son Edward, following the family tradition, took the pseudonym 'Carrick' after he left *The Mask*, specialising in similar areas. He was mainly involved in historical research and photography, although the form 'Carric' does appear at least once in *The Mask*.) This device of setting up pseudonyms as plausible theatrical characters and, at the same time, constantly stressing their artificiality creates a type of alienation effect which adds to the meta-theatrical quality of the periodical.

Personae: Masks of Impersonality

The obsession with masks is, of course, very much a product of the aesthetic concerns of the period. *The Mask* could have acted as a title of a periodical dealing with almost any aspect of aesthetics or philosophy between 1880 and 1910. The fact that Craig's publication dealt mainly with theatre is almost a convenient coincidence. Trumpeted as the ultimate artifice at the turn of the century, masks appear in almost every domain of art. In *The Birth of Tragedy* Nietzsche did much to construct an aesthetic theory with the mask as its symbol and method. His anti-humanist and very unclassical reading of ancient Greek drama proposed the mask not only as a carrier of meaning but as the ultimate creator as well. Nietzsche's 'every genius deserves a mask' presented the mask not as a barrier that hides and conceals but rather as a liberator that reveals. This apocalyptic quality of the mask is what made it attractive to late Romanticism and filtered through to Craig's version of Modernism. Yeats's poem 'The Mask', written in 1910 is just one example of this fascination with the mask:

THE MASK

'Put off that mask of burning gold
With emerald eyes.'
'O no, my dear, you make so bold
To find if hearts be wild and wise,
And yet not cold.'

'I would but find what's there to find,
Love or deceit.'
'It was the mask engaged your mind,
And after set your heart to beat,
Not what's behind.'

'But lest you are my enemy,
I must enquire.'

'O no, my dear, let all that be;
What matter, so there is but fire
In you, in me?'[11]

The elevation of the mask to a metaphysical realm is something which is a constant theme throughout the aestheticist 1890s. Oscar Wilde's essay 'The Truth of Masks' expounds a detailed analysis of how the 'appearance' of a performance is just as important, if not more, than the text. In a detailed presentation, which includes the work of Godwin, he explains how historicist reconstruction (including the re-introduction of masks) can only enhance the meaning of a play. Oscar Wilde goes further, however, to claim that the mask – the ultimate symbol of 'appearance' – is there not to conceal but to reveal. The mask becomes the emblem of apocalyptic art. The essay ends:

> For in art there is no such thing as a universal truth. A Truth in art is that whose contradictory is also true. And just as it is only in art criticism, and through it, that we can apprehend the Platonic theory of ideas, so it is only in art criticism, and through it, that we can realise Hegel's system of contraries. The truths of metaphysics are the truths of masks.[12]

With the distinction between artifice and reality blurring through the manifestations of aestheticism, the mask is seen as pure artefact, not merely mediating reality but also creating it. Having broken the distinction between art and reality, the mask then acts as the catalyst that dissolves the barrier between the artist and the artefact. Squeezing all three parameters – reality, art and the artist – into one, the mask presents itself as the absolute symbol. The artist no longer sees himself/herself as the separate subject. Subjectivity and individuality no longer impede the creative process but enhance it. The artistic process itself gives birth to both the artefact and the artist. Oscar Wilde's essay 'The Critic as Artist' proposes a model where not only do the personal and the aesthetic fuse into one, but the critical and interpretive functions are also woven into the creative process. Using the proto-Craigian form of the didactic dialogue he writes:

> ERNEST: I would have said that personality would have been a disturbing element.

---

[11] W. B. Yeats, 'The Mask' (1910), rpt. in *Collected Poems* (London, 1978), p. 106.

[12] Oscar Wilde, 'The Truth of Masks' (1891), rpt. in *Intentions and The Soul of Man* (London, 1969), pp. 269–70.

> GILBERT: No; it is an element of revelation. If you wish to understand others you must intensify your own individualism.[13]

The Mask is that which will filter the personal into the aesthetic. Gilbert (i.e. Oscar Wilde) continues:

> Yes, the objective form is the most subjective in matter. Man is least himself when he talks in his own person. Give him a mask, and he will tell you the truth.[14]

Like many of his contemporaries Craig used the mask (and in his case *The Mask*) as a device that would both hide and create himself, play and tell the truth. Maud Ellmann writes in *The Poetics of Impersonality*:

> Eliot and Pound both show that it is impossible to overcome the self, but this does not mean that their work is merely a disguise for their biographies. Their poetry should be regarded neither as their mirror nor their hiding-place, but as the laboratory for the fabrication of themselves.[15]

The Mask provided Craig with a workshop for creating and expressing his ideas, as did Pound's shorter poems, collected under the significant title *Personae*. At the same time, it moulded and formed Craig's identity as an artist. Craig fabricated himself as much as he fabricated his art form through *The Mask*. Disguises, pseudonyms, masks all acted not so much to hide as to create his artistic identity, which is the only identity he acknowledged anyway.

In this context, theatre acts as the ultimate workshop for the fabrication of the artistic psyche. Taking place in space rather than in time and stressing the materiality of its nature, the stage provides an arena that can (re)create not only reality but also the artist himself. Unlike much of the whole Modernist experiment in writing, which acts as a metaphor of this whole process, the theatre can actually enact it. The establishing of the director is crucial in this context. As perceived by Craig any relation of the 'Artist of the Theatre' to the production itself could only be a monodramatic one. His Moscow production of *Hamlet* subjugated every other aspect of the production to the play's protagonist; likewise Craig's director can view the stage as that space which extends, develops and finally defines his artistic self. One example of such a merging of self and artifice in a procedure that gives birth to both

---

[13] Oscar Wilde, 'The Critic as Artist', in *Intentions and the Soul of Man*, p. 162.
[14] Ibid., p. 191.
[15] Maud Ellmann, *The Poetics of Impersonality* (Brighton, 1987), p. 198.

categories is an early Russian Constructivist performance. Entitled *Vladimir Mayakovsky*, it was written, directed and acted by the poet himself. The few accounts of this production recall the poet/actor/ director asking the audience 'to darn the holes of his soul' and then proceeding with a long monologue about himself (despite the laughter he had aroused). Konstantin Rudnitsy records the event in *Russian and Soviet Theatre: Tradition and the Avant-Garde:*

> In the centre of the production was the author of the play, who had turned his piece into a monodrama... It was an unbroken monologue divided into separate parts which were just distinguishable from each other by intonational nuances. Only Mayakovsky himself moved about on the stage, dancing and reciting, and revealing no desire to relinquish one effective gesture or to tone down one note of his splendid voice.[16]

This shameless exposition and obsession with the 'artistic self' was of course, indulged in all in the name of impersonality. Pasternak wrote of that same performance:

> How simple it all was! Art was called tragedy. And so it should be called. The tragedy was called Vladimir Mayakovsky. The title concealed a brilliantly simple discovery: that the poet is not the author, but the subject of lyric poetry, which addresses the world in the first person. The title was not the name of the author, but a description of the content.[17]

Through Nietzsche's re-reading of Dionysus all art was to be called tragic: that process that through ecstasy displaces and loses the self. The artistic experience would always include birth, death and resurrection. Tragic art would initiate the ritualistic baptism of the artist. This 'simple discovery' justified this whole project philosophically. The only way to achieve complete impersonality would be to expose oneself to the extreme. By the same token Craig's periodical could have been called *Edward Gordon Craig*. Short of doing that, *The Mask* has to be accepted as being as much about Craig as it is about the art of the theatre, if on a Craigian stage the two can be separated. It is with his journalistic endeavours as it was with his theatrical projects, which stressed the monodramatic dimension of a production.

It is interesting that similar projects were undertaken by other schools of performance of the period. Again, Craig uses *The Mask* to metaphorically enact much of the experimentation that was actually taking place on stages elsewhere in the world (in many cases inspired by

---

[16] Konstantin Rudnitsy, *Russian and Soviet Theatre: Tradition and the Avant-Garde*, trans. Roxane Permar (London, 1988), p. 14.
[17] Ibid. p. 184.

his own work). The received 'failure' of his Moscow *Hamlet* left him with one stage only where he could experiment with his monodramatic obsessions: *The Mask*. Whether as substitute, extension, symbol of the material stage, *The Mask* presents Craig with an arena where he can fulfil most of his ambitions, artistic and otherwise, if not in a concrete way, at least to enact them in a symbolic way.

'You philosophize like a poet'

The above phrase from one of Dostoevsky's[18] letters (borrowed by Sologub in his theoretical works on theatre) implies the style that such a narrative adopts. Sologub calls upon the epigram to justify his somewhat whimsical and haphazard writing.

> Perhaps the transition in thought here may seem rather abrupt – but I am not arguing rationally (not that I am incapable of doing so) but simply propounding my one idea, 'I philosophize like a poet'.[19]

Likewise Craig could revise the epigram as 'You philosophize like an Artist of the theatre'. Not having to remain faithful to one particular narrative thread throughout *The Mask*, Craig employs almost any style he wishes. Ranging from historical to expository writing, his text exhibits his ability to move very smoothly from style to style. Having built up quite complicated characters for his pseudonyms, he maintains the pretence by presenting each of them with very different styles.

Such stylistic exuberance makes *The Mask* very exciting to read and/or experience. There are many instances where Craig, under a pseudonym, writes a letter to himself and then proceeds to answer it under yet another name with a style to match. This schizophrenic discourse imposes the suspension of belief strategy on its readers in a very powerful manner. The readership/audience of *The Mask* is probably aware of the fact that the 'authors' are one and the same person[20] and Craig uses this as another instance to play more 'theatrical' tricks on his readers:

> ... And if I may express a second wish, it is that you do not start your letter with, 'Dear Horace... I know you are Gordon Craig in another mask... and so I will begin by saying "Look here, Craig, my first quarrel is with you... why the deuce, etc. etc".' Don't, I beg, begin in that gracious tone. For even if I am not Gordon Craig, I have been

---

[18] Quoted in Lawrence Senelick, *Russian Dramatic Theory from Pushkin to the Symbolists*, University of Texas Press at Austin (Austin, 1981), p. 136.

[19] Ibid.

[20] See Lee Simonson, *The Stage is Set* (London, 1932), pp. 345–50, where amongst other things Simonson attacks Craig for his thin disguises.

> working a good deal longer at this craft than you, and to be a
> whipper-snapper (if only in manner) does not become you any the
> better just because you hail from America.[21]

Jokes like the above are more of the stage than they are of the written page.
At times it seems almost as though Craig gets carried away by his own
rhetoric. Certain passages read as if he really *believes* he can be all the different masks he embodies. In an introduction, signed by himself, he writes:

> It took me some time to see that a group could make a Foolish Drama
> with far better ease than I could alone. I now sit round a table...I and
> Tom and It...and having brought out different notes or parts of MS.,
> we talk over and over. What anyone of us does not like...objects
> strongly to...we cut out. Only what we are all agreed upon – be it in
> a scene – only that do we leave in.[22]

The '*we*' of this quotation is far less obvious than that of the previous
one. Reading it we are led to believe, following Craig's example, that it
really does involve more than one person.

'Philosophizing like a poet' also allows Craig to be as whimsical
and eccentric as he pleases with his narrative. Applying modes as
diverse as aphorisms, epigrams or fairy tales Craig uses quite a degree
of poetic licence in his text. One of the oldest narrative techniques for
poetic philosophizing is, of course, the dialogue. Craig constructs dialogues to put forward his ideas on the theatre rather as Wilde wrote
dialogues to promote his ideas on aesthetics. All his dialogues on the art
of the theatre are printed in *The Mask*. Although they add a dramatic
element to the writing, dialogue narratives (that are not meant to be
performed) also display a transference of dramatic action onto the page.
It is not purely coincidental that Plato, one of the first to employ the
philosophical dialogue, was a fierce opponent of theatrical art. As a
narrative the dialogue is one of the purest classical modes. It is conservative, didactic, and enacts in words the action that should take place on
a stage. In short, it two-dimensionalizes the three-dimensional quality of
the stage, giving prevalence to the written word over the other more
physical aspects of the theatre. The dialogue stresses theatre as literature
rather than as praxis. For someone who was concerned about the
'tyranny of the word' on the stage, it seems odd that he was also
enraptured with the intricacies of the written word. If we treat the whole
Mask project as a transference of Craig's urge to direct and materialize
his ideas on the theatre, his narrative indulgences appear as a logical

---

[21] *The Marionette*, Vol. 1, No. 9 (Florence, 1918).
[22] *The Marionette*, Vol. 1, No. 3 (Florence, 1918).

consequence. For reasons which have been presented throughout this analysis, *The Mask* was the only contsant 'stage' Craig could work on. As a periodical it only allowed for innovation in certain fields. Layout, presentation and narrative were areas where Craig could be as experimental and adventurous as he wished. And the more *The Mask* became a surrogate performance the more baroque the narrative got. The narrative devices were to be the 'set' of this meta-theatrical performance.

All these highly literary and writerly devices underline the fact that, for a man who was vehemently anti-Shavian and anti-theatre of ideas, with *The Mask* Craig produces a quasi-Shavian 'drama of ideas' of extreme verbosity. Just after Shaw's *Man and Superman*, *The Mask* is Craig's *Puppet and Uberpuppet*. And just as Shaw, in a drama like *The Apple Cart* alternates scenes of prose and pure theatre, so Craig runs *The Mask* as a verbal debate while dreaming of pure theatre.

Certain aspects of the work presented in *The Mask* demanded rigorous academic research, i.e. the work on Oriental theatre or the Commedia dell'Arte. Usually the scholarly work was done by others. Craig was involved in much of the research, but did not necessarily take much pride in that aspect of *The Mask*. Facts did not interest him. He writes:

> We are here on earth to live, not to die. We happen to die, but it doesn't make it any less certain that we are here to live; to create, not to kill.
> Now the historian has always done his very best to kill us. Oh, I know how fascinating a book of facts and dates can be. But a clerk can do that work. It does not need a real dead alive historian. What I object to is all the *evidence* of the historian; that's what kills.[23]

Displaying a common Modernist scorn of history Craig conceives it as boring, irrelevant and not aesthetic enough. Accuracy, fact and historicity do not have a primary interest for him. Consequently his studies of Oriental theatre or of the Commedia were only useful as potential material for adopting and appropriating. Ironically, of course, much of the material presented in these areas was full of facts and historical evidence. As this was not the main issue, however, the people conducting such research for *The Mask* were given very little credit or simply none at all. *The Mask* was to be a solo performance.

Women as Masks:
Dorothy Nevile Lees, Isadora Duncan, Ellen Terry

In actual fact, far from being a one-man show, *The Mask* was, in the mechanics of its preparation and production, a collective project. In a

---

[23] *The Marionette*, Vol. 1, No. 1 (Florence, 1918), p. 21.

typically Craigian way, the contribution of Dorothy Nevile Lees has generally been neglected. Lees's role in the whole *Mask* project was very formative indeed. Her scholarly contributions, especially on the Commedia dell'Arte, were very valuable and made much new material accesible to the English-speaking public. When Craig was away, as he often was, on trips in Europe or Russia, she would assume the role of the editor. She shared many pseudonyms with Craig.[24] Like an understudy, she would step in when Craig was busy doing other things. Her role was never publicly acknowledged by him, and it is mainly due to Lorelei Guidry's introduction to her *Index to The Mask* that we are aware of her. Considering his fervent anti-feminist stance, it is surprising she was allowed to be seen to participate at all. As long as Lees remained hidden behind another mask, Craig's phallocentric notions on art and the artist weren't threatened. The assumption was that he too was only acting as a medium for the 'artistic genius'. Having succumbed to the cult of impersonality, Craig might have believed that he actually did not exist as a separate entity and was only functioning as an agent of artistic genius. His metaphorical disappearance, though, led to a very literal one for Dorothy Nevile Lees. Despite all her work and devotion there is very little trace of her among the by-lines of *The Mask*. If anyone was practising 'impersonality' it was her.

In 1917 Lees acted to save the Arena Goldoni from requisition by the authorities due to the war. The troops eventually requisitioned it, but all the equipment and the belongings of the school were saved. While all this was going on Craig was in Rome, delivering instructions from there. As his son Edward Craig records 'D. N. L. had done a marvellous job':

> Then came more startling news: D. N. L. announced that she was expecting a child by him. As usual when confronted with such a situation, he felt quite lost, for he had been incapable of coping with emotional situations all his life. Without D. N. L's help *The Mask* could not have existed – for the last nine years she had dedicated her life to him and his work; she had helped to finance *The Mask* during one or two difficult times. Now he would dearly like to help her but he was not in a position to do so – he had just written to Elena begging her to come over with the children, telling her of a wonderful scheme involving the use of marionettes that he wanted them all to work on, and it was all he could do to find enough money for their fares.[25]

---

[24] Dorothy Nevile Lees shared the most important pseudonyms with Craig, including that of the editor Semar and John Balance. One of her more exotic pseudonyms was Pierre Rames (Semar spelled backwards).

[25] See Gordon Craig, *Edward Craig*, p. 301.

It is interesting to note that despite Craig's son's attempts to restore Dorothy Nevile Lees' 'presence' in the whole *Mask* project, she still remains D. N. L. She is referred to as a 'helper', as a useful person for Craig to have had around. Craig's general attitude is attributed to some vague notion of 'emotional deficiency'. This is tolerated, even expected, from an 'artistic genius'. Misogyny and the artistic act go hand in hand in this framework. At the end of the quotation we see that Craig is eager for Elena to arrive to put her to work as well on his new 'wonderful scheme'. This is not merely a case of using the personal to interpret the artistic. It is the scheme of things itself that allows such approaches. By definition the artist would be masculine. Together with most Modernists Craig conceives of the artistic act as phallic (Pound's 'poetry writes in phallic direction'). The artist has the right to reinvent himself only on the image of man. The artistic process becomes an engendering process as well. In an article entitled 'A Word about Schopenhauer and the Feminist Movement', John Semar gives us his philosophical background:

> One only need look at a woman's shape to discover that she is not intended for either too much mental or too much physical work.
> Women are directly adapted to act as the nurses and educators of our early childhood, for the simple reason that they themselves are childish, foolish, and short-sighted... in a word, are big children all their lives, something intermediate between the child and the man, who is a man in the strict sense of the word.[26]

This gives Craig the philosophical justification to totally consume the contribution of women like Dorothy Nevile Lees. If they are something 'between the child and the man', with no separate and distinct identity, it seems only natural that their efforts be appropriated by men. The irony, of course, lies in the fact that Craig's mother Ellen Terry was one of the most dynamic and iconoclastic women of her time. Much of Craig's resentment and fear may stem from this fact.

Craig, in many ways, defined himself against his mother. The figure of the great Ellen Terry, whom he adored, followed him all his life. He had enough difficulty as it was collaborating with male artists. His suspicions and phobias were particularly sensitized when it came to women collaborators. As he wrote to Isadora Duncan:

> Woman as a rule being the most material packet of goods on this earth, makes a good effort to kill the desire for an Ideal... and is trying to break the man of his worship of King-monarch – Stars and Gods – that he may have no other gods than Her. And she will succeed until she

---

[26] *The Mask*, Vol. 7, No. 1 (Florence, 1914), p. 3.

reaches the artist, and then she will utter a shriek and like the sphinx will throw herself off the cliff...[27]

This is a letter to a woman who had revolutionized dance, and who had defied the moral code of her time to have a child with Craig. It is significant that it was Oedipus who killed the sphinx. Craig's obsession with *Hamlet* has been investigated with emphasis on the monodramatic dimension of his interpretation. Craig found many parallels in the play. He saw himself as *Hamlet* and his mother as Gertrude. In the *Index to the Story of my Days* he writes:

> I too had lost a father. I too saw my mother married to another ... I was always haunted by this father who was, yet no longer was there.[28]

Craig's personal obsessions seem to become justified theoretically within the framework he was using. His misogyny appears naturalized and whatever his problems with his mother were they are displaced in a model that allows for his every whim and caprice, not only in the form of tolerance but celebration and elevation to an ideal. *The Mask*, as a stage for him to bear his soul, and as a technique to do it by, aestheticizes Craig himself in a scheme that fuses the personal with the artistic and historical. The Arena Goldoni generates the Arena Craig.

Craig's inability to collaborate with other artists is common theme in all studies of his work. This fact stresses his *monodramatic* mania which derives from both artistic and personal preoccupations. Francis Steegmuller wrote on this:

> He obsessively insisted on his 'independence' – but much of what he called 'independence' was fear of the world...Edward A. Craig links his father's fear and his defensive arrogance to the pall of illegitimate birth. The fears that prevented Craig from working with others were reproduced in his private associations.[29]

Whether deriving from the personal or the public spheres, Craig was a monomaniac. As an 'artistic genius' behind a mask he had the right to appropriate and consume the work of others – and it became all the more necessary if these others were women. His attempts to work with Eleonora Duse proved disastrous. The most outstanding disaster in these

---

[27] Craig-Duncan Collection, The Dance Collection, The Library for the Performing Arts at Lincoln Centre, New York, p. 272.

[28] EGC, *Index to the Story of My Days* (London, 1957), p. 162.

[29] See *Your Isadora: The Love Story of Isadora Duncan and Gordon Craig*, ed. Francis Steegmuller, Random house and the New York Public Library (New York, 1974), p. 12.

terms was his relationship with Isadora Duncan. A passionate love affair went sour soon after she had had their daughter. Isadora Duncan and Ellen Terry had much in common. Both were renowned, non-compromising artists, and both had had children to the outrage of the society around them. Had Craig collaborated with Isadora Duncan artistically the results might have been very interesting indeed. As it was, much of Craig's writing on movement seems influenced by Isadora Duncan's experiments in dance. However, Isadora Duncan was too much like Ellen Terry, and, despite their mutual love and desire, the possibility of an artistic partnership seemed inconceivable: similar attempts to work with his mother received mixed reviews. Isadora Duncan writes in *My Life*:

> I adored Craig...but I realized that our separation was inevitable. To live with him was to renounce my art, my personality, nay perhaps my life, my reason. To live without him was to be in a continual state of depression, and tortured by jealousy, for which, alas! it now seemed I had good cause... All this drove me to fits of alternate fury and despair. I could not work, I could not dance...I realized that this state of things must cease. Either Craig's Art or mine – to give up my Art I knew to be impossible...I must find a remedy.[30]

The Mask was definitely a monodramatic project. Craig, whether as masked-playwright, or ventriloquist, or puppet, or master of ceremonies was the centre of the whole affair. *The Mask* existed to present both his art and himself, since he worked within a model that did not differentiate between the two. *The Mask* was to expose and articulate Craig's ideas *and* Craig's psyche. It was to be the workshop that could mould the art of the theatre and its artist.

In moulding his artistic self through *The Mask*, Craig was characteristically exemplifying a Modernist preoccupation. This artistic self, like his *Ubermarionette* was to be impersonal, with no history or psychology. In pursuing the cult of impersonality, like his literary counterparts Craig ends up articulating a totalizing discourse. In Craig's case this expressed itself in the figure of the all-powerful director. Craig's flirtations with fascism express his search for an ideological model that can accommodate such a figure. However unlike Pound (and Eliot in many respects), he was not 'modern' enough to reach eschatological solutions and become a wholehearted advocate of fascism.

In Modernist theatre this loss of the artist in the art form follows a twofold direction. In general, experimentation in total theatre can be seen deriving from two very distinct theoretical backgrounds. The first

---

[30] See Isadora Duncan, *My Life* (New York, 1927), pp. 208–209.

31. Frontispiece by Stefano della Bella for *Li Buffoni* (1641) by Margherita Costa, Vol. 10, No. 1, p. 1a, 1924.

is rooted in idealist extensions of a Judaeo-Christian tradition and manifests itself in apocalyptic and mythopoeic modes. The artist of such a theatre exists only to be 'sacrificed' in a ritual that aspires to collective notions of consciousness and sub-consciousness. History for this model is replaced by metaphysics. The high priest of this expression of performance theory is Artaud. The artist of this model is the sacrificial scape-goat. Artaud's madness is not at all coincidental in this framework (nor is Pound's). On the other hand, the second tradition, as epitomised by Brecht, is consistently secular in its commitment to history. The ideology that reconstructs the artist is seen as a political one. The role appointed is also 'impersonal', as the artist now exists to promote and exemplify his commitment to history. Both approaches reconstruct the role of the artist: one in the body of the sub-conscious, the other in the body-politic.

Craig falls between these two traditions in total theatre. Not extreme, nor modern, nor political enough to embody either, *The Mask* enacts the tensions of somehow being trapped. A performance that is not really a performance, modern but not modern enough, political but not really: are all traits of *The Mask* that make the periodical fascinating and at the same time dictate its sometimes distressing limitations.

Craig has been rightly hailed as one of the 'prophets' of twentieth century theatre. His legacy can be traced right through the historical avant-grade to theatre practitioners like Brook and Grotowski, and in aspects of the more recent performance art and intercultural projects. Indeed, it is felt more in terms of influence, inspiration and appropriation, rather than through specific techniques or practices. It is *Craigism* or *Craigiana* – the whole mythology that fuses his personal, biographical details with aspects of his theatre theory – that seems to have had an impact on the generations of theatre innovators that were to follow. *The Mask* is one of the first attempts to construct such a *Craigiana*. Scripted and directed by the man himself, this quasi-theatrical periodical/performance was to be one of the first constructions of the Craigian myth. A myth, however, that at once reveals its historical sources and gestures towards the huge impact its subject would have on the future generations of twentieth-century theatre makers.

BIBLIOGRAPHY

PRIMARY MATERIALS

Edward Gordon Craig, *The Page* (London, 1899).
    The Gordon Craig Book of Penny Toys (Hackbridge, 1899).
    Woodcuts and Some Words (Hackbridge, 1899).
    Henry Irving, Ellen Terry: A Book of Portraits (Chicago, 1899).
    Bookplates (London, 1900).
    The Art of the Theatre (London, 1905).
    Isadora Duncan: Six Movement Designs (London, 1906).
    The Mask (Florence, 1908–1929).
    Portfolio of Etchings (London, 1908).
    Portfolio of Etchings (London, 1910).
    On the Art of the Theatre (London, 1911).
    Towards A New Theatre (London, 1913).
    'A Living Theatre' (Florence, 1913).
    The Marionette (Florence, 1918).
    The Theatre Advancing (London ,1921).
    Puppets and Poets (London, 1921).
    Scene (Oxford, 1923).
    Woodcuts and Some Words (London, 1924).
    Books and Theatres (London, 1925).
    Nothing, or the Bookplate (London, 1925).
    Hamlet (Cranach Press, 1929).
    A Production, 1926 (Oxford, 1930).
    Henry Irving (London, 1930).
    Ellen Terry and Her Secret Self (London, 1932).
    Index to the Story of my Days (London, 1957).

SECONDARY MATERIALS ON EDWARD GORDON CRAIG

Arnott, Brian, *Edward Gordon Craig and Hamlet* (Ottawa, 1975).
Bablet, Denis, *Edward Gordon Craig* (Paris, 1962).
Beacham, Richard C., 'Brothers in Suffering and Joy: the Appia-Craig Correspondence', in *New Theatre Quarterly*, Vol. 4, No. 15, (1988), pp. 268–88.
Craig, Edward, 'Gordon Craig and Herbert von Herkomer', in *Theatre Research*, Vol. 10, No. 1 (1969), pp. 7–16.

Gordon Craig: The Story of His Life (New York, 1968).

Craig, Ellen G., *Edward Gordon Craig: the Last Eight Years 1958–1966 – Letters* (Andoversford, 1983).

Fletcher, Ifan Kyle, and Arnold Rood, *Edward Gordon Craig: A Bibliography* (Society for Theatre Research, 1967).

Franklin, Colin (ed), *Gordon Craig's Paris Diary, 1932–33* (North Hills, 1982).

Guidry, Lorelei, *Introduction and Index to The Mask*, Vol. 16 (New York, 1968).

Ilyin, Eugene, 'How Stanislavsky and Gordon Craig Produced Hamlet', in *Plays and Players* (March, 1957), pp. 6–7.

Innes, Christopher, *Edward Gordon Craig* (Cambridge, 1983. Second edition, Amsterdam, 1998).

Leeper, Janet, *Edward Gordon Craig: Designs for the Theatre* (Harmondsworth, 1948).

Marker, Frederick, and Lisa Lone, *Edward Gordon Craig and The Pretenders* (Carbondale, Ill., 1982).

Marotti, Ferrucio, *Edward Gordon Craig* (Bologna, 1961).

Newman, Lindsay, *Gordon Craig Archives: International Survey* (London, 1976).

'Reinhardt and Craig?' in Max Reinhardt. *The Oxford Symposium*, Margaret Jacobs and John Warren, eds. (Suffolk, 1986).

(ed) *Black Figures. 105 Reproductions with an Unpublished Essay by Edward Gordon Craig* (Wellingborough, Skelton, 1989).

(ed) *The Correspondence of Edward Gordon Craig and Count Harry Kessler, 1903–1937* (Leeds: Institute of Germanic Studies, University of London, 1995).

Rood, Arnold, *Gordon Craig on Movement and Dance* (New York, 1977).

'E. Gordon Craig, director, School for the art of the Theatre', in *Theatre Research International*, Vol. 8, No. 1 (1983), pp. 1–17.

and Donald Oeslager, *Edward Gordon Craig: Artist of the Theatre* (New York, 1967).

Rose, Enid, *Gordon Craig and the Theatre* (London, 1931).

Senelick, Laurence, 'The Craig-Stanislavsky Hamlet at the Moscow Art Theatre,' in *Theatre Quarterly*, Vol. 6, No. 2 (1976), pp. 56–122.

'Moscow and Monodrama: The Meaning of the Craig–Stanislavsky Hamlet', *Theatre Research International*, Vol. 6, 1981.

Gordon Craig's Moscow 'Hamlet': A Reconstruction (Westport. Conn. 1982).

Walton, J. Michael, ed., *Craig on Theatre* (London, 1983).

INDEX

Other titles in the Contemporary Theatre Studies series:

This book is part of a series. The publisher will accept continuation orders which may be cancelled at any time and which provide for automatic billing and shipping of each title in the series upon publication. Please write for details.